INSIDE YELTSIN'S RUSSIA

INSIDE YELTSIN'S RUSSIA

Corruption · Conflict · Capitalism

John Kampfner

First published 1994
Cassell Publishers Ltd
Villiers House
41/47 Strand
London
WC2N 5JE

British Library Cataloguing-in-Publication Data
A catalogue record for this book is available from the British Library

ISBN 0-304-34463-X

Designed by Patrick Knowles

Typeset by Litholink Ltd, Welshpool, Powys, Wales
Printed in Great Britain by Mackays of Chatham

To Lucy and Alex

Contents

Preface

My own personal adventure began in 1978. The era of stagnation, the geriatric rule of Leonid Brezhnev, still had a few more years left to run. The four of us in my sixth-form Russian class were on our way to Moscow and Leningrad. We were told to stock up before we went on small gifts, postcards of double-decker buses and bobbies, and tapes of Genesis and Deep Purple. I was given numbers of friends of friends whom I'd been warned to contact from phone booths, not from the hotel. For two weeks we sat in our bright red Icarus buses, a ubiquitous sight on the tourist trail, and stared down at the dowdy men and women with their string bags going through their daily ritual of queuing for whatever was available, a slow-moving river of grey. I met the people I had intended to see, a young artist and her mother, a teacher and her husband, and gave them some books I had brought. Every potential topic of conversation was embarrassing. I couldn't mention which countries I had been to recently or what films were all the rage in London. They had never been outside the USSR and never thought they would. Few Western movies made it to Moscow. I asked them where they went out to in the evenings. They didn't. The hotels and restaurants were for foreigners, black marketeers and the odd birthday or wedding celebration. Educated and enquiring people, they had not had the opportunity to do very much with their lives. I was struck not so much by the fear as the frustration.

Our hotel, the Orlyonok, the Little Eagle, was run by the Komsomol, the Communist Youth League. Every night at 6 p.m. we were ordered to sit at the same long table, where we would be doled up gristly cutlets, congealed rice and tinned cabbage. I was intrigued. If the time never changed, why were the cutlets always cold? This was the first of the great riddles of the Soviet command economy that I was to encounter. Everything was regulated by the *plan*. Yet there was a market of sorts, outside the hotel. Every day four young men, the same four young men, stood in the slush asking if we had anything to sell. Oleg – at least, that was what he called himself – was not your average young Muscovite. He spoke English with an American drawl. His use of language was straight out of a textbook. His designer jeans and moccasin shoes suggested he was in a different economic league from his peers. Did I, he asked, want to change money? Did I want to sell any of my tapes? (How did he know

I had any?) Did I want to buy a fur hat? I knew it was illegal and highly dangerous to buy and sell, so I suggested a swap: a pair of trainers for a hat made from rabbit fur. It was a good deal. We shook hands. I thought nothing more of it.

I returned to the USSR several times. The following year I went on a bus that took fifty of us from London to Odessa and Kiev, camping with Soviet holidaymakers. Four years on I was back again as an interpreter for a group from Cornwall. I hardly felt as if I had been away. Little seemed to have changed.

In 1985 I was sent on my first journalistic posting, for Reuters. This was the early Gorbachev period, when barriers were beginning to be broken down. On the first Saturday I persuaded a French colleague to accompany me on a walk around the town, to reacquaint myself with Red Square and the streets around it. It was a sultry evening; Muscovites had abandoned the city for their country *dachas*. Barely half an hour into the walk, we were ambling past the Hotel Metropol, when somebody shouted my name. I turned round but didn't recognize anyone, and moved on. Suddenly a man tapped me on the shoulder, a tall man in shiny black shoes and a white suit. Before me stood the spitting image of Al Capone. 'Hi John,' he said in English. 'It's great to see you back in Russia.' I apologized, but said I had no idea who he was. 'Surely you haven't forgotten, John? How's the hat? Enjoy your posting, John.' He turned his shoulder and sauntered back to his friends, young men in polo shirts and sunglasses and with a distinctly un-Soviet swagger. I had forgotten about that little episode. If his aim had been to unsettle me, he did a very good job.

Six years on, in 1991, I was back again full-time, now for the *Telegraph*. This was the period of Boris Yeltsin, of the birth of a new state after seventy years of Communist rule, of coups and uprisings. But for me the most startling change was the discovery of money. I was most certainly witnessing a revolution, but a revolution not for the purists. I saw Oleg once more, or at least I thought I did. There were so many like him now. He (if it was he) was as dapper as ever. I never found out what he was doing, but his BMW and bodyguard provided me with enough clues. He slipped into his car and sped off. I will never know if he recognized me. I tried to put together the various strands. That he had been colluding with the KGB from the early days was beyond doubt. Black marketeers simply could not have existed otherwise. He had probably got himself into trouble at some point and thereafter, in return for a quiet life, provided his new employers with information and a share of the profits. Now he had become a businessman, one of thousands, living a life of threats, deals and big spending. Of all the people I had met on that first trip to Moscow, he was the one who had benefited most from the changes.

The old Communist elite, the *nomenklatura*, managed the transition with consummate ease. Anyone who did well under Communism had all the prerequisites for doing well under capitalism. I had seen this already in the former East Germany, where the most ambitious under Honecker's regime – the majority of opportunists, not the small number of genuine ideologues – had no trouble making the grade after unification. In Russia, the old system was based on *blat* and *svyazi*, influence and connections. Under Communism very few people had become wealthy by Western standards; privilege at least ensured a minimum of inconvenience – special shops, special housing, special schools, special medical care, even a chance of doing the unthinkable and going abroad, albeit on an organized tour.

As Gorbachev took on the Party in the late 1980s, as he allowed the criticisms that had been on the minds of many to be aired freely, so the financial straitjacket was gradually lifted. Two processes were taking place simultaneously. Radicals led by Yeltsin and Sakharov were challenging the political status quo, defying Gorbachev to go beyond attempting to reform a party that was unreformable. At the same time, the very same people who were pillars of that establishment were themselves looking to move on. The Komsomol became a young businessmen's club. The KGB sought ways of making money. Members of the ruling Politburo forged links with emigré entrepreneurs in the West to help them sell off the USSR's reserves of precious metals. The Communist ship was sinking: survival entailed not jumping off first, but staying on board for as long as possible and using the privileges and contacts that came with membership to point the way to pastures new.

In *Inside Yeltsin's Russia* I seek to explain that ideological differences played a part, but not the most significant part, in the power struggle that dominated Yeltsin's first years in power. Politics was largely a means to an end, and that end was economic control. For members of parliament, the government, the presidential apparatus, civil servants, military chiefs, industrialists, and anyone who played a role in the old system and wanted a taste of the new, it was about seizing whatever they could. Capitalism and privatization opened up a myriad opportunities for self-enrichment. An entire nation was put up for sale – its property, natural resources, intellectual reserves. Communism, with its lack of political culture and civic society, its dependence on oppression and its material shortages, had bred and nurtured avarice and criminality; but civic responsibility and civil justice had always been alien concepts in Russia. Here there had always been two kinds of law, one for the rulers and one for the ruled. Graf Alexander Benckendorff, security chief under Nicholas I, described it most succinctly: 'Law is for the underlings.'

The symbiotic relationship between the Soviet elite and organized crime that flourished under Brezhnev reached its apogee in capitalism. For those of us who witnessed the first stirrings of democratic opposition in the late 1980s, the Sunday morning rallies that would attract tens of thousands of decent people, the retrenchment of the elite came as a bitter disappointment. Yeltsin had promised a moral crusade, a new type of politics, no longer isolated from the people and corrupted by privilege; but within a year of his taking outright control of the Kremlin, that dream had been shattered. The enthusiasm for the political process, which exploded in 1989 with elections to Gorbachev's first parliament, dissipated with alarming speed.

Nobody believed Yeltsin had a panacea. One of the characteristics that has enabled Russians to withstand adversity is their scepticism. But what sustained his support was the realization that the alternative would have been considerably worse. Everyone was groping in the dark for a model to shake Russia out of a century of misrule. *Perestroika*, Gorbachev's vision of slow and gradual change, had run its course. The failure of the coup plotters in August 1991 opened the way for Yeltsin. He did not need much convincing to put his faith in a group of young, Western-influenced economists in their thirties and in their vision of a radical move to the market. It did not take long for the conservatives to rally opposition, harnessing the discontent and disorientation felt by millions. At the heart of the fight was the perennial question of Russia's place in the world, one that had occupied nineteenth-century thinkers, the Slavophiles and the Westernizers alike, but had been submerged under the veneer of Soviet internationalism. Through a majority in parliament, and with the Vice-President, Alexander Rutskoy, as a figurehead, the hardliners became an ever-present threat that all but paralysed the government and instilled in it the fear that any day it could be toppled and all its reforms could be undone.

How did it all go wrong? Could it have been any different? Was the revolution destined to be hijacked? Was there a revolution at all? Does Russia now have the worst of both worlds? In this book I seek to answer those questions.

Inside Yeltsin's Russia is divided into three parts. The first part, a prologue, focuses on the antics of a young lawyer who managed to work his way into the very heart of the Kremlin, a man who played each side off against the other, and who epitomized more than anyone else the depths to which both sides had sunk. General Dima is a metaphor of modern Russia at its smartest and sleaziest. Part II describes the early Yeltsin years, from his fights with the party to his accession to power and on to the demise of his young government. It shows how money, real money, changed people's lives. The third part describes how and why the power struggle reached its peak in the battle for the White House, how the old elite and the criminals regained their influence, and how the President did little to stop them.

Much of the material is taken from my own experience in Moscow and around the country and from articles I have written on the basis of that experience. Several longer pieces for the *Daily* and *Sunday Telegraphs* and the *Telegraph Magazine* I have adapted and included as small cameo chapters – on Valentin Pavlov, the former Prime Minister; Lev Kerbel, a much-decorated sculptor; Mikhail Kalashnikov, the inventor; Stanislav Glebov, a cousin of Yeltsin's in the President's home town; and Alexander Rutskoy on the campaign trail. In each case I have endeavoured to switch from the big picture to the very specific experiences of an individual trying to come to terms with the changes. The multi-millionaire businessmen and disc jockeys, the army veterans and transvestites, say as much about the era as Yeltsin and Rutskoy do.

For the personal accounts of the political battles, I have relied in part on interviews I conducted with prominent politicians and their aides towards the end of my posting at the end of 1993 and early 1994, as well as a trip back to Moscow in April and May 1994. Some of my interviewees have asked to remain anonymous. Those who are freely quoted, and to whom I am most indebted, are: Yegor Gaidar, Mikhail Poltoranin, Grigory Yavlinsky, Valery Zorkin, Yuri Boldyrev, Galina Starovoitova, Sergei Baburin, Vladimir Isakov, Oleg Rumyantsev, Arkady Volsky, Sergei Yushenkov, Gleb Yakunin, Andrei Illarionov, Alexei Golovkov, Pavel Voshchanov, Nikolai Gulbinsky, Andrei Fyodorov and Dmitry Yakubovsky. Brief details on these individuals, and on many others besides, are given in a list of 'Dramatis Personae' for the reader's quick reference.

I am grateful for considerable insights from well-connected Russian journalist colleagues. Where I found a particular detail hard to verify, I have said so. For background information, I relied on the usual sources: the main Russian and international news agencies and Russian newspapers. These have been named only in cases where the information is not generally accepted as having long been in the public domain.

Inside Yeltsin's Russia is not intended as the definitive word on the Yeltsin era. No writer can make such a claim, not even the President himself, because many of the details behind the historic events are still shrouded in half-truth and secrecy. For those with extensive knowledge of Russia, I hope to have shed new light on specific incidents and offered perhaps a different overview, one that deliberately shuns the simplistic labels of left and right as so often applied in the West. For general readers with a less focused interest in the country, I hope to have conveyed the period as I saw it – a lunge from one dramatic development to another. I have concentrated on the developments that I regard as being formative for the period, which, as the subtitle suggests, was marked by three leitmotifs – corruption, conflict and, above all else, the advent of capitalism. While many of the characters do not emerge with credit, I have not intended the book as an indictment of Yeltsin. With others in charge it could have been so much worse. Russia is finding its way, slowly. Many, Russians and foreigners, have sought to see the changes through the narrow prism of historical determinism. Russia, they say, is not fit for democracy. That it is fundamentally different, that it must seek its own path, is a truism; but it does not follow that the path must necesssarily lead to autarchy. That my Russian friends lived through the same experiences as I did with such engagement and equanimity makes the transformation all the more remarkable.

Acknowledgements

E ach generation of Moscow correspondents makes the same mistake, departing with the satisfaction of believing that they have seen the best of it. Gorbachev and *perestroika*, we were told, could not be beaten. I would like to think that two 'coups', the collapse of the USSR and Communism, and the birth pangs of the new Russian state, marked a new peak, but experience teaches that we should never be so sure. Yet for all the great historical landmarks, I will treasure with equal pleasure the *other* experiences. Of our many Russian friends, I will list my very closest who gave my wife Lucy and me such fond memories: Pyotr Kochevrin; Olga Timyanskayá; Olga Kapitonova; Artyom Troitsky and Svetlana Kunitsina; and Vera Nanivska.

Throughout my posting, and the subsequent work on the book, the help of many in the Russian press corps was invaluable. These included Dmitry Ostalsky and Sergei Parkhomenko, editor-in-chief and political commentator respectively of *Sevodnya*; Svetlana Sorokina, presenter of Vesti (Russian Television news); Boris Grishchenko, co-director of Interfax; and Misha Voznesensky, Far East correspondent of Vesti. At Izvestia I was particularly grateful to Andrei Ostalsky, Irina Demchenko and Mikhail Berger.

Among the foreign press and diplomatic corps, for camaraderie and cooperation I would like to thank Oliver and Rosie Wates at Reuters; Ben Brown and Geraldine Ryan, Kevin Connolly, Bridget Kendall and Nick Worrall, Lucy's colleagues at the BBC; Peter Conradi and Roberta Bonometti at *The European*; John Lloyd of the *Financial Times* and Marcia Levy, our neighbours in town and at the *dacha*; Miranda Ingram at the *Daily Mail*; Jeremy Nicholl and Lola Toptchieva at Katz Pictures, for some unforgettable trips together to the provinces; Jonathan and Ruth Steele, John Rettie, and David and Harriet Hearst at the *Guardian*; Meg Bortin, outgoing editor of the highly successful *Moscow Times*; Catherine Phillips in St Petersburg; and Jo Durden-Smith in Nikolina Gora. My neighbours and colleagues in 'Sad Sam', Dan Schneider and Justin Bourke at the *Christian Science Monitor* and Celestine Bohlen and Steve Erlanger at the *New York Times*, shared many hours of soul-searching about the future of Russia. The British Embassy was most hospitable and helpful, led by Sir Brian and Lady Delmar Fall, Francis and Gill Richards,

David and Catherine Manning, Noel and Jean Jones, Richard Bridge and Philippa Leslie-Jones, and Christopher and Brigitte Granville.

To Nigel Wade, foreign editor, who brought me on to the *Telegraph* in 1989 and supported me throughout, and to Max Hastings, editor-in-chief, who entrusted me with two of the most exciting postings of the late twentieth century, I am most grateful. I am indebted to both for granting me a sabbatical to work on the book. On the *Daily Telegraph* foreign desk I received unfailing guidance, advice and good humour from Teresa Jeffrey, Paul Hill, Pat Prentice and Patsy Dryden. I was especially fortunate to have been indulged with so much space and scope on the *Sunday Telegraph*, first by Frank Taylor and latterly by Ivo Dawnay; on the leader pages, my thanks go to Lord Deedes and Christopher Hudson, on the magazine to Nigel Horne and George Darby.

While my colleagues in London had to cope with me at the end of a telephone line, the long-serving and long-suffering Moscow-based staff lived through the events with me, and my warmest thanks go to them – Nellie Vinogradova, Tolya Chivilyov, Ira Dorucheva and Katya Svergun, as well as Nina Andreyevna. Alan Philps, my successor, with whom I first worked in Moscow at Reuters, was most helpful during my trip back to Moscow in spring 1994. For fixing up some of the interviews then, I am grateful to Lena Yakovleva. My warmest thanks go to our close friend, Constance Richards, for putting me up during my recent stay.

Sean Magee, my editor at Cassell, displayed admirable trust by taking me on and agreeing to a fast publication, and never flinching even when the deadline approached and he had not seen a word of text. His relaxed but steadfast approach provided just the foil I needed. I am similarly grateful to Clare Howell, director of general non-fiction, and to the others at Villiers House. Special thanks to Gillian Bromley for an excellent job of copy-editing, and to Alison Whalley at Katz for her help with the photographs.

Such were the offers of help during the frantic final few months of writing, I ended up with an army of volunteer 'readers' of my penultimate draft. These included Simon Scott-Plummer at the *Telegraph*, Gordon Clough at the BBC and my old friend Patrick Napier. Another of the group was Tim Whewell of the BBC. Tim's wife, Rachel Osorio, spent many weeks transcribing the tapes from my interviews and using her sharp knowledge of Russia as yet another back-up for me. Their friendship in Moscow and London was much valued. Another 'reader' was Helen Womack of the *Independent*, whom I first met back in 1985 with her husband Kostya Gagarin. Both were bedrocks of support during my two postings in Moscow.

My love and thanks go to my parents, Fred and Betty Kampfner, my brother David and sisters Judy and Helen, and Lucy's parents, Sir Eric and Clare Ash, and their family.

Pride of place, however, goes to four people. First, to Marcus Warren, my colleague and friend, who showed that it is possible for two journalists to work amicably within ten yards of each other, seven days a week for three years, in the most turbulent and fraught of situations. His help on the book was limitless, his advice spot-on. My greatest thanks of all go to Nick Weir-Williams, my brother-in-law and head of Northwestern University Press in Illinois, who guided me through from my first mention of wanting to write a book through to publishing date, acting as my de facto agent throughout. Then, of course, comes Lucy, who despite being a contemporary in London and at Oxford I was fated to meet in, of all places, Moscow. Two years later came our red-headed spark, Alex Ayuna, who lit up many a day and charmed all who met her.

Dramatis Personae

Aizderdzis, Andrei — Member of parliament/businessman, shot dead in April 1994

Anpilov, Viktor — Leader of hardline Communist/nationalist group Working Russia

Baburin, Sergei — Prominent opposition/nationalist politician

Barannikov, Viktor — Security Minister December 1991 until sacked for alleged graft July 1994

Barkashov, Alexander — Leader of neo-fascist group Russian National Unity

Barsukov, Mikhail — Head of Kremlin Regiment

Birshtein, Boris — Prominent businessman based in Switzerland, friend of political elite

Boldyrev, Yuri — Corruption investigator March 1992 until pushed out March 1993

Bonner, Yelena — Widow of Andrei Sakharov, prominent activist in Democratic Russia

Burbulis, Gennady — Right-hand man of Yeltsin until mid-1993; the 'Grey Cardinal'

Chernomyrdin, Viktor — Prime Minister from December 1992

Chubais, Anatoly — Deputy Prime Minister, in charge of privatization

Dudayev, Dzhokhar — President of self-styled republic of Chechnya

Fyodorov, Boris — Finance Minister January 1993 to January 1994; outspoken monetarist

Fyodorov, Svyatoslav — Eye surgeon, multi-millionaire entrepreneur

Gaidar, Yegor — Architect of radical reform, twice in government, head of Russia's Choice

Gerashchenko, Viktor — Central Bank chairman

Glazyev, Sergei — Foreign Trade Minister until hounded from post, joined opposition

Golovkov, Alexei — Assistant to Burbulis, prominent member of Russia's Choice

Golushko, Nikolai — Security Minister August 1993 to February 1994

Govorukhin, Stanislav — Film-maker turned nationalist politician; activist in Democratic Party

Grachev, Pavel — Defence Minister

Gulbinsky, Nikolai — Press secretary to Rutskoy, became confidant of Yakubovsky

Gusinsky, Vladimir — Multi-millionaire banker turned media mogul

Illarionov, Andrei — Deputy head of government's Working Centre for Economic Reforms

Ilyushin, Viktor — Head of presidential secretariat

Isakov, Vladimir — Prominent nationalist member of parliament, one-time deputy speaker

Kalashnikov, Mikhail — Inventor of automatic rifle that bears his name

Kerbel, Lev — Sculptor who made his name creating monuments to Lenin and Marx

Khasbulatov, Ruslan — Speaker of former parliament, one of leaders of October uprising

Kobets, Konstantin — One-time military adviser to Yeltsin

Kobzon, Iosif — Communist-era pop singer turned big-time entrepreneur

DRAMATIS PERSONAE

Sukhanov, Lev	Long-time member of Yeltsin's apparatus
Tarpishev, Shamil	Yeltsin's tennis coach
Terekhov, Stanislav	Head of Officers' Union, militant nationalist group within army
Travkin, Nikolai	Reformist turned populist critic of Yeltsin, leader of Democratic Party
Tsaregorodtsev, Alexei	Aide to Yeltsin, transferred to Rutskoy's camp
Volsky, Arkady	Communist technocrat, self-styled leader of centrist opposition
Voshchanov, Pavel	Yeltsin's spokesman until early 1992
Yakovlev, Yegor	Editor *Moscow News*, head of television until sacked by Poltoranin
Yakubovsky, Dmitry	Ambitious lawyer who became friend of both sides in power struggle
Yakunin, Gleb	Dissident priest, activist in Democratic Russia
Yanayev, Gennady	Vice-President to Gorbachev, coup figurehead
Yavlinsky, Grigory	Radical economist, maverick politician, leader of own group in Duma
Yazov, Dmitry	Defence Minister under Gorbachev, one of coup leaders
Yerin, Viktor	Interior Minister
Yushenkov, Sergei	Radical aide to Yeltsin, member of Russia's Choice
Zhirinovsky, Vladimir	Leader of extreme right-wing Liberal Democratic Party
Zlobin, Konstantin	Spokesman for old parliament until uprising
Zorkin, Valery	Chairman of Constitutional Court until late 1993
Zyuganov, Gennady	Leader of re-legalized Communist Party after 1992

Part I

1
General Dima

I was told to flash my headlights on approaching the car park. Vitaly would be there to meet me at 9.45 p.m. sharp. I did as I was told. I had always wanted to meet Dmitry Yakubovsky.

The destination was a café on the road to Uspenskoye, the route the Communist elite took from their Kremlin offices to their suburban *dachas*, the country homes where the rich and powerful could enjoy their privileges shielded by high fences from the reality that was the Soviet Union. The road had changed little over the years. The surface was attended to every month, police patrols stood watch at each turn-off. Every lane led to a different *dacha*, a little palace where the parties would go on all night, the revellers would gorge themselves on food and drink, and conspiracies would be hatched. The locals called it Moscow's Switzerland. It was an extravagant claim, but the rolling hills leading down to the Moscow River provided a gentle relief from the drabness of the capital. With the onset of privatization, old privilege was being forced to mix uneasily with the emerging monied class. New and even more luxurious residences were springing up all around.

Shortly after passing through Barvikha, the hamlet preferred by Mikhail Gorbachev in his day and later by Boris Yeltsin, I found Vitaly – or rather, he found me: he had jumped out of his unmarked Lada before I had turned the corner. We shook hands, he told me to follow. Minutes later, the village of Zhukovka behind us, we stopped. The metal gates opened backwards, very slowly. Two dozen men, walkie-talkies in hand, loitered around. They told me to leave my keys in the car. They would park it between the bullet-proof Mercedes and the more humble decoy vehicles.

This had been one of the homes of Vladimir Kryuchkov, KGB Chairman and chief conspirator in the August 1991 coup. After his arrest, Kryuchkov was never allowed to return to his bungalow. Many of these *dachas* came with the job, passed from one group of favoured sons to the next. Now it was Dima Yakubovsky's turn.

Yakubovsky had been asked to help destroy the opposition to Yeltsin. The venture was fraught with risk. His task was to expose the Vice-President, Alexander Rutskoy, and his cohorts, for corruption. Rutskoy and his backers in parliament believed that within months they would bring Yeltsin down; the President had been losing his grip and his aides were petrified. In the battle for loyalty, and the financial rewards that came with it, Rutskoy was forging ahead. Threats and dirty dealings had become a normal part of political life. In this bitter battle for primacy nothing was beneath Yakubovsky, or his foes.

'General Dima' began hustling at a young age. The son of a military engineer, he was born in 1964 in Bolshevo, a village outside Moscow. After national service he took a correspondence course in law, working part-time as a porter in the local railway station to make some money on the side. He tried hard to get into Leningrad's top military engineering academy. But, like many young men in the Soviet Union, he had a problem. He was rejected because of one wretched word in his internal passport, the entry under the fifth heading, 'nationality'. His mother was a Jew.

With the help of friends of his father, he was accepted at the Supreme Military Command School for Missile Troops in Perm, a town in the Urals. It was not quite as prestigious as the Leningrad academy, but it was a good start. Yet within a year Yakubovsky had been thrown out of the school for 'low moral attitude'. He recovered from that blow and by his mid-twenties had been taken on by the Moscow City Prosecutor's Office. Despite more complaints about his brash behaviour he moved on to a junior job in the Union of Lawyers. A good career beckoned for this ambitious young man, one who wanted to do more than push paper. This was just the kind of man the 'new' Soviet Union needed late in 1989, as the Communist world was collapsing around Gorbachev's feet.

Yakubovsky was starting to know the right people. But it took a stroke of luck, and genius, to get himself noticed. He stumbled upon a directory of telephone numbers of Politburo members. One day, with nothing better to do, he dialled a few. If mere advisers answered, he hung up. Several months later, he dialled the number of Marshal Dmitry Yazov, the Defence Minister, and was startled when Yazov picked up the phone himself. This was a few months before German unification, and many in the Soviet military were becoming twitchy about the status of property held in what would soon no longer be the GDR. Yakubovsky sold Yazov the idea of earning real income, real Deutschmarks, from the army's vast real estate holdings in East Germany. Billions were at stake. Yazov said it was worth a try, spoke to some senior generals, and within days Yakubovsky was flying out on a secret directive, in Yazov's personal plane, in charge of the investigation. On his return, he went to see Anatoly Lukyanov, the Chairman of parliament and Gorbachev's right-hand man. Lukyanov's son-in-law happened to be head of personnel at the General Staff, and a friend of Yakubovsky's. Young Dima now had the job, full-time.

Many Soviet assets in the former East Germany were never accounted for. Many in the top brass of the Western Group of Forces were suspected of making handsome profits as the army withdrew. Despite numerous complaints in parliament, the full truth was never revealed. Yakubovsky travelled to and fro on his secret missions, until on one flight a few months later he was ordered to turn back. The order, it transpired, had come from Gorbachev, who had become embarrassed by the property scam. Gorbachev had already agreed terms with Chancellor Kohl for selling the assets and didn't want some young upstart interfering. Yakubovsky by now knew too much and was considered a liability by those who had been on the make. He was spirited away to Switzerland by a friend, a former government minister who was now making a merry million in the fertilizer trade.

Yakubovsky's adventures were only just beginning. Now, barely twenty-five and in charge of his own firm for the first time, he lived a charmed life. Limousines, women, a large house in Basle – he seemed to have everything he could possibly need. But he was bright, and realized that these pleasures were transient. What he needed far more were friends in high places. By the early 1990s that meant businessmen, and rich ones at that. In Switzerland he brought himself to the attention of a certain Boris Birshtein, a man who through his wealth would come to play a pivotal role in Russia's power struggle. In time, Birshtein would summon members of the Russian leadership for meetings, not the other way round.

Back in 1979, when Birshtein emigrated for Israel, he did not seem destined for fame and fortune. The most he had achieved in Soviet Lithuania was to become manager of a textile factory. But within a few years in the West, his company Seabeco had grown into a major trading empire. The mid-1980s were a time when the smartest Communist officials were looking to become involved in capitalist companies to provide little nest eggs for themselves. The trouble for these *apparatchiki* was that there were precious few friendly faces in the West who were willing to do their work for them. Birshtein turned himself into a go-between, and became indispensable. Wherever there was a trading opportunity, the licences were granted to him. Among Birshtein's friends were several leaders of the August coup. Gennady Yanayev was its figurehead, an inveterate drinker of small intellect. Nikolai Kruchina was smarter. He was a top-ranking official who had administered the Communist Party's finances.

As the coup failed and the whistle was about to be blown on the party's illegal dealings, Kruchina jumped from his apartment window to his death. He was said to have committed suicide, but some wondered whether he hadn't been pushed. Kruchina knew better than anyone else about the Party's foreign bank accounts, its funding of foreign Communist Parties and 'friendly firms', its sell-off of most of the country's gold reserves and other natural resources. Even before the coup leaders were arrested, the party hacks began to panic. The men and women at the Central Committee worked the shredders around the clock to destroy much of the incriminating evidence. Outside on Old Square, thousands of demonstrators shouted 'put the Party bandits on trial'. Gennady Burbulis, Yeltsin's number two, ordered the building sealed. But it was too late. Millions of dollars had already been smuggled abroad and the documents to prove it were no more.

The coup did not damage Birshtein. The new political elite, he reckoned, would be just as keen on his services as the old one. He was proved right. The first two to befriend him were Rutskoy and Viktor Barannikov. Barannikov had been put in charge of the Security Ministry, the new name for the old KGB. His brief was to push through radical reforms in a security agency loathed by the people and distrusted by Yeltsin. Barannikov did not carry out his orders.

Biershtein returned frequently from his Swiss headquarters to Moscow, where he had been given a large house on the prestigious Kosygin Street, once the preserve of the Central Committee. His firm, Seabeco, had become one of the main channels through which raw materials were exported from the former Soviet Union to the West at dumping prices. It was a lucrative business for him and for the men who controlled the ministries. Birshtein was welcomed in other former Soviet republics too. He was seen as an economic messiah, put in charge of government committees and asked to handle their gold reserves. He was happy to oblige. He also tried his hand at peacekeeping in ethnic conflicts, flying Rutskoy and himself to the republic of Moldova on his private jet to put an end to fighting there.

Young Yakubovsky, by this point, had settled in Canada. Wife number four was found, and he was not yet thirty. By now he had made a small fortune, enough to pay more than $3 million for a house in the opulent Toronto neighbourhood of Bridle Path. It wasn't quite to his taste, though, and for another $1.5 million he had the place shelled out. A further $1.5 million went on new furniture. But, as with many Russian emigrés, he was finding life abroad a touch dull, and he was only too thrilled when an old friend from Moscow got in touch. Yakubovsky had met General Konstantin Kobets back in early 1990. Both were standing for the Russian parliament. Both failed at the first hurdle, but Kobets made it to a run-off. Yakubovsky organized his campaign, Kobets won and was grateful for the help.

Kobets had distinguished himself during the coup and was made Yeltsin's personal adviser on military matters. The President said he needed someone to keep tabs on the officers in the army and the KGB. He wanted to ensure that neither organization fell for Rutskoy's promises. Did he know of anyone who could do the job? Kobets said he did. He phoned Yakubovsky who said he would be delighted to return, but on one condition. Kobets had to fly out to Zurich to fetch him, to guarantee his safety.

Yakubovsky was an instant hit. He was given a *dacha*, a bullet-proof Mercedes, diplomatic immunity and a licence to carry firearms. He was appointed a colonel. So popular was he that it was proposed to create for him a super-ministerial post, to coordinate the Ministries of the Interior, Defence and Security.

Yeltsin realized something was wrong. He was a past master at inventing jobs and filling them with his old chums, but he knew little about young Dima. Yakubovsky's appointment to the top job was one of a pile of papers on his desk for signing. Yeltsin scrapped the new job and refused to confer on Yakubovsky the rank of general that he had been promised. Even so, everyone had got used to calling him General Dima. Once again Yakubovsky was proving too hot to handle. Yeltsin ordered an investigation.

A few days later, Yakubovsky's car was stopped at gunpoint by police as it left the *dacha*. Purely by chance he was not in the car at the time. It was not clear who ordered the intimidatory tactics, but they worked. Yakubovsky got the message. He was driven into town a few hours later in a clapped-out old Volga to avoid being recognized. He tried frantically to get hold of Vladimir Shumeiko, a Deputy Prime Minister, a man keen to push himself and Yakubovsky up the hierarchy. Shumeiko was in Washington with other ministers, lobbying the International Monetary Fund for aid. Yakubovsky got through on the phone. 'Don't worry, Dima,' Shumeiko told him. 'I'll fly to Moscow, go to the President, and sort everything out. Go to Toronto and rest.' Yakubovsky slipped out that night. He thought he'd be back in Russia within a week. But Barannikov was by now playing a double game. He had already put the word out that Yakubovsky was a Canadian spy. Yakubovsky was marooned in Toronto.

The year 1992 was drawing to a close. Opposition was mounting to Yeltsin's reforms. Rutskoy had allied himself openly with the hardliners in parliament and their chairman, Ruslan Khasbulatov. They were baying for the blood of Yegor Gaidar, the acting Prime Minister and architect of the changes that they were calling shock therapy. Yeltsin was forced to sacrifice Gaidar and to give up the emergency powers parliament had granted him a year earlier. But the hardliners were still not satisfied. They wanted to change the constitution to trim Yeltsin's powers. The battle lines had been drawn.

The first line of attack in the power struggle was corruption. Accusations flew of kickbacks, underhand trading, links with organized crime. Rutskoy, who had been appointed to head a team investigating crime and corruption, told parliament he had eleven suitcases full of evidence. It just so happened that they all involved his enemies. What documents he showed were flimsy. Both sides searched frantically for material to compromise the other.

Yeltsin's new chief investigator was not known for his purity. Andrei Makarov, a rotund lawyer of limitless ambition, had shot to fame in

Gorbachev's time by defending the public enemy number one, Yuri Churbanov. Churbanov was son-in-law to Leonid Brezhnev, under whose leadership corruption was turned into an art form. There was hardly a Communist official during Brezhnev's era of stagnation who was not on the make. Then, however, the sums were generally small. Churbanov was First Deputy Interior Minister. He was found guilty in 1988 of accepting over $1 million in bribes, mainly in a cotton fraud in Uzbekistan. His misfortune was to coincide with Gorbachev's clampdown on corruption. An example was set. Despite Makarov's best efforts, Churbanov was sentenced to twelve years in a labour camp. One of Makarov's first tasks on his appointment to the Kremlin was to persuade Yeltsin to pardon Churbanov. Yeltsin was happy to oblige. So much for his attacks on party privilege.

Yeltsin had given Makarov free rein to deal with his enemies. Makarov knew that only one man was up to the job. Only one man had the *kompromat*, the compromising material. The problem was, nobody knew where Yakubovsky's loyalties lay. Wasn't he, after all, known to be a friend of Rutskoy and Barannikov?

This was decision time for Yakubovsky. He had been visited by both sides at his Toronto retreat, each begging him for his services. He thought long and hard. It was touch and go. Yeltsin had only recently won a referendum, but once again he was looking a spent force. The army's loyalties were unclear. Still he opted for the President.

It was a top secret operation. The date was Friday, 23 July 1993. Makarov boarded a presidential jet and flew off with several members of Yeltsin's personal guard to Zurich. There they collected Yakubovsky. As the plane was preparing to land at Moscow's government airport at Vnukovo, a detachment from the elite Alpha division, which was loyal to Yeltsin, surrounded the tarmac. 'If they'd found me they would have killed me without a moment's hesitation,' Yakubovsky recalled. 'Too much depended on me.'

He was put inside an armoured Mercedes and taken straight to the Kremlin. Identical limousines took different routes to keep potential pursuers off the scent. Yakubovsky was installed in a three-roomed suite of offices, with a birchwood table big enough to accommodate his computer, hundreds of folders and the trays off which he ate his meals. He began collecting material on Barannikov and Rutskoy, his former friends. He was forbidden to transfer any of the material on to floppy disks. All the material had to stay in one computer. He would sleep either in his office or at one of Yeltsin's guesthouses. Once, when working late in the Kremlin, he was seen by a guard walking up and down in his underpants. There were no frills to Dima.

After working through the weekend, Yakubovsky announced he had come up with the goods.

Yeltsin, meanwhile, was on holiday in Valdai, in the forests of Novgorod, to the north of Moscow. Some of his supporters were worried that, true to form, he had chosen to take time off at a particularly tense period. Parliament was plotting another of its constitutional coups against him. The small bunch of radicals who still stood behind him in the legislature applied to see him urgently. They were led by Sergei Yushenkov. Yeltsin was not particularly pleased at being disturbed, but they had told him it was a matter of national security. 'He was fresh off the tennis court, after a game with his tennis coach and friend Shamil Tarpishev,' Yushenkov recalled. 'Yeltsin was all sweaty, and still in his shorts. We sat down on some garden chairs and we told him he was losing grip of the country, that the enemy was advancing, that another coup was being planned.' They told him Barannikov was now in the hands of the opposition and had to go. Yeltsin listened, thanked them for their concern, but said little.

He did agree to cut short his holiday to return to the Kremlin to meet Yakubovsky. There he was given startling *kompromat* against Barannikov. According to Yakubovsky, Barannikov's wife, Lyudmila, had gone on a shopping spree in Switzerland together with the wife of a deputy interior minister. The trip had been paid for by Birshtein – Rutskoy's millionaire friend. Yeltsin was shown receipts from their Zurich hotel, their return business-class air tickets and more than £200,000 worth of purchases of perfumes, fur coats and watches.

It was devastating news for Yeltsin, who had continued to trust Barannikov. During all the President's tribulations with parliament earlier in the year, the minister had stood staunchly at his side. Or so Yeltsin thought. Radicals in his administration had been urging Yeltsin to get rid of him for a long time. Under Barannikov's leadership, they said, the Security Ministry had fostered extreme right-wing groups and done all that it could to undermine reform.

Four days after Yakubovsky's arrival in Russia, Yeltsin sacked Barannikov. Fortunately for him, he found a convenient pretext. A contingent of Russian border guards had just been murdered by Afghan-trained Muslim rebels in Tajikistan. The Russian Security Ministry was responsible for the border, and Barannikov had apparently failed in his task. Nobody believed for a moment that this was the real cause of his dismissal. Barannikov told his staff at a farewell meeting later that day that he had been brought down on the false allegations of 'faggots'. The men at the KGB were sad to see him go.

Barannikov guessed the evidence must have been the work of Yakubovsky who, he realized, must be back in the country. He was determined to flush him out. The hunt was on. Word reached Yeltsin's entourage that Khasbulatov was about to announce that a 'wanted criminal' was being hidden in the Kremlin. The Prosecutor General,

Valentin Stepankov, an opportunist who had fallen in with the hardliners, was preparing to sign a warrant for Yakubovsky's arrest on charges of unauthorized entry into the country. Word had it that the Security Ministry had prepared a cell for him in Lefortovo jail, where dissidents were incarcerated in the old days.

Yeltsin's men panicked. Yakubovsky had to flee. They assumed the airports were covered. The best way would be to travel incognito by train to Armenia, whose sympathetic government had promised to lay on a plane to get him to the West. Yakubovsky was bundled into a presidential car, which then set off for the Kursk railway station and a train heading for the southern town of Rostov-on-Don. An entire carriage had been taken over by presidential officials and men from Alpha. But as they made their way from the car to the train, the party spotted a journalist from a Moscow newspaper. He had gone to the station on a completely unrelated pretext, having been invited by the police to write about the night-time beat, their battle against down-and-outs, drunks and petty thieves; but he recognized the small delegation, realized he was on to something, and pursued them. Yeltsin's men dashed back into the car and sped across the city trying to lose him. They holed up for a night at a special government retreat, and set off next morning in two BMWs, with false number plates, on an epic journey south. They took a circuitous route along country roads, through the town of Voronezh, into Ukraine, where one of the cars ended up in a ditch. The flustered guards dragged it out in the dead of night, continued back into Russia, to Rostov, and on to the Black Sea resort of Sochi. From there they flew to Armenia; but their problems were not over yet. They tried to fly to Turkey but were refused permission to use its air space. Next option was Iran – but they didn't have visas. So they went to the United Arab Emirates, stopped there overnight, and finally flew on to Frankfurt and then Zurich. Dima had escaped.

Yakubovsky had uncovered some *kompromat* against Yeltsin's enemies, but not as much as the presidential team would have liked. The Yeltsin pack turned its attention to Rutskoy, the self-styled champion of the downtrodden Russian, who had risen in popularity by fulminating about the giving away of Russia's wealth to evil foreigners. It just so happened that two of the main intermediaries in that process were his friend, Birshtein, and Yakubovsky. One of the companies involved was even headed by Rutskoy for a while.

Russia's raw materials were being sold off for a song. It was the quickest and safest way of making millions in the new capitalist environment. Many of the people involved in this trade were out-and-out criminals. Others were ministers, or the friends of ministers, who had set up special funds on behalf of the Russian government. These were supposed to be charitable institutions, financed partly by the state. The most prominent was called *Vozrozhdeniye*, Renewal. Its declared aim was to export metals and use the profits to buy foodstuffs and other basic goods for the poorest in society. Yeltsin was involved at the very beginning, but quickly extricated himself from the web. Rutskoy stayed around longer, but also handed it on. More than 150 commercial structures were associated with *Vozrozhdeniye*, but little of the money ever seemed to go on social welfare. Nobody could quite account for the money.

Shortly after Yakubovsky's dramatic escape, Yeltsin's investigation team called a press conference. Television schedules were suddenly changed to broadcast the conference live – a privilege usually afforded only to the President himself. Sensations were afoot. Makarov lost no time. He accused Rutskoy of stashing away millions of dollars in a Swiss bank account, courtesy of *Vozrozhdeniye*, which he said was running 'an independent economic empire'. Makarov also claimed he had been played a tape of a telephone call between Yakubovsky and Stepankov, in which the Prosecutor General had suggested getting Makarov 'medical treatment'. This, Makarov said, corresponded to 'a plan for my murder'. Yakubovsky, he said, had reported to Toronto police that a shot had been fired into the indicator light of his BMW in his driveway. Close by the car was a letter warning him against 'disturbing AV', as he had done 'Uncle Vitya'. AV were the initials of Rutskoy's first name and patronymic (the Russian second name); Vitya was a reference to Barannikov. Or so Makarov said.

The scandal was used by Yeltsin as an excuse to suspend Rutskoy from office. To dress up the decision as impartial he also ordered that Shumeiko be temporarily removed from the government. Shumeiko had been the main target of the opposition in its counter-claims that many ministers and members of the presidential staff had been involved in corrupt practices.

In the latest instalment of his autobiography, *The View from the Kremlin*, Yeltsin referred to Birshtein, Yakubovsky and the other actors in this tale. With touching innocence, Yeltsin described how on 22 May 1993, in the midst of the corruption fight, Barannikov invited him to his *dacha* to discuss something urgent. Yeltsin was reluctant, but agreed. He believed Barannikov was still one of his. There he was introduced for the first time to Birshtein. Yeltsin was not particularly impressed by what he saw. Barannikov took the hint and said Birshtein had to go, his plane was waiting. As Yeltsin took his leave shortly afterwards, he noticed that Birshtein had not left. The meeting, he wrote, had forced him to do some serious thinking about the powers behind the shadow economy, about the possibility of making money cleanly in Russia. The line beween honest and dishonest business, he concluded, was hazy.

The appearance before me of such a magnate as Boris Birshtein was indicative of the severity of the problem. In order to cross that ethical line, in order to run that red stoplight, under Russian conditions you don't necessarily have to peddle pornography, sell drugs, or deal in contraband cheap goods. Why fool around with such nickel-and-dime stuff? It's easier to buy one government official after another. Birshtein tried to get to the very top – and he almost made it.

Within weeks of suspending Rutskoy, Yeltsin disbanded parliament and ordered elections to a completely new body. The siege of parliament, the White House, had begun. It was hardly surprising that Barannikov rushed to Rutskoy's side.

In December 1993 Yakubovsky was told it was safe to return to Russia again. It was two months since Yeltsin's successful assault on the rebels. The ringleaders, Rutskoy, Khasbulatov and Barannikov, were safely in Lefortovo prison. As he arrived in Moscow, Yakubovsky was asked why he had chosen to come back. 'Why should I live in Canada?' he replied. 'There's nothing for me to do there.' A new political career was on his mind.

What nobody realized at the time was that within two months, the rebels would be freed in an amnesty passed by the new parliament. The pendulum had once again swung against Yeltsin. He thought the elections would produce a more submissive parliament. He had not reckoned on the public mood and the popularity of the men with the simple nationalist slogans – Vladimir Zhirinovsky, the leader of the increasingly powerful far right, and the Communists, who had shown they were not a spent force. Shortly before his triumphant march out of jail, Rutskoy was cleared of the accusations levelled at him.

How did it get to this, that the leader of a former superpower had to rely on the financial ferreting of a young adventurer? Had the government of Russia no other means of seeing off its opponents?

The Rutskoy affair marked the peak in the corruption battle. That it failed spoke volumes for the moral standards of public life. There was hardly a Russian who did not believe that most politicians, pro- and anti-Yeltsin alike, had used their positions in office to enrich themselves. With each accusation, the interest diminished. Everyone knew that the few real attempts that had been made to get to the heart of the problem had been baulked. It was not in the interests of the President, the government or parliament to dig too deeply. The only reason for accusing someone was to score a political point. It no longer mattered whether a particular signature was real or fake. If it was fake it proved little, as nobody in his right mind would put his own name so obviously to bank transactions. There were many more subtle ways of transferring money. If it was real, then it would hardly make the culprit worse than the rest, only unfortunate for being caught out. In any case, there was nothing illegal in having a foreign bank account, or receiving money from another individual. The law was stacked against the investigator. Evidence from telephone tapping or other forms of undercover work was inadmissible in the courts. Nobody who was anybody was ever formally charged.

Yakubovsky's mistake was to have betrayed his erstwhile friends in circles where personal loyalty had always played a bigger role than political conviction. Despite the dangers, however, he resolved to stay in Russia. He became a virtual prisoner, languishing in luxury at his *dacha* but far removed from the political scene. It was at this point that my visit to the *dacha* took place. Dima was trying to make a comeback, and I was intrigued to find out whether he was really as much of an opportunist as he had been made out to be.

I was led up the stairs by the guards. The place was much smaller than I had anticipated. For all Yakubovsky's years in the West, it smacked more of money than taste, with its Soviet-era leather chairs, loud table lamps and state-of-the-art Japanese hi-fi. There was not a picture in sight, only one photograph of Masha, his latest wife, and one of him in the army. Dima had to make do in his gilded cell. He couldn't simply go for a walk in Moscow, it was too dangerous. Wherever he was driven, he was accompanied by a phalanx of protectors.

He was not short of company. Sitting at the dinner table as I arrived were five men and a woman. They did not introduce themselves. After some enquiries, they called themselves business associates. They were also awaiting Dima. They offered me some vodka. I thanked them but declined. I told them I was driving. The assembled let out a roar. 'We don't worry about such things here,' one of them said. 'We've got the police sewn up.'

I recognized one of the guests. Nikolai Gulbinsky averted his gaze. I had first met him in the White House in September 1991, at which time he was press secretary to Rutskoy, no less. I knew Gulbinsky had fallen out with Rutskoy and had fallen on hard times, but I didn't appreciate how effortlessly he had slipped into the enemy camp.

Dima entered. He was in a fluster. Looking at his squat figure in jeans and sweatshirt, his face even younger than his years, it was not hard to imagine Yeltsin's scorn when word got to him that Yakubovsky was about to become a general. Dima cracked a few jokes, yelled at a servant to take his shoes away, closed the partition door to the dining table and slumped on to the *chaise-longue*. A blonde girl in a very mini skirt and very high heels snuggled up next to him. 'I want you,' they groaned to each other. 'What are you up to nowadays?' I asked, trying to hide my embarrassment and put the meeting on to a more serious note. 'Sex,' he replied, as his hand reached up her skirt. Dima was out to impress his friends. They giggled on cue. I went through the stories of his antics in the Kremlin. It was all a joke now, all very simple, he replied. Rutskoy had had to be dealt with, he said, because 'He is full of shit.'

'I came to help the President and the country. I hid. I wasn't here. I was dead throughout all that time, I was like a cosmonaut in space,' Yakubovsky continued. Why was Barannikov sacked? 'He betrayed Yeltsin, he went to the other side.' None of the trouble would have happened if Rutskoy had confined himself to flying planes. 'The quiet time ended when the prick lost the referendum. They screwed up the case against him. You can't get someone simply for holding a Swiss bank account. But don't think he's innocent just because the case was dropped. Russia's not a logical place. It's screwed up. The only thing Russians care about is bread and circuses. Politics is shit. Rutskoy is like a used condom. One should be put on his head, the other lower down to stop him from breeding. I like that line. I could sell you the rights, you know.' What about his friendship with Barannikov and Rutskoy? He wouldn't answer.

Yakubovsky switched moods. 'What you don't realize is that in the summer of 1993 Russia had become ungovernable. It was the law of the jungle, us against them. If I hadn't got rid of Barannikov, imagine what would have happened. The uprising in parliament, with the full force of the KGB behind it. That would have been the end of us all.'

I asked Yakubovsky about his consultancy work. Several top Russian banks had taken him on and were paying him up to $20,000 a month. 'What I earn is enough to live on. They pay me for my knowledge.' Somebody interrupted him. 'Shut up, you faggot,' he yelled. 'Am I a faggot? Definitely not. There are so many prats and poofs around. I respect Yeltsin but he doesn't act resolutely enough. The country has been out of control for years. They fucked over our Tsar and since then there's been no order.'

I touched a raw nerve when I asked about his safety. 'I could teach you to shoot in five minutes,' he retorted. 'Why do I need bodyguards?' He beckoned me to the entrance of his bedroom alongside, told me to stand still and not flinch. He then did a couple of karate chops, leg kicks and other contortions. His socks just missed my head. 'Why do I need to walk around Moscow's streets? People invite me to their homes, I get driven straight up to the entrance, or I invite them here. Yeltsin surrounds himself with jerks. If I were in power, I'd restore order within a week.' Yakubovsky was yesterday's man, a metaphor for an era everyone hoped had passed. But he knew too much about too many people to be left in peace.

Part II

2

The Magic Touch

In May 1991 it all seemed so different. It was a time of uncertainty, anxiety, but also a time of no little hope, invested in one man. It was midnight inside the Arctic Circle, and the sky was still bright. This was Murmansk, the most northerly industrial city in the world. We were following the campaign trail of Boris Yeltsin, the people's champion. The Communist hardliners were retrenching, goading Gorbachev to clamp down on the democratic experiment he had begun. Joint army and police patrols had been deployed on the streets of major cities. The military was reasserting its muscle in the Baltics. In Moscow, barely a day passed without a warning of a coup.

Murmansk was quintessentially Russian grey. The snow would lie on the ground for ten months a year and the sun seldom shone. Only during the 'white nights', the few weeks that passed for summer, did the city come to life. Yeltsin had chosen his moment. As we checked into our hotel the streets were still bustling, the town's two passable restaurants were still serving. Competition, however, had not yet set in. 'They're both crap,' said the receptionist when invited to recommend the better. 'Norway's not far away.' Not that many of the locals had been there. Murmansk's 500,000 inhabitants earned twice the national average at the time, compensation for having to live in the frozen wastes. But money wasn't the issue. There was little to spend it on, apart from getting drunk. There was a yearning for change across the generation divide, from factory workers, to pensioners, to officers at the naval base. This was fertile Yeltsin territory.

Hundreds of people went to the airport to greet him, at his first port of call on a trek across the country. They had not been herded in by their trade unions, as was the practice in the old days; they had come out of genuine curiosity. Here was a man who had shaken off humiliation at the hands of the Communist elite. Here was a real *muzhik*, a real Russian man. He did not let them down, his voice growling into the microphones: 'I will be President. There is no alternative.'

First stop next morning, bright and early, was the Murmansk Fish Processing Factory, down by the harbour. The plant was one of the largest of its kind in the Soviet Union, and one of the city's biggest employers. Yet not one of Murmansk's fish shops had any fresh fish in them, only the odd tin of sprats on a good day, and row upon row of tins of mango juice from Cuba. Nobody had ever seen a fresh mango down in these parts, let alone an apple or orange. This was all part of the Soviet 'economic miracle', part of a system in which Yeltsin had made his career but had late in life learnt to loathe. Once again, the crowds lined the street, slipping in the mud from the snow that had only just melted and craning their necks for a better view. 'Boris Nikolayevich, you are our last hope,' they shouted as he entered the factory. This was a clarion call heard all across Russia that year.

Inside, the management had prepared a display of fresh shrimps, herrings and turbot, elegantly arranged on a lace-covered table. They could do all sorts here with fish, as testified by the tubs of cranberry-flavoured fish oil, low-cholesterol pastes, even fish chewing gum. None of it was much use. The guest of honour moved quickly to the cavernous factory floor, skipping persistent offers to try the produce. Instead he began to interrogate the managers: why were the goods not reaching the shops? It was the most obvious of all questions and it lay at the heart of so much misery. Why did the people of Murmansk, and every other city, town and village in the USSR have to queue for hours, string bags under their arms, every day of their lives in case *anything* might become available on the streets? The answer was equally simple. More than 90 per cent of the fish caught in Murmansk's port, one of the most important in the country, was handed over to the central ministries in Moscow. The bureaucrats ordered that as much as possible be exported to the West for hard currency. They kept most of the money for themselves and made a hash of distributing the rest.

A year on, I would see the absurdity of the system from the other end of the chain. I was in Muynak, what had once been a thriving port on the Aral Sea in newly independent Uzbekistan. Almost all the townfolk there had worked for years in the fish canning factory. Then, thanks to a showcase project devised by the Kremlin in the early 1980s to divert the rivers, to irrigate new cotton fields and meet absurd production targets, the sea shrank. It was an act of ecological vandalism in which the Communist leaders excelled. Muynak ended up more than twenty miles from the shore, leaving the workers with no fish and no jobs. The bureaucrats came up with a brainwave they thought would solve the problem. The fish caught in Murmansk would be transported to Muynak – a five-day odyssey in grimy trains and lorries across thousands of miles from the Arctic to Central Asia – to keep the factory in production. That little idea kept the people of Muynak going for several years.

Not only did the Murmansk plant have no say in where its produce went, it could not even decide for itself what kind of machinery to use. Now it was lumbered with Japanese-built state-of-the-art conveyor belts, but with no yen or dollars to pay for the spare parts. All the factory wanted to do was to control its own affairs. 'We're trying to become self-managing,' screamed Yuri Manakov, the deputy general director, above the din of the machines. 'We don't like begging for help.' Yeltsin nodded and promised to help.

A fortnight later, on 12 June, Yeltsin trounced the opposition in Murmansk, as he did across Russia. In truth, the competition was not particularly tough, but it was still a remarkable vote of confidence for a man hounded out of the Politburo by Gorbachev and the hardliners he was seeking to impress. Yeltsin won 58 per cent of the vote, well ahead of Nikolai Ryzhkov, the former Prime Minister, who was known as the 'weeping Bolshevik' for his tendency to burst into tears when criticized in parliament. Third out of the six candidates was Zhirinovsky, a complete unknown at the start of the campaign, who secured a remarkable 8 per cent of the vote with his promises to reduce the price of vodka and make Russia a great power again (in that order of importance).

The election victory was a vindication of Yeltsin's crusade to clear his name. He had been picked out of provincial obscurity by Gorbachev and appointed to head the Moscow city Communist Party in 1985. Like other good Gorbachev men, Yeltsin was expected to criticize old Party habits, ruffle a few feathers, and stop there. That was the new way. Improving life meant improving the Party. This was the policy behind Gorbachev's slogan of 'socialist choice', reform guided from above. Yeltsin, the novice in the capital, did not grasp the subtle distinction. He had learnt that the main reason why none of the shops had anything decent in them was because the goods were being siphoned off before they got to the shelves. He marched unannounced into shops, demanding to see the goods hidden under the table. He then had the bosses sacked. He started to use the word 'mafia' in public. He was breaking all the conventions, challenging the unwritten code between the party, which was supposed to run the country, and the crooks, who were in charge of the streets. The system had suited both groups, as long as the number of people involved remained small and nobody flaunted his wealth in public. Gorbachev's slow moves to the free market benefited the elite, as it ensured that they and they alone would control who was beginning to make money, and who was not.

One of Yeltsin's first associates was Mikhail Poltoranin. Here was a man cut from the same cloth as Yeltsin: burly, tough, jaded after a life of intrigues within the party structures. Poltoranin was a senior correspondent at *Pravda* when he befriended the Moscow Party boss in 1986. He soon concluded that Yeltsin's haranguing of corrupt officials, his trips on buses and trams, were more than a populist touch. 'He would arrive at a factory during the night shift and head straight for the toilet. He worked from the assumption that the toilets reflected the state of the enterprise. Word got around and suddenly everyone was upgrading their toilets,' Poltoranin recalled. Yeltsin moved on to the quality of cutlery in canteens. 'They began getting rid of the old aluminium spoons and forks, replacing them with better quality nickel ones. They trouble was workers would nick them. It was a disaster for the public catering services.' During all the shortages of the 1980s, any item at the workplace that was in short supply in the shops, such as lightbulbs, would disappear.

Soon after they met, Yeltsin made Poltoranin editor of *Moskovskaya Pravda*, the Moscow Party newspaper, which then started to publish Yeltsin's speeches in full. To millions Yeltsin was seen as a startling departure from the past. He was already the talk of the streets. But at the Central Committee they were being bombarded with complaints by Party workers and factory bosses about the upstart. For Gorbachev it was all very inconvenient. He didn't appreciate somebody else hijacking his assault on the old vested interests, and doing it with considerably more vigour. As the denunciations and the pressure grew, so Yeltsin's health deteriorated. He decided he had had enough and wrote to Gorbachev, advising him of his intention to resign. Gorbachev didn't respond. Yeltsin forced the pace further, using a Central Committee meeting in October 1987 to speak out against the *nomenklatura*, the ruling elite. Shortly thereafter he collapsed under the strain. On Gorbachev's orders he was dragged out of his hospital bed and made guest of honour at a special session called to carry out his political execution. Speaker after speaker champed at the bit to outdo one another in the viciousness of the charges levelled against Yeltsin. He was derided as an unbalanced demagogue, ambitious, immature, mistrustful and untrustworthy, a traitor. He was demoted to the job of First Deputy Chairman of Gosstroi, the state construction organization – virtual banishment for a man so important. But denouncing the faith did not come easily for a man who had risen through the Party ranks. Despite the humiliation, Yeltsin tried to apologize to his comrades and win back their favour.

The experience left a wound that would never heal. Accounts of Yeltsin's original speech and the follow-up meeting spread like wildfire across Moscow. They had not been reported in the official press. The more outrageous each rumour was, the more it was believed and the more Yeltsin rose in public esteem. Here was a dissident from the heart of the establishment. It took some time for Yeltsin to recover his strength of will. He survived the emotional confusion and the tedium at Gosstroi only through the loyalty of many of the staff. Yeltsin came to rely on a close-knit community, on the camaraderie of close friends. It was a habit he would take with him to the Kremlin. It would dictate his work patterns, and his appointments. He would remember old friends and stick by them through thick and thin, often when political exigencies dictated otherwise.

Poltoranin was tainted by his alliance with Yeltsin and forced to leave *Moskovskaya Pravda* for a more lowly job with the Novosti news agency.

Within a couple of years he would join up with Yeltsin again. Another of the original stalwarts was Alexander Korzhakov. He had been assigned from the KGB's Ninth Directorate, responsible for the security of top leaders, to become one of Yeltsin's bodyguards in 1985, and rarely left his side. Korzhakov soon realized that the KGB was one of the forces most hostile to Yeltsin, that it would do virtually anything in its power to disable him, politically or physically. When Yeltsin was expelled from his Moscow job, Korzhakov offered to stay on, without pay if necessary. From that moment on, Yeltsin put his personal security entirely in the hands of Korzhakov. The mutual distrust between Yeltsin and the KGB was intense. Korzhakov drove Yeltsin around in his Niva jeep, guarding him with a dedication well beyond the requirements of professional service. Yeltsin rewarded his fealty by consulting him on many a major decision. 'While outwardly he seems very simple, behind this simplicity is a sharp mind and an excellent and clear head,' Yeltsin wrote.

Apart from Korzhakov, the disillusioned Yeltsin of 1988 relied on two men. One was Lev Sukhanov, who would linger in the background throughout Yeltsin's career; the other was Alexei Tsaregorodtsev, who would later go on to work for Rutskoy. These men helped pick Yeltsin up, persuaded him to return to the offensive, to take part in some of the many anti-Communist demonstrations that were taking place in Moscow and other big cities. Yeltsin joined the growing band of radicals at some of the rallies, denouncing Gorbachev's 'half-measures' and calling for a radical transformation of the party. Demonstrators at these gatherings would be hauled away by police for unfurling the white, blue and red tricolor of pre-revolutionary times. Whenever Yeltsin did appear, the crowds flocked to see him.

One of Gorbachev's 'half-measures' was his plan in 1989 for the Soviet Union's first real parliament, the Congress of People's Deputies. With the Party proving more intransigent than he had bargained for, Gorbachev's aides came up with the idea of creating a discussion forum that would alter the political balance and provide him with more muscle with which to beat the hardliners. It was a brave enough step, but Gorbachev didn't want it to go too far. Most of the 2,250 seats in the new parliament were rigged in favour of traditional Communists. Yet where the radicals took on the established candidates, they invariably won – and the most spectacular victory was Yeltsin's, in beating the director of the Zil car factory, Yevgeny Brasov, nine to one, in the single open constituency for the whole of Moscow. The dirty tricks campaign in the media, coordinated by the Politburo, backfired. Yeltsin was back representing the city, and he and the radicals finally had a chance to talk directly to the people.

In its first year, parliament had almost the entire Soviet population glued to their television sets night after night to watch unedited broadcasts of proceedings. This was democracy in action for the first time. Yet in that period Yeltsin rarely shone. His speeches paled in comparison with those of Andrei Sakharov, the father of the dissident movement. New figures were also making a mark, such as Anatoly Sobchak, a lawyer from Leningrad, and Gavriil Popov, an economics professor from Moscow. Sakharov embodied the spirit of the opposition, but he was frail. The radicals were not short of thinkers. They needed a tough and uncompromising leader to fight their battles. Yeltsin, for his part, needed a broad political base and an articulate political cause upon which to pin his personal bitterness against Gorbachev.

The meeting of minds took place in the House of Cinema, the headquarters of the film-makers' union, in July 1989. The occasion was the inaugural meeting of the Inter-Regional Group, an umbrella organization for the radical 'deputies', as members of parliament were known. Those two days provided one of those rare interludes when optimism appeared justified. The group combined sharp intellects, a sense of purpose and an awareness of the possible. Decisions were taken democratically, but not chaotically. When it came to a vote on the group's leader, Yeltsin easily won; but it was deemed more appropriate to share the job. Yeltsin was joined by Sakharov, Popov and Yuri Afanasyev, another party stalwart and late convert to radicalism. Other, younger figures, such as Arkady Murashev and Sergei Stankevich, had come to the fore through grass-roots discussion clubs. It was Afanasyev who won the loudest ovation with his closing speech. 'Gorbachev is justifiably regarded as the man who launched reform,' he said, 'but the time has passed when he can remain the leader of both *perestroika* and the *nomenklatura*. He has to make a choice.' Gorbachev never did.

For Yeltsin, the Inter-Regional Group marked acceptance by the intelligentsia of Moscow and Leningrad, most of whom had hitherto distrusted him. He was too much of a provincial hillbilly for their liking. On coming to power Gorbachev had allowed them to chat and write away in their kitchen salons without too much obstruction. But by the end of the 1980s the agenda had moved on. Gorbachev's unwillingness, or inability, to go beyond the strict bounds he had set to *perestroika* had forced the liberals to turn to Yeltsin, a man they had previously dubbed a populist and demagogue. It was not a natural meeting of minds, but an alliance necessitated by political reality. This complex web of relationships was to lie at the heart of Yeltsin's future successes and failures.

Manezh Square, a large expanse beneath the walls of the Kremlin, on a Sunday morning was the place to be seen. With each challenge to Gorbachev – from the striking miners, from the Baltic states, from parliament itself – the crowds grew larger, the calls for change became more brazen. From the top of a rickety battle bus parked in front of the Hotel Moskva, the radicals would address crowds in their tens of thousands, a sea of banners, each more caustic than the last. It was a time for people-spotting. Members of the cultural world were joining the bandwagon, self-consciously at first. Yevgeny Yevtushenko would start reading his poems. Taboos were picked off, one by one. It was now a commonplace to call for the Party's monopoly on power to be broken. With each concession he made, Gorbachev infuriated the Party orthodoxy and only encouraged the radicals to press for more.

Whatever his popularity at home, Yeltsin was still scoffed at in the West. He was seen as an adventurer, a destabilizing factor. Here was a man who had felt himself out of place when he moved from his home base of Sverdlovsk, in the Urals, to Moscow. Already in his late fifties, he knew little about the outside world, having made only a few brief trips abroad, usually to 'fraternal' socialist countries. Here was a man who acted on impulse, the very antithesis of the more manageable Gorbachev.

Yeltsin had no real team to speak of, only a collection of individuals whose numbers increased as his political revival gathered speed. Some of his antics at home, and travels abroad, led to disaster. The most infamous was his 'bourbon tour' of the United States in September 1989. Yeltsin had been invited by a Californian institute on a lecture tour that was to take in eleven cities in a mere seven days. He experienced all the reactions of a first-time tourist: jet-lag, disorientation and naïve awe. He was bewitched by the Statue of Liberty which he overflew by helicopter. After a ten-minute visit to a supermarket in Houston, Yeltsin staggered out in shock. 'When I saw those shelves crammed with hundreds, thousands of cans, cartons, and goods of every possible sort, for the first time I felt quite literally sick with despair for the Soviet people,' he wrote. At least he was brave enough to admit it. One Soviet general visiting Britain a few months later suggested the supermarket he had just been shown might have been stocked especially to please him. So often had it been practised, from the time of the Tsars, that Russians had a word for the window-dressing that accompanied leaders' visits: *pokazukha*.

Yeltsin had already been rumoured to be a big drinker. The reputation did his image among Russians no harm, but in the relatively austere American context a more circumspect approach was called for. Pavel Voshchanov, a political commentator for a leading newspaper, *Komsomolskaya Pravda*, was a new recruit to the team. He was one of only five aides who accompanied Yeltsin across America. They were approaching the end of the trip, which had received a cool reaction from a sceptical American media, not enhanced by reports of Yeltsin staggering drunk into a breakfast meeting. The official version was that he had had difficulty sleeping and was under the influence of heavy tranquillizers.

The small Yeltsin team was staying at the home of a rich entrepreneur on Miami Beach.

When we arrived, this man's daughter greeted us and said we should help ourselves to the food and drink. The official functions had finally ended at about 11 p.m. We got back to the flat and one of our group suggested we take the whisky out of the fridge and go sit by the sea. We took a bottle of Jack Daniels and some fruit and went to the beach. We were completely exhausted. Yeltsin and the others saw us from the hotel and came down to join us. The five of us stood by the sea and drank. When it was time go back in I started looking around for somewhere to leave the bottle. I didn't want just to dump it on the beach. There were no rubbish bins, so we decided to leave it all – the plastic cups, the remains of the fruit and the empty bottle – on a bench and in the morning someone would clear it away. A few days passed and articles started appearing in the American press about how we had boozed our way across the States.

Voshchanov believed that the Americans and the KGB could have been in league in disseminating a sensationalized version of the story. Still, it said something about the visitors' lack of elementary caution.

In Washington, the Bush administration meted out rough treatment on the visitor. Yeltsin was desperate to be seen in the Oval Office with the President. When he was told a meeting was not on the cards he lost his temper in the grounds of the White House. He was spirited instead through a side door to meet Brent Scowcroft, the National Security Adviser, while Bush 'dropped by' to chat for a few moments – the traditional way of dealing with embarrassing guests. After the meeting Scowcroft described Yeltsin to his colleagues as a 'buffoon'.

The problems with his Western audiences persisted for several years. While Gorbachev was away in Japan in April 1991, Yeltsin travelled to Strasbourg to address the European Parliament. By then he was already Chairman of the Russian Parliament, theoretically the chief representative of more than 150 million people. But he was treated to a harangue from Jean-Pierre Cot, a French socialist who, like many in Europe, believed Yeltsin was undermining Gorbachev's 'social democratic dream'. A distraught Yeltsin tried to interrupt him, to put his case. 'If you don't want to face unpleasant questions, don't come to a democratic parliament,' retorted Cot. At the end of the trip, Yeltsin went to Paris. He sat impatiently on his hotel bed waiting for the call from the Elysée Palace for an audience with Mitterrand. The French President was at that very moment entertaining Anatoly Lukyanov, a man who a few months later would betray Gorbachev. Andrei Fyodorov, Deputy Foreign Minister at the time, was with Yeltsin. The French trip had a long-term effect on him, he said. 'He kept on saying to me: "Why don't they understand me? I'll be President whether they like it or not." '

Shortly after Yeltsin's return from America late in 1989, Moscow was abuzz with rumours that he had survived another assassination attempt.

Late one night a soaked and bedraggled Yeltsin appeared at a police post guarding the approach to the *dachas* of several top people. Vadim Bakatin, the Interior Minister, was asked by parliament to report on the incident. He concluded that Yeltsin had told police he had been on his way to visit friends. He had chosen to walk the last part of the journey on foot and sent his driver home. Suddenly he was bundled into another car by unknown assailants and flung into the Moscow River, emerging some 300 yards downstream. The police helped Yeltsin dry out his clothes, and his family collected him later. Yeltsin asked the police not to report the incident, but the next day Bakatin made his report public. There were considerable discrepancies between Yeltsin's initial story and the official version. Yeltsin told parliament there had, after all, been no attack. 'That is my private life,' he concluded cryptically. In the first volume of his autobiography, *Against the Grain*, Yeltsin said he had been knocked off the bridge in what he called 'an organised, premeditated act of provocation'.

Everyone in the adjoining village of Nikolina Gora had his own version. Yeltsin, they said, was carrying flowers. Were they for a lover? Did the jealous husband find out and seek revenge? A variation on the flower theme was that Yeltsin was hoping to present them to Ryzhkov, who was celebrating his birthday with friends; but as he approached the *dacha*, he was summarily despatched by Ryzhkov's bodyguards. Yeltsin might have alluded to this version when he said in his autobiography that he did not reveal the true cause because it could have led to strikes in his defence. Ryzhkov was Prime Minister at the time. The only point on which each story fully coincided was, naturally, drink.

Yeltsin's small team was so short of experience that he was willing to accept anyone who knew his or her field. Galina Starovoitova first started working with him in July 1989. An ethnographer by profession, she was a member of the Inter-Regional Group and an avowed radical.

> I phoned him up and said, 'Boris Nikolayevich, there's something I'd like to discuss with you.' He told me to come round immediately. We spoke in whispers in his office. We knew Gorbachev had got the KGB to bug Yeltsin's office. Naturally Gorbachev was very frightened of him. I arrived and offered Yeltsin my services. I suggested that I could write or help him prepare his speech for the forthcoming party conference.'

Starovoitova became Yeltsin's chief adviser on nationalities.

The entourage consisted of two distinct groups. One was irreverently dubbed the 'Sverdlovsk mafia', old chums from his Party fiefdom days; the other was the Moscow set of younger, more radical deputies. Everyone was cultivating his own patch, jockeying for influence. Unlike

Gorbachev and previous Party leaders who had an established hierarchy and committees of experts to choose, Yeltsin just had his friends and followers. The structures were built up from scratch. The more his political stock rose, the greater the tension became between the two camps.

One man straddled the divide. Gennady Burbulis was known as 'the Grey Cardinal'. Rarely was a politician to arouse such vehement reactions. Yeltsin met him first at the Inter-Regional Group, even though Burbulis hailed from the President's home town, where the man who was to become the chief ideologue of radical anti-Communism spent many years teaching Marxism–Leninism at Sverdlovsk's polytechnic. Burbulis had great designs for himself and his boss, while Yeltsin was impressed by his sharp mind and organizational skills.

Many of the radicals were young, brainy, and untainted by long careers in Communist administration. On a personal level, Yeltsin felt ill at ease with them. He was not a great socializer. He was a family man and a bit of a loner, and he had little to do with his political allies after hours. He preferred the company of the people he had worked with in his Party days. Viktor Ilyushin had known Yeltsin since 1975. A former welder, he had been head of the Party organization in a district of Sverdlovsk where the city's most important factory, Uralmash, was based. He moved on to work with Yeltsin in the Moscow Party, but when Yeltsin was sacked Ilyushin was sent off to Afghanistan to serve as a political adviser to the government Moscow had installed there. He returned to his mentor in 1990.

Yuri Petrov was another member of the clan. Dour, efficient and without a hint of radicalism, Petrov was Yeltsin's personal choice to succeed him as First Secretary in Sverdlovsk. He too was 'exiled', as Ambassador to Cuba. Yeltsin brought him back to become his Chief of Staff in 1991. A third old-timer on whom Yeltsin came to rely was Yuri Skokov, but he came from Moscow. Skokov was the archetypal factory director, having spent his entire career in the military–industrial complex up to the time Yeltsin met him in 1987. Yeltsin saw him as open to new ideas of management and ready to shake up old work practices. He didn't enquire particularly about his politics. These men had little time for the Inter-Regional Group, but they went along with it because it was providing Yeltsin with a platform, and in Yeltsin they saw a vehicle to further advancement.

In the Soviet parliament, Yeltsin was as yet making little headway. However, the next phase in Gorbachev's gradual reforms was to prove more propitious for him. Each of the fifteen republics was to have its own parliament, while Russia, on the national level, would have a Congress that would meet about twice a year to discuss major constitutional issues. From its ranks would be elected a smaller standing parliament, the

Supreme Soviet. The new legislatures would have a strictly limited remit, but this time no seats would be set aside for Communist organizations.

The elections to the Russian parliament in March 1990 were, within a Communist context, as fair as could have been hoped for. The Yeltsin team was to argue in future years, during its battle with parliament, that it was no more legitimate than the Soviet parliament had been. That claim was spurious. Certainly, some individuals who had failed to make it in 1989 and who were genuinely second-rate did succeed in 1990; certainly they were elected in a different era; but the process itself had been more or less democratic. Yeltsin chose this time to stand in his home Sverdlovsk constituency. Again he won more than 80 per cent of the vote.

Overall, the parliament was balanced evenly between Yeltsin supporters and Communists. What was particularly worrying for Gorbachev was that many of the Communists were just as opposed to him as they were to Yeltsin. Yeltsin's successes in the previous years had shattered the veneer of consensus in the Party. It was becoming acceptable to criticize Gorbachev from viewpoints other than the radical. Many were attacking him openly for abandoning the satellite states of Eastern Europe. His dilution of Party authority was now seen as an act of treachery.

As was to happen so often in the latter years of his rule, Gorbachev got his calculations woefully wrong. Local elections were held at the same time as the vote for a new Russian parliament and radicals swept the board. Popov, the professor, took charge in Moscow and Sobchak in Leningrad. In the Baltics and in the republics of Armenia and Georgia, independence-seeking Popular Fronts were victorious. Democratic Russia, a group to which all the prominent radicals belonged, became the most important political force in opposition to the Communist Party.

Gorbachev believed the subordinate republican parliaments would carry little weight. After all, what was Russia within the mighty Soviet Union? As a republic, it might account for more than half the Soviet population and over two-thirds of its territory, but the Russian Federation had never carried any political clout. That was now about to change. Gorbachev had inadvertently given Yeltsin a perfect platform.

Burbulis had ousted all the challengers and had become Yeltsin's undisputed right-hand man. Yeltsin needed little persuasion to put himself up as Chairman of the new parliament. He needed to win over a simple majority of the deputies – no mean feat. Burbulis coordinated the campaign. Gorbachev, his economic strategy in tatters, his own reputation at an all-time low, tried desperately to stop his rival. The President's team wooed uncommitted deputies, even resorting to supporting the candidacy of a particularly nefarious old-timer. Ivan Polozkov had made his name in the southern city of Krasnodar by closing down 300 cooperatives. These first examples of the tentative 'social market' Gorbachev hoped to build were too much for Polozkov. He called them a social evil, a 'malignant tumour'. But for Gorbachev in this state any opponent of Yeltsin's would do. First he tried Polozkov, who failed at the first hurdle, then another less extreme candidate. Yeltsin finally won out at the third attempt, by the narrowest of margins. He had returned to the very top.

Within minutes of the result being announced, Yeltsin left the Kremlin through the Spassky Gates and marched on to Red Square. As he made his way down the hill towards the hotel where the deputies had their offices he was mobbed by crowds. His supporters cut across all age barriers, but most noticeable were the elderly. 'Boris Nikolayevich, save us, save us. In God's name help us!' cried one woman as she knelt at his feet. Korzhakov, his bodyguard, picked her up. 'Don't get upset, granny,' he said. Yeltsin, his faced etched with embarrassment, slipped away.

At his first press conference, Yeltsin cut a formidable figure. Sitting on the dais of the Grand Kremlin Palace, where the Russian Congress held its sessions, his voice booming across the hall, he promised Gorbachev he would seek cooperation, but warned him the Russian Federation now had a leader of its own.

For all the bluster, all the responsibility thrust upon him, Yeltsin took a strangely detached view of the Supreme Soviet. He had little time for the intricacies of parliamentary life. He would often leave the chairing of sessions and committees to his number two, Khasbulatov. It was a task Khasbulatov took to with ease. His control of parliament was impressive, more for its slyness than its authority. Khasbulatov's biggest handicap was his nationality. Being a Chechen was in the eyes of most Russians synonymous with being a crook. The small autonomous republic in the northern Caucasus had for years been associated with shady elements. Chechens reigned over Moscow's farmers' markets and street stalls, controlling many of the criminal operations. Yet he was just the kind of person Yeltsin needed in the chamber, and Yeltsin saw no reason to distrust him.

The rules, the structures of parliament, were formulated as the deputies went along. Yeltsin needed a body to formulate policy. It was given the unwieldly title of the Supreme Consultative Coordinating Council, comprising several of the country's top academics and politicians. To the surprise of many, Yeltsin appointed as its head Burbulis, not a more well-known figure such as Sobchak. To the public Burbulis was an unknown quantity; to Yeltsin he was indispensable. He would act like a sponge, assimilating the best advice from all around and filtering it into bite-size chunks for his master. Usually he would take credit for the ideas, even if they weren't his. Throughout the early Yeltsin years, Burbulis would be moved from one job to another, many of them created by Yeltsin specifically for him, irrespective of the official hierarchy.

Yeltsin's cooperation with Gorbachev went in fits and starts. He thought he had struck a *modus vivendi* with the Soviet leader when

Gorbachev agreed to co-sponsor a radical economic programme devised by a young economist, Grigory Yavlinsky. The 500 Day Programme was flawed on many points, but for its time it was a notable breakthrough. Gorbachev at first supported the working group, but just as the project was nearing its conclusion, he disowned it. He had been threatened by army chiefs and hardliners in the Politburo that he was taking the country to the brink, that the time had come to rein in reform and stamp out the radicalism that was threatening to take over the political agenda.

As Gorbachev rejected the plan, Yeltsin was nowhere to be seen. He was taking time off increasingly often and absenting himself from important meetings. His health had once again become a problem. Earlier in the year he had hurt his back in a plane crash. He had been touring Spain and was flying between Cordoba and Barcelona when his small aircraft developed technical problems. It made a crash landing in heavy winds at a remote airstrip and hit the ground hard. Yeltsin was taken to hospital where the doctors said that if they didn't operate he could be crippled for life. The operation was successful and within a few days he was able to walk, aided with a corset. He was extremely grateful to the Barcelona surgeons, and would come to rely on them many times in the future. According to one deputy who was travelling with him, Yeltsin did not receive one phone call or telegram from his political colleagues while in his hospital bed. His supporters put it about that the KGB had sabotaged the plane.

A couple of weeks after the crash he was back in Moscow. Just as he was most needed in parliament to extract something from the aborted 500 Day Programme, Yeltsin aggravated his spinal injury again when his Volga car was rammed in the side as he was being driven to work. Once more, the incident had elements of mystery. The official police report showed discrepancies. On the day of the accident police said Yeltsin had not been injured, but later they changed their version to speak of slight concussion and bruises. Yeltsin appeared in his office the next day sporting a large bruise on his head and complaining that concussion had affected his eyesight. But he never mentioned his back.

The trouble with Yeltsin's parliament was that it had no legislative clout. The great optimism of 1989 and early 1990 was disappearing as Gorbachev appeared to abandon the reformers and move towards the hardliners. Yeltsin's own legislature was unable to enact reforms on its own. Both sides expended considerable time fighting a 'war of laws', each cancelling the other's decisions. Russia had already declared its 'sovereignty'. Russian laws now took precedence over Soviet laws on Russian soil. But it counted for little. Gorbachev was still very much at the helm. He had strengthened his own powers by having parliament appoint him to the new post of President. But he didn't dare to put himself to the popular vote. It took the dramatic warning of a coup by Eduard

Shevardnadze, the Soviet Foreign Minister, in front of Congress in December 1990, to alert the world to the seriousness of the Communists' regrouping.

Yeltsin had spent some time the previous summer cultivating the leaders of the Baltic states. Take as much sovereignty as you can swallow, he had told the republics. When Gorbachev allowed the hardliners to send troops to Vilnius and Riga, the capitals of Lithuania and Latvia, in January 1991, in a belated attempt to stem the tide towards independence, he presented his radical foes with a great opportunity. Yeltsin was back in his element, travelling to the Baltics and promising support for their struggle. He was in an enviable position, with almost none of the responsibilities of office but a powerful platform from which to attack Gorbachev. Yet to many hardliners in his own parliament, Yeltsin was going too far. They were happy for the Russian parliament to be used against Gorbachev, they were happy for some notion of nationhood to be developed for the old Russian state. But that was where it stopped. They saw no reason to undermine the Communist Party even more, and no benefit in encouraging the centrifugal tendencies across the Soviet Union.

Sergei Baburin was a lawyer, just turned thirty, from Siberia. A cross between Trotsky and a devil in a medieval icon, with his goatee beard and white streak in his hair, he stood apart from the rest. Like many ambitious young men of the time, the dean of the law faculty at Omsk University joined the radical movement. When he criticized Gorbachev on television, the head of the local broadcasting company was sacked. Baburin shared Yeltsin's contempt for the complacent Party bureaucrats, but towards the end of 1990 their paths began to diverge. Baburin became one of the Russian leader's more charismatic critics. 'I went into open opposition when Yeltsin went to the Baltics and appealed to the UN to do battle with Moscow and appealed to army conscripts not to obey orders,' he said. 'This was the moment when he overstepped the boundaries of what might be termed "permissible mistakes".'

Yeltsin, as he would later admit, was about to make two more mistakes. He had almost never received fair press coverage, and when he finally managed to gain a long interview on national television in February 1991, he got carried away. For almost all the programme he patiently fended off tough questioning. In the last five minutes he let rip. 'I warned in 1987 that Gorbachev hungers for absolute power. He has shown this already and has brought the country to dictatorship. I distance myself from the policy of the president and advocate his immediate resignation and the handing over of power to a collective body, the Council of the Federation.' This was Yeltsin's first open call for Gorbachev to go. There was now little holding him back. Addressing a small opposition meeting a week later, he proclaimed: 'Let's declare war on the leadership of the country, the leadership which has led us into this quagmire.' Even for some of the radicals this was too much. They knew that however much they disliked his 'half-measures', such unbridled attacks on Gorbachev only played into the hands of more invidious forces. Yeltsin had shown himself at his most belligerent and unpredictable.

Yet on the streets he could do no wrong. A crowd of up to a quarter of a million flooded Manezh Square and overflowed into adjoining streets, all the way to the Bolshoi Theatre. A tape of Yeltsin's 'war' speech was relayed. Messages of support were read out from the Baltic leaders, from the miners in Siberia. One elderly woman held up a giant banner which read: 'Yeltsin, the truth, the hope, the love of Russia' alongside a small cut-out of the Madonna and Child. Next to her stood a woman with a placard that said: 'Saddam Gorbachev'. 'It's us against the criminals,' said a retired lieutenant-colonel, a Party member of forty years standing. 'If they do anything to Yeltsin, we'll march in front of the tanks.'

Yeltsin's foes in parliament had forced an emergency Congress, with one motion on the agenda, no confidence in Yeltsin. Yeltsin's strategists, led by Burbulis, saw that the best way out of the crisis was to increase Yeltsin's powers and make him less dependent on the legislature. Now was the time to create a new post: President of the Russian Federation. This was the most direct of all challenges to Gorbachev, the creation of a job that would directly mirror his, but one that would carry more moral authority by being subject to popular election.

On the eve of the Congress, Democratic Russia had called its supporters on to the streets. Gorbachev responded by deploying 50,000 Interior Ministry troops. More than 100,000 people risked injury to come to Yeltsin's support. Both sides called for restraint, and the march ended peacefully. Said one deputy, Nikolai Travkin, 'We have crossed the threshold of fear.' Travkin was a new breed of politician, a labourer who had kept his distance from the established groups. Now, he was solidly behind Yeltsin. But within a year he and many others like him would turn their backs on the Russian President.

Such was the strength of support for Yeltsin on the streets that the no-confidence threat soon dissipated. The Yeltsin camp struck back, putting to the vote its plans for a change in the constitution to allow for presidential elections. It was passed overwhelmingly. The dramatic turnaround in his fortunes was due largely to three people. One, naturally, was Burbulis, with his behind-the-scenes scheming. Another was Khasbulatov, for guiding proceedings in one direction. The third was a certain Alexander Rutskoy, a disgruntled Communist and military man who had split the Communist caucus in parliament in two. The final decision on whether Russia needed a president of its own was to be decided by a referendum. The question was inserted cunningly on the back of a separate referendum Gorbachev had called to seek approval for his plans to revise the structure of the Soviet Union. Both questions received the required majority, but the day was more Yeltsin's than Gorbachev's.

Andrei Sakharov had died in December 1989, three years after Gorbachev had phoned him to tell him he was free to return to Moscow from internal exile in the city of Gorky. Sakharov had always looked upon Yeltsin with apprehension, but he realized the democratic cause would be lost without him. His widow, Yelena Bonner, was a prominent member of Democratic Russia. Her word counted for much and she did not pull her punches. Among the guests at a gala at the Conservatoire marking the seventieth anniversary of Sakharov's birth were Gorbachev and Yeltsin. Yeltsin was being pulled by his two camps in two directions. Some were telling him to try to work with Gorbachev, others had advised him to go for broke. Having regretted opting for the latter approach a few months earlier, Yeltsin now chose conciliation. He, Gorbachev, and the leaders of eight other republics agreed during days of secretive talks at a government residence to a new peace deal. The 'Nine Plus One' arrangement was vital for Gorbachev in that it urged striking miners, a force that could destroy Gorbachev, to go back to work. The republics agreed to complete work on the Union Treaty, a more devolved version of the USSR. This would be followed within six months by elections to all national organs of power, including Gorbachev's presidency. Yeltsin was roundly criticized by radicals for throwing Gorbachev a lifeline, effectively endorsing government economic policy.

Bonner saw the deal as a carve-up. She heaped criticism on Gorbachev and his support for the criminals at the heart of the Communist establishment. 'Until the party freely gives up all its wealth to the people who really earned it – everything down to the last worthless rouble – Stalinism will still triumph.' Turning her attention to what she called the pseudo-democrats, she said: 'Don't call yourselves friends of Sakharov, those of you who latched on to him after Gorbachev phoned him.' Everyone knew that she had in Yeltsin in mind. Few people on the democratic wing had ever spoken about him like that in public.

The more the opinion polls indicated an outright Yeltsin victory, the more the state-run press heaped invective on him. A bizarre plot had been uncovered involving a shady British businessman and a Deputy Russian Prime Minister in a deal to sell roubles for dollars at preferential rates to buy consumer goods. The Briton fled, the Russian quit. Yeltsin said he knew nothing about it. Such were the figures involved that the episode said more for the inexperience and foolishness of members of Yeltsin's 'shadow' government than for its criminal intent. Nevertheless, the deal was used by ministers in Gorbachev's government as 'evidence' of a Western plot to subvert the economy. It made for snappy reading, but nobody took it too seriously. Nor did they lay too much store by a 'psychological analysis' of Yeltsin by three self-styled professors published in *Pravda*. Based on a study of three recent speeches, the study concluded he was an unpredictable megalomaniac who was personally inadequate and aggressive.

Yeltsin and his backroom team knew that the readers of *Pravda* and other unreconstructed publications were beyond conversion. But there were millions of apolitical, sceptical and anxious voters out there to be won. He was looking for a Vice-President to join his ticket and broaden his appeal. Popov and Sobchak had been considered, but they were too radical. Khasbulatov deserved a reward, but his nationality wouldn't help. Skokov was mooted. Burbulis was the favourite. Instead Yeltsin turned to Rutskoy, the man who had helped him out in parliament a couple of months earlier. Yeltsin's inner circle had collected in one room in the White House to await his verdict. When it came, they were shocked; Burbulis was hurt. Once they had had time to reflect on it, however, several of them praised Yeltsin for making what seemed an inspired choice.

Handsome, tough and young (he was forty-four at the time), Airforce Colonel Rutskoy was a perfect vote-catcher, a perfect Russian patriot. Born in Soviet Ukraine, the son of a tank commander, he had lived wherever his father served. His parents settled in Kursk, a provincial town in southern Russia. Rutskoy joined the local air club before qualifying as a fighter pilot, a prestigious calling for a young man. He made his way steadily through the ranks and was happy to do his duty in Afghanistan. Six years into the war he was shot down and suffered a fractured spine. He was retrieved by Soviet soldiers. He fought off the prospect of life in a wheelchair and by 1988 he was back, flying daily sorties into enemy territory as Deputy Air Force Commander of the 40th Army. Hit by a surface-to-air missile, he ejected and was hunted for five days by *mujahedin* guerrillas. He was wounded in a shoot-out and was a prisoner of Pakistani intelligence for six weeks. They offered him the chance of defecting to Canada. He doggedly refused and was eventually swapped for a Pakistani agent. He was twice awarded the Hero of the Soviet Union medal.

Rutskoy had known little outside military life when he plunged into the political maelstrom of the late Gorbachev years. He became a founder member of a nationalist group called *Otechestvo*, Fatherland. He failed to get into the Soviet Congress, beaten by democratic forces in the Kuntsevo region of Moscow. His campaign stood out for its cheap nationalist sloganizing. But he made it to the Russian parliament, where he became chairman of its committee on veterans' affairs. His work there opened his eyes to the obduracy of the Party officialdom, which rode roughshod over the needs of veterans and invalids. Rutskoy denounced Gorbachev for sending the army into Vilnius and Riga. But his ultimate contribution to the Yeltsin cause was to take away 200 deputies from the official Communist Party and into his breakaway group, Communists for Democracy. For this betrayal he was expelled from the Party.

Yeltsin and Rutskoy split the election campaigning between them, trying to take in as many of Russia's eighty-nine regions and republics as possible. Even in the conservative agricultural areas the joint ticket won easily.

They gathered at the Kremlin's Palace of Congresses – leaders of the republics, ambassadors, leaders of all religious faiths, politicians from across the spectrum – for the inauguration. The accent was on the Russia of pre-revolutionary times. Khasbulatov introduced the new President of the Russian Federation. Yeltsin was nervous. His voice quivered. Gorbachev sat in the front row, a forced smile on his face. Hand on heart, Yeltsin declared: 'The President is not a God, not a monarch, not a miracle worker. He is an ordinary citizen, vested with special responsibilities.' Russia would take its place as a civilized society, he said. 'Unfortunately we realized later than other civilized countries that a state's strength is proportionate to the well-being of its people. We have paid a huge price for that mistake.' As he finished, a military choir sang the new Russian national anthem, with the sound of cymbals, church bells and a full orchestra resounding through the vast hall. Gorbachev wished Yeltsin well in a short speech. In a symbolic gesture of reconciliation, the two men walked to the centre of the stage, shook hands and took their leave together. 'Tolerance and wisdom must not desert you,' said Patriarch Aleksiy II, the head of the Orthodox Church. 'A sick society needs love and patience.' The Patriarch was the symbol of the new – or rather old, pre-Communist – values. He made the cross over the new President, Yeltsin bowed, and they embraced. The emotion also got the better of Rutskoy. 'If I hadn't accepted Yeltsin's offer to join his ticket, it would have been tantamount to treachery,' he declared.

3

The Revellers

I t was a balmy Sunday night, a few days after Yeltsin's election victory. I was walking down Chekhov Street when I heard loud music. In Moscow at that time, outward signs of exuberance were rare. Revelry was confined to the home or the *dacha*. Apart from hotel restaurants and bars, access to which was controlled by the mob, and squalid basement beer counters that closed in the early evening, there was still nowhere for people with money to enjoy a drink or two, nowhere half decent to go out to on a whim.

The noise that night was something different. It was coming from the back courtyard of the Lenkom, the Theatre of the Lenin Komsomol. Despite its name, the theatre had become one of the more fashionable venues in town. There was rarely an empty seat in the house for the performances that regularly stretched the limits of Gorbachev's *glasnost*. The theatre's director, Mark Zakharov, had sprung to fame after suggesting on television that Lenin should be removed from his mausoleum on Red Square and given 'a decent Christian burial' next to his mother and sister in Leningrad. Profanity! Sacrilege! screamed the Communists. Among the cultural cognoscenti Zakharov instantly became a person to be seen with.

Russia's intelligentsia had always regarded itself as a cut above the rest. The very idea of going commercial, of mixing with businessmen, was considered infra dig. Or so I thought. I was to learn that night that the cultural world was becoming just as materialist as the rest of the population. The party was tantalizingly loud, but inaccessible, invitations only. I persuaded the doorman to let me in. My mouth fell open. Hundreds of young men in Italian double-breasted suits and women in diamonds were singing and dancing, drinking French champagne and eating the best caviar.

The purpose of the *Zadvorki*, the Courtyard Party, was to raise money to build a monument to dead children 'from Hiroshima to Chernobyl'. It did not seem the highest priority for a country reduced to accepting food parcels from abroad. The memorial, needless to say, was never built, but the 800 guests had a good time. The entertainment continued until sunrise. First to appear was Oleg Gazmanov, a swarthy teenyboppers' idol with his mixture of Cossack dancing, on-stage somersaults and Michael

Jackson hip routines. Then came a fashion show from the avant-garde designer Valentin Yudashkin, a speech by Stankevich, who by now was a very dapper Deputy Mayor of Moscow, and a welcome from Zakharov. 'My friends,' he said, 'that well-known astrologer Nostradamus predicted that a state in the northern hemisphere, founded after a revolution in October, would last for exactly seventy-three years and seven months. Well, time is up. I wish great success to our new Russian President.' They drank to that.

The highlight of the night was the auction. 'Do I hear 50? Yes, 100, 150.' Nikolai Karachintsev, a leading actor, was relishing his new vocation. He was selling off a very ordinary bottle of Stolichnaya vodka. In the shops it would go for a few roubles, well below £1. But stylish Russians were drinking imported vodka, from Sweden, Germany, Britain, America, anything but their own. Suddenly one man in the audience waved his podgy hand and shouted: 'What's all this rouble rubbish? Let's get on to dollars.' Everyone cheered, some threw their notes into the air like confetti. For one bidder it was a disaster. He was made to look decidedly un-cool with his carrier bags stuffed with roubles, as his rivals nonchalantly picked off the odd greenback from their wallets.

I had stumbled upon the *nouveaux riches*, the New Russians as they came to be known, at play for the first time. In thirteen years of travel to the Soviet Union, never before had I, a privileged Westerner, felt like a pauper at a rich man's ball. Westerners were deemed to be richer than locals, as if by right. Dollars meant access to a netherworld of special shops with their blacked-out windows and guards at the door. Even the most obvious of gifts, perfume from the duty-free, a model of a London bus or a four-pack of beer, were snapped up. The process was demeaning for all concerned but it had its purpose: to ensure that contact between Russians and foreigners would be as awkward as possible. Foreigners, with their distinctive number plates, would drive in the lane reserved for Party bosses. The smallest of Volvos or Volkswagens were gawped at. Of course, there were always the few who had long enjoyed such access, top Party and KGB functionaries and their families, but they would keep that to themselves.

Nineteen ninety-one was the year when *homo sovieticus* met money.

These people had it, and flaunted it. Some came from the criminal underworld, running the illegal casinos to which their friends in the Politburo turned a blind eye. They were usually easy to recognize, surrounded by henchmen in leather coats or loud sports jackets. The head of the Tambov mafia, a small town to the south of Moscow, was there. He had carved up a small area of the capital for himself. He was showing his face to bring some influential people into his camp. There was not a hint of self-consciousness in that courtyard. The man with the podgy hand won the auction for the vodka bottle, at a cost of $250. It was a startling sum to pay. Those Russians who did have hard currency, and there were precious few of them, would never in their wildest dreams spend it on food or drink. But Shura Skodo had enough to spare. He made his first money in the late 1970s, importing computers. He was well connected. He had to be to do what he was doing. He and a handful of others took advantage of Gorbachev's early legislation permitting cooperatives. His income snowballed from there. He invested some of his profits in the film industry, and became a sponsor of the arts. 'There's black money, grey money and white money,' Skodo explained. 'I'd say about 60 per cent of the donations tonight are from joint ventures and cooperatives. Of course there is a criminal element because a lot of gangsters use occasions like this to offload some of their money. But if you're collecting money you can't ask too many questions or demand to see people's passports.' It was impossible in the old days to make purely 'white' money when the laws were stacked against anyone who showed initiative. Only in December 1991 was the article that defined the buying or reselling of goods for means of making profit as 'speculation' removed from the statute book.

It was already light. The first shift was making its way to the factories. Money spent, drink drunk, the *Zadvorki* was winding up. For those with enough energy, a boat was being laid on to take them up and down the Moscow River, more champagne and vodka provided. On to the stage for one last time came Time Machine, a band that started out in the 1970s and retained its popularity well into the 1990s. They played their most famous hit *Novy Povorot*, New Direction. The song was considered subversive in Brezhnev's time, hinting as it did in the most oblique way about the need for change. That it had caused controversy now seemed quaint. It had become the youth anthem in those days, calling to a youth for whom new opportunities now beckoned. As the party-goers dispersed, an enormous red, white and blue hot-air balloon appeared, blazoned with the word *Rossiya*. The organizers couldn't get it to lift off the ground. Eventually it rose a few feet, snagged on the corner of the theatre and fell limply to the ground. It was not the best of omens for the new Russia.

Artyom Grigoryan was digging up divots with the force of an industrial excavator. He was one of the first local members of the Tumba golf club. 'It'll take some time, but I'm getting there,' he said, as he lunged at his second shot, which skidded 50 yards along the ground. Grigoryan's designer jeans were getting scuffed. Even in the height of the Moscow summer, the ground was a touch soggy. The Tumba had opened in 1988, the brainchild of a Swedish ice hockey star and a Russian entrepreneur. With a down payment of £12,000 followed by an annual fee of around £1,200, membership was confined mainly to the Japanese and South Korean business fraternity, the super-rich and the super-keen. The nine holes were constructed on an old rubbish tip behind a cluster of embassies, near the Mosfilm film studios, on grass that was brought in refrigerated trucks from Finland. It is not the world's most picturesque or challenging course.

But it was a start, and Grigoryan was happy to take advantage of the sizeable discount on offer for Russians to join. He had learnt the basics of the game during a business trip in America, where he picked up a set of clubs. Grigoryan came from a well-to-do family, and had been a model Communist, a member of the Komsomol, the youth wing of the Party. By the early 1980s, as Brezhnev was doddering about, missing pages from his speeches and turning the country into a laughing-stock, no self-respecting young Komsomol man took the ideology seriously. Being a member was like going to public school. The Komsomol provided both *blat* and *svyazi*, influence and connections.

Grigoryan joined the Komsomol's prestigious foreign arm, the KMO, the Committee of Youth Organizations. The KMO had close links with the KGB and was responsible for propagating Soviet ideology around the world, especially in developing countries. Grigoryan's beat was the frontline states of Africa. As opportunities for making money beckoned, anyone in the KMO was well placed. The organization owned property and had good connections. Grigoryan developed links with South African businessmen on the quiet. As soon as Russia recognized South Africa, Grigoryan was off making deals and enjoying the good life in Sun City.

He and I would play tennis, in his indoor club up the road or outdoors at the Coalminers' Club in eastern Moscow. Trade union officials had never really taken to the sport, and the club was one of the first to be opened up for outside membership. One Saturday morning on the adjacent court two men were knocking up. Standing on the sidelines were their armed bodyguards (occasionally they doubled as ballboys). Grigoryan had done well. He came to own his flat in a prestigious high-rise block, one of seven buildings of the Stalin era modelled on wedding cakes that tower over Moscow. His consultancy work with the South Africans enabled him to go out whenever he wanted, to drive a Volvo and to pop off to the Canary Islands for long weekends with his friends.

When I returned to Russia in early 1991 the foreign community in Moscow was still considered the most wealthy contingent in town, the most attractive target for bribe-hungry traffic police and others on the make. Only a tiny number of Russians had broken into this league. A few BMWs and Mercedes began to appear, their owners skulking in the back to avoid being recognized. The first shop selling imported Western clothes for roubles appeared, but it got into trouble for faking the label for Levi jeans. Russians were looking around to sign up joint ventures with Western partners. Every day came a new first: the first pizza, the first sex shop, the first pub, the first independent radio station – the first self-declared millionaires.

Every gimmick was worth a try. Hundreds of reporters assembled at the International Trade Centre, a sleazy leftover from the Brezhnev era that had been off limits to 'ordinary' Russians, to see German Sterligov, a 24-year-old university dropout turned entrepreneur, announce the creation of the Russian Club of Young Millionaires. 'Millionaires have fewer rights than any other section of Soviet society,' Sterligov declared. 'We are considered thieves in our own country.' He had named his private commodities brokerage after his dog, Alisa. The brokerage was a simple and clever idea, taking advantage of the old economic rules to make new money. Because the centralized system had been so hopelessly inefficient, each factory would have a *tolkach*, a sort of travelling salesman, who would traipse across the country to negotiate back-hand deals to buy raw materials or spare parts, often in a barter system. This avoided the bureaucracy but was laborious. Sterligov set himself up as a middle man.

For an annual subscription of 500,000 roubles, Sterligov said his club provided financial and legal advice to help members defend themselves from prying bureaucrats and protection rackets. He boasted several members, but said they had insisted on anonymity. We all sniggered. The man had to be a fraud or a dupe. In fact, he was a bit of both. He made his first million roubles in a month. It was big money for the time. Sterligov's ground floor office was the stuff of fantasy for young Russian men. Gaggles of mini-skirted secretaries were on hand, staring admiringly into his newly installed Japanese computers or perched on the edge of his newly installed Austrian-built executive's desk and lighting his newly bought American cigarettes. Marlboro Country had arrived, and Sterligov had obviously seen the advertisements.

The role models for these young men were America's zillionaires – the Donald Trumps, the Michael Milkens. Russia's new generation of aspiring entrepreneurs had all seen the film *Wall Street* on bootlegged videos and admired the ruthlessness of the corporate raiders, the junk bond dealers, the men in the red braces and fast cars. They tried to emulate them, working eighteen hours a day, talking money, and picking up their trophy wives. A new vocabulary sprang up. For bucks and greenbacks read *baksi* and *grini*. The most prestigious calling was to be a *broker*, *diler* or *biznesmen*.

Sterligov tried to make his way up society. He bought himself an ice-hockey team. He tried to hand over a stuffed boar's head to the Queen to mark her birthday, but the guards at the British Embassy refused to accept the gift. Within months he encountered his first threats. Sterligov sent his wife and children abroad, to keep them out of harm's way. The police and the KGB came from time to time to look at his books. It wasn't so much that he was making money, and flaunting it, both of which were bad enough; far worse, he wasn't sharing it out, through the long-established channels.

The KGB had always had a vested interest in business. Even in the 1970s it was taking a cut from the *valyutchiki*, the black marketeers who would hang about Western hotels. The system was ripe for exploitation. The rouble–dollar rate was so ludicrous that tidy profits could be made by anyone playing the game. The black market rate of the dollar rose inexorably. Anyone who had access to hard currency, who could buy, sell and buy again, was on his way to a fortune. The trouble was that few of the transactions escaped the KGB's attention. They would leave the dealers alone as long as they became informers, and handed a proportion of the money over. If a trader refused, or simply wasn't liked, he would be taken away and thrown in prison.

Artyom Tarasov was one of the first seriously rich businessmen. He made millions of dollars in real estate and commodity deals and was forced to flee Russia. He too paid the price for seeking a high profile. The KGB was after him and he spent increasing amounts of time out of sight in the south of France. He moved to London, to Mayfair, naturally. He was accused of smuggling hard currency out of Russia and knew that if he set foot on home soil he would be in for trouble. Only a long time later, when many others had become richer than he, did Tarasov return to Russia, to stand as an independent member of parliament in December 1993. He was elected and the matter of his first millions was quietly dropped.

Svyatoslav Fyodorov was a safer bet for the Communist establishment. A veteran member of the Central Committee, he was one of the first entrepreneurs that the Party was proud to show off. An ophthalmologist, he set up one of the world's foremost eye surgeries and pioneered revolutionary but controversial operating techniques. He became a multi-millionaire. When not travelling, which was rare, he would lounge in his executive's chair and monitor dozens of operations going on at any one time from a bank of giant video screens on his wall. With his remote control he would hone in on a particular eyeball being slashed and bark instructions from his squawk box to the surgeon. Fyodorov was no faint heart. From time to time efforts were made to force him to hand over part of his foreign currency earnings, but he had enough influence to fend them off. Fyodorov was approached as a possible Prime Minister by Yeltsin's team in the autumn of 1991. He turned them down. His attention was focused elsewhere. 'It's all about the property business now,' he would say.

Konstantin Borovoy was a different proposition, an outsider to the club. Borovoy ruffled feathers. A graduate of the less than prestigious Moscow Institute of Railway Transport Engineers, he became a teacher of applied mathematics. In 1990 he established the Moscow Commodities Exchange, the first in the country, and became its chairman. His declared personal fortune, in excess of $2.5 million, was enormous at the time. His was the most famous face of Russian capitalism. He was constantly on television, and was also on the agenda of visiting Western politicians. He was affable and extravagant. But things began to go wrong when he claimed in mid-1993 that his exchange had been taken over by criminal groups, who were fixing prices for their own profit. A few months later he was sacked as president of the exchange's board and thrown out of his opulent offices opposite Old Square. He claimed to have been the target of two assassination attempts. 'The exchange is controlled by the mafia,' he said. 'When this is revealed and these people go to prison, I don't want to be with them.'

Capitalism, in its crudest guise, was coming of age in the Russia of 1991. The moves were still tentative, but the process had begun. What set many of these young men apart – there were almost no women – was their ambition and nihilism. Apart from making money, the only thing that mattered was spending it. The drug was alluring. The first television advertisements were usually for banks, telling gullible and despairing viewers that money brought semi-naked girls, fast cars and happiness. In the Situations Vacant columns a new code was devised for aspiring secretaries. *Bez Kompleksov*, without complexes, it would say. If you're not ready to sleep with your boss, don't bother applying.

It was a glorious summer, 1991. Moscow was deserted at weekends; everyone had gone off to their *dachas*. Yeltsin was an exception, hard at work in his office, signing the first decrees of his presidency. I was lying with some friends on the beach at Nikolina Gora, the in place for the children of the elite who wanted to try out their new speed boats. They called it a beach. It was really the dirty Moscow River. But it would have to do. It was the place to be seen. The *nouveaux riches* eyed each other's Ray-Bans or Christian Dior swimsuits, their cars and ghetto-blasters. For the unaccompanied, discreet escorts lay sunning themselves seductively. One party was picnicking on *shashliks*, kebabs, listening to *Evropa Plus*, the fashionable radio station. It was time for the news. Yeltsin, the announcer said, had banned all Communist organizations in the workplace and in public organizations.

Battle with the old guard had commenced. Rarely in those months did a day pass without another warning of a coup. 'Good old Boris,' shouted one of the gilded youth, and got back to his lunch with the confidence of one who knew that, Communism or no Communism, he would not fall on hard times.

4

The Hedgehog

Valentin Pavlov thought he knew a thing or two about money. One evening, in January 1991, he turned up unannounced on television and ruined millions of peoples' lives. Currency reform, he said, was vital if the nation was to survive. Pavlov's greatest contribution as a member of Gorbachev's government, first as Finance Minister, then as Prime Minister, was to spark panic buying among a despairing population by proposing to raise prices on a range of goods. The measure solved nothing. Prices bore no relation to reality, because there was almost nothing to buy in the state stores. It was the black market that dictated terms. When Ryzhkov quit in a flood of tears, Gorbachev displayed his knowledge of economics by promoting Pavlov to premier. The omens were not good. The oil boom that had sustained Brezhnev had disappeared. The West was moving on into a post-industrial era. The Soviet Union still used the abacus, and produced goods that nobody wanted. It had lost most of its trade links with its former satellite states. Inflationary pressures were building up; there was too much money chasing too few goods. With almost nothing to find in the shops, and no proper banks to speak of, many Russians kept their money in their mattresses. Such were the waiting lists that it would take ten years to buy a Lada – unless you knew somebody who could help, of course.

Pavlov told viewers he was taking out of circulation fifty- and hundred-rouble notes. This was essential, he said, to mop up surplus cash which had got into the hands of speculators, who, he said, would be the only people carrying around large amounts of cash. Pavlov and Kryuchkov, the KGB chief, were obsessed with the idea that the West was scheming to bring down Gorbachev by flooding the market with fake roubles. The victims of the Politburo's latest paranoid whim were, as ever, ordinary people. Savings banks were inundated the following morning by people forlornly trying to offload their money.

Parliament was never dull when Pavlov was around, his portly frame squeezed into his seat at the front. Sometimes he would be seen huddling with his fellow comrades, Kryuchkov, Yazov and Boris Pugo, the Interior Minister. Pavlov's crew cut set him apart from the rest. He was known as the hedgehog.

Pavlov liked the word 'emergency'. He threatened striking workers with armed intervention. They were even striking in Belarus, one of the

41

most docile of republics. Pavlov called on parliament to back a 'state of emergency' or 'special regime' to deal with vital sectors of the economy, such as energy and transport. He and Kryuchkov warned parliament that Gorbachev was being tempted into another Western conspiracy. Yavlinsky, still smarting from the rejection of his 500 Day Programme the previous autumn, had gone off to Harvard for a brainstorming session with some of America's top academics. He came back to Moscow with a new scheme, called the Grand Bargain, much too radical for Pavlov's liking. The Prime Minister was scornful: 'I know a few gentlemen from Harvard University,' he told deputies. 'They do not know our way of life. We can hardly expect them to explain everything to us.'

Gorbachev considered Pavlov a useful foil. Whenever anything went wrong, Gorbachev would shrug his shoulders and point to his ministers. But Pavlov and his comrades were nothing if not consistent. They had been quite open in their efforts to push Gorbachev towards taking more 'emergency' measures and were growing frustrated at his unwillingness to do so. Throughout the spring and summer the gang, led by Kryuchkov, would consult one another informally at their various *dachas*.

The first plan was to persuade parliament to grant Pavlov special powers, including the right to issue his own decrees. It was a brazen attempt to usurp the President's powers. The plan was hatched while Yeltsin, the man most likely to force a fight, was away in America. At first Gorbachev tried to laugh it off. It took him three days to respond seriously. He ordered parliament to vote down the idea. 'Comrade Pavlov did not think it through,' Gorbachev told them. They heeded his word. The 'constitutional coup' was over. But Gorbachev took no action against Pavlov, who he said, was 'a good economist' but 'inexperienced' in politics.

A month later, and three days after Yeltsin's decree banning the Party from the workplace and public bodies, *Sovietskaya Rossiya*, the most prominent hardline newspaper, published an open letter from several senior members of the political and military establishment. It was entitled 'A Word To the People' and its language was portentous:

> Our motherland, this country, this great state which history, nature and our predecessors willed us to save, is dying, breaking apart and plunging into darkness and nothingness . . . our home is already burning to the ground. The bones of the people are being ground up and the backbone of Russia is being snapped in two.

On 29 July Yeltsin went out to Gorbachev's *dacha* in Barvikha together with Nursultan Nazarbayev, the leader of Kazakhstan, to hammer out details of the Union Treaty between the central authorities and the republics. Yeltsin warned them that Kryuchkov, Yazov, Pavlov and

Lukyanov – a large part of Gorbachev's cabinet – were up to no good. He also told them he knew Gorbachev's telephones were bugged. Gorbachev laughed. Popov, the Mayor of Moscow, had already warned the US Ambassador, Jack Matlock, that a coup was in the making. Matlock told Gorbachev that Washington was worried. Gorbachev thanked him for his concern but told him everything was under control. Gorbachev had never felt better. He went off to Foros, his new mansion in the Crimea, to rest in the sun and work on his speech for 20 August, the day the Union Treaty would be signed and the Soviet Union would be transformed into a looser relationship between the republics.

As soon as Gorbachev's back was turned, Kryuchkov stepped up his secret meetings. The bottom line was that the Union Treaty had to be stopped. Each gathering took place in a different KGB sanatorium and involved a slightly different group of Politburo members, military top brass and Party officials. Pavlov was a regular participant.

The group resolved that they would give Gorbachev an ultimatum, a choice they believed he would find hard to refuse: agree to our clampdown, or we'll do it without you. All that was demanded of the President was that he stay at the beach and pretend to be ill. With the coast clear, the radicals locked up, and good old-fashioned Party rule re-established, he could return to Moscow. After all, Gorbachev had feigned ignorance about the army's intervention in the Baltics the previous January.

Kryuchkov and his allies formed a Committee for the State of Emergency. On the afternoon of 18 August they sent a small delegation down to Foros, led by the head of ground forces, General Valentin Varennikov, to inform Gorbachev of their intentions. According to Pavlov, Gorbachev was angry, but refused to commit himself either way.

> He [Gorbachev] decided to play a game in which he could not lose. If he stayed there and the state of emergency worked, he would come back to Moscow later, having recovered from 'illness', and take charge. If it didn't work he would come and arrest everyone and once again as President he would take charge. In either case he would show the people that his hands were squeaky clean.

Gorbachev's refusal to go along with them sent the plotters reeling. They had a broad concept of what they needed to do, but the planning was rudimentary.

On the eve of the coup, Pavlov was a bag of nerves. He had spent the whole afternoon drinking. In the evening he and the rest of the gang were summoned to the Kremlin by Kryuchkov to put their signatures on the state of emergency declaration that would go into effect at 4 a.m.,

19 August. Many of them hesitated. Kryuchkov, convinced himself that only stern measures could stave off the Armageddon that was lodged firmly in his head, warned them that the USSR was heading for civil war. They dutifully fell into line, but, fearful of the consequences, many of them developed sudden 'illnesses' to keep them out of harm's way. Pavlov spent most of the night drinking with Yanayev in his Kremlin office. Yanayev was in despair. He was about to become Acting President and had no idea what to do. He was found drunk at his desk the next morning, several hours after assuming 'power'. Pavlov had been driven home in a stupor, but was roused early the next morning by a doctor sent by Kryuchkov. Both were ordered to sober up, fast, and get back to work.

Yeltsin was eating breakfast in his *dacha* when the news came in. He despatched Rutskoy and Khasbulatov to the White House, taking country roads to try to avoid detection. Rutskoy broadcast directly to the armed forces from a makeshift radio station, Khasbulatov to the citizens. As Yeltsin arrived, the only queue larger than the one hoping to talk to him was that of deputies hoping to be baptized by a priest in case this was to be their last day. Everyone took a role. The Cossacks were there in full regalia, as were private security men in black jumpsuits, awaiting orders. Burbulis was in charge of strategy, operating with Yeltsin from his third-floor 'war room', writing decrees and issuing orders. Korzhakov, as ever, was at the President's side, protecting him with a briefcase which when unzipped turned into a bullet-proof shield. The volunteers, Afghan veterans among them, assembled their little mountains of weapons under secretaries' desks – guns, grenades, Molotov cocktails at the ready. Each entrance to the labyrinthine building was guarded. Iron railings, concrete blocks, pieces of furniture, they piled anything bulky on to the flat roof in the hope of preventing a helicopter landing by paratroops. But, despite the defection of a few tank commanders, the defenders knew it would take only minutes to overrun them. The attack might come any time. Even if there were no frontal assault, the special forces might come in with gas through the ventilation shafts.

Burbulis suggested that Kozyrev be sent abroad to coordinate with Western governments. A small team was sent to prepare a government-in-exile from 'Point X', a bunker thirty feet underground and thirty-five miles outside Sverdlovsk, built to withstand an American nuclear attack.

At 6 p.m., as the resistance inside the White House gathered pace, Pavlov convened a full cabinet session. All but one of the ministers endorsed the declaration by the coup leaders, an act of betrayal that Gorbachev would later find hard to acknowledge. Pavlov was still under the influence and went home as soon as cabinet was over, complaining of high blood pressure. He felt his job was done. He and his wife were driven to the *dacha*. As the world watched the dramatic developments unfold, Pavlov stayed tucked up in bed, nursing his head.

Even after failing to arrest Yeltsin and his supporters, the coup leaders could have neutralized the opposition early on by sealing off the White House and cutting most national and international communications. Even inside the KGB itself, the most basic measures hadn't been taken. Several months earlier Yeltsin had hived off a few dozen officers in an attempt to create his own rival, *Russian*, security service. The man in charge, Vladimir Ivanenko, had an office on the same floor as Kryuchkov. Throughout the coup he was free to come and go, and he freely passed what information he could glean back to Yeltsin's people at the White House. Yeltsin was told that differences among the coup leaders were emerging, with Kryuchkov insisting on an attack but others running scared, especially from the second morning when the crowd outside the White House swelled.

Tragedy turned to farce. The young conscripts ordered into the city on the first morning had no idea why they were there or where they were going. One tank took the wrong turning at an overpass outside my office building. The spotty young commander tried to turn round on the slip road and crashed straight into a correspondent's Mercedes parked at the side. He got out, surveyed the mess and looked as if he was going to cry. Kryuchkov's plan was to use only elite cadres. With the help of airborne troops and KGB contingents, the Alpha Group would blast their way through doors with grenade launchers. The crowds would initially be dispersed with tear gas and water cannons. Once this had been achieved, the building would be shelled.

The White House was an oasis of defiance in the rain. But apart from the small area around the building, Moscow on those three days hardly bore the signs of a city under siege. Most people went to work as normal, ignoring calls by Yeltsin's authorities for a strike. Several of my acquaintances clammed up, returning to their outspoken selves only after the second night when the coup began to peter out. Some had wept when they saw the original announcement on television, but realized they had best keep their heads down. In the ministries and in the regions, the most sensible sought to avoid comment and wait until one side emerged on top. Afterwards they tried to cover up their equivocations.

The initiative seeped away from the plotters in a haze of drink and confusion. They took fright when the air force commander, Marshal Yevgeny Shaposhnikov, threatened to launch an airborne counter-attack on the Kremlin if they stormed the White House. In the middle of the second night Kryuchkov phoned Burbulis, then Yeltsin. The coup was unravelling. The plotters were about to flee to Foros to plead with Gorbachev.

Pavlov knew his time was up. He waited for them to come and get him. The guards arrived at his *dacha* the day after Gorbachev returned to Moscow. Pavlov was reunited with his fellow plotters in the Matrosskaya Tishina (Sailor's Rest) prison in eastern Moscow.

On the day of Pavlov's arrest, a still-shaken Gorbachev was invited to the citadel to give his version of the coup and offer his ideas for a new start, taking into account the three days that had transformed the country. But on his return to Moscow Gorbachev was lost in a time-warp, still espousing faith in a Communist Party most of whose leaders had betrayed him. That parliamentary session should have been a moment of reconciliation. Gorbachev's poor judgement and Yeltsin's smiling spite ensured that it was anything but. Yeltsin was angry that Gorbachev had failed explicitly to thank him and parliament for saving him. Yeltsin allowed the deputies to mock Gorbachev, only occasionally tapping his pen gently on his microphone to call for calm. At one point Yeltsin strode over to Gorbachev, who was standing at the lectern, and, towering over him, gave him a document. 'Read it out,' the deputies yelled. It was the minutes of the cabinet meeting chaired by Pavlov. Gorbachev read them slowly, his voice dropping and shaking, trying to defend one or two of the ministers who, he said, had assured him afterwards that they had behaved honourably.

Eventually Gorbachev gave in. 'I think the correct approach would be for the entire government to resign,' he said. Yeltsin had not finished. Was he going out of his way to inflict the kind of humiliation he had received from Gorbachev back in 1987? Yeltsin addressed parliament, a smile stretched across his face. 'On a lighter note, shall we now sign a decree suspending the activity of the Russian Communist Party? I will now sign it,' Yeltsin declared, his voice booming. He began putting pen to paper. 'Boris Nikolayevich, Boris Nikolayevich,' Gorbachev beseeched him. Yeltsin cast a cursory glance at his long-time adversary, smiled and signed. The hall rose in unison, clapping and cheering. Yeltsin then turned to the hall and clenched his fist as Gorbachev was looking away. It was Yeltsin at his best, and worst. Gorbachev had said he would *never* come clean on some of the details of the coup. Many Russians wonder to this day what he had to hide. The coup leaders' assertions that Gorbachev had misled them testified more to their crass failures of judgement than to his cunning. Gorbachev, after all, had almost never given a short and straight answer to any question.

I had met Pavlov several times before, so a couple of months after the coup I phoned his wife, Valentina. She invited me round. It was no ordinary flat, and Alexei Tolstoy Street was no ordinary address. *Nomenklatura* property was easily recognizable, by its red brick exterior, its watchful guards, and by the absence of urine in the lifts and dirt on the hallway carpets. No attempt had been made to force Valentina out of the flat. She was fearful for her husband, convinced that someone would 'do away with the defendants' to prevent unwelcome secrets coming out at the conspirators' forthcoming trial. She said she never asked him about the details of his work. On that fateful Sunday night, the eve of the coup, he suddenly rushed to the office, telling her only he had some important business to finish off.

She had been allowed to visit him once in the first weeks thereafter, for just over an hour on his fifty-fourth birthday. Initially, he and his fellow defendants shared cells with ordinary remand prisoners, with relatives permitted to send one food parcel weighing up to 20 lb per month. 'I send him sausages, cheese and garlic, to disinfect his stomach,' she said, sobbing intermittently. 'Plus *salo* [a type of fatty bacon-cum-lard]. He loves that.' It was a formative experience to see how the Soviet mighty had fallen.

As time went on, Valentina became more confident. Conditions for the defendants improved inside the prison. The Pavlovs' state *dacha* was taken away – it had come with the job – but she was left alone. Her son, who worked for Vneshtorgbank, the Soviet Foreign Trade Bank, was doing very well for himself in Luxembourg. He came back to Moscow once in a while to visit. The relatives of the dozen conspirators would meet collectively with the lawyers to discuss tactics. Sometimes they would demonstrate outside the prison gates, a motley collection of women in furs and their supporters, hard-nosed Communist sympathizers with bloodshot eyes. They lobbied hard for the men to be released on bail ahead of the trial.

After seventeen months in jail, on 26 January 1993, Pavlov was released. A few others had been freed earlier on grounds of ill health. They had been charged with treason, a crime that allowed for the death sentence. They were forced to give up their internal passports and told not to leave Moscow without permission. The decision to let them go aroused no reaction among the public. It was as if everyone had forgotten about the coup. Life had moved on.

I phoned Valentina that evening. 'Give him time to have a shower,' she said. Pavlov had certainly lost some weight, but he looked all the better for it. He had much he wanted to explain. There had been nothing underhand in his behaviour before the coup, he said. He acknowledged that several meetings had been held in July and August to discuss a state of emergency. But the participants had merely gone over well-trodden ground. 'All this had already been worked out in March,' he said. Gorbachev's deployment of troops then to stop the pro-Yeltsin march had been a dress rehearsal. 'The very word "plot" is slightly naïve. Why would we have gone to see Gorbachev and discussed all the problems with him?'

The trial began in April 1993. Tons of documents had been pored over by the lawyers; 120 witnesses had been summoned. But as the men appeared before the military tribunal of the Supreme Court, it was not hard to sense that they had already seen the last of their prison cells. Within a month the judge had suspended the trial, upholding a defence application demanding the dismissal of the entire prosecution team. The court said it would ask parliament to debate 'serious violations' by Stepankov, the chief prosecutor, and his deputy and chief investigator, Yevgeny Lisov. The two had had a book, *The Kremlin Coup*, ghost-written in their names. Stepankov's lust for money outweighed any concern that publication would reveal many previously unknown details of the coup and dealt with material that would in most countries be considered *sub judice*. He had already made a bob or two earlier by organizing access for Western correspondents to the accused in prison and negotiating the serialization of the book with foreign magazines.

Pavlov had shed his apprehensions within weeks of his release from prison. He saw no reason not to dabble in politics again, as he demonstrated by joining Kryuchkov and several co-defendants as they linked arms down Moscow's main street, Tverskaya, in another of the ritual anti-Yeltsin demonstrations. They made their way to Manezh Square, the venue for the pro-democracy rallies of old, and as Pavlov was about to mount the podium, he recognized me and gave me a bear-hug. 'Comrade, nice to see you here.' I was both chuffed and embarrassed. I slid away.

The trial dragged on. The longer it took, the more likely it seemed the case would collapse as Yeltsin's position was steadily undermined. The defendants took it in turns to go off sick. On each occasion, the proceedings were abandoned. The judge, Anatoly Ukolov, warned them about contempt but took no action. Even when the court did convene it made little progress. After each statement by a witness or the prosecution, each of the defendants and each of their lawyers had the right of reply. These responses could take the form of speeches, with the lawyers vying to outperform each other with their wit and erudition, delivering soliloquies on the subject of 'when is a coup not a coup?.' The attorneys all came from the top drawer of the Soviet legal world. Their Western-cuts suits stared out at the ill-fitting Soviet variations worn by the hapless prosecutors opposite.

Suddenly, in late 1993, it all went wrong for the defendants. Yeltsin had attacked the White House and smashed the opposition. The leaders of 'coup two' had just been put in jail. The leaders of 'coup one' would no longer be given such an easy ride. 'The atmosphere's completely different now,' said Pavlov, as he paced the corridor during a break. 'The people in the Kremlin are pressurizing the judge to hurry things along.' But the elections of December and the discomfiture of the radicals put an end to their anxiety. The new parliament, the State Duma, passed an amnesty pardoning the leaders of both coups.

Pavlov was back to his old self. Some of his colleagues, Lukyanov among them, returned to politics; some sought peace at their *dachas*. Pavlov joined the business world – the group he had accused, when he was in office, of being in the pay of the CIA. The coup was rewritten in the minds of millions as a little local mistake, as an over-ambitious attempt by basically good men to get to grips with the country's problems. The 'failures' of the Yeltsin regime somehow vindicated or excused their actions. Yazov, the Defence Minister, was the only one who seemed genuinely sorry for what he had done. Pavlov was anything but contrite.

I asked Pavlov to describe his first meeting with Yeltsin. It was in 1986.

We shook hands, but neither of us introduced ourselves. Everyone would assume that we should all know who everyone is. I'd heard his name mentioned, but I didn't know that was him. I can't claim he made any special impression on me. The only thing that struck me was that when he shook hands he didn't look you in the eye. That's not a very pleasant characteristic. Later I began to take more of an interest. We met a second time in the same place, and this time he looked over his shoulder as he shook my hand. That's the kind of thing you do in the company of enemies.

Pavlov became an adviser to a small, 'very private' bank, called Rublyovsky, and also headed two small commercial firms, one in consultancy, the other in investment. Valentina had worked throughout her husband's captivity in the property and real estate firm she had formed, with the help of friends. Their son had moved on from the Foreign Trade Bank to a joint venture commercial bank. All in all, they were not doing badly. They had 'privatized' their town flat and clubbed together with old chums to join in a condominium project for new *dachas* near Zvenigorod, just beyond Yeltsin and company.

As if on cue, Pavlov went through the motions of complaining: most of the politicians were the same, nobody was dealing with the economic collapse or the rise in crime. 'It's all games to them. The current politicians try to tell us businessmen what to do, but they've no idea, so we in turn ignore them.'

'You know,' he concluded as we parted, 'People thought that we Soviet politicians didn't know anything about economics. Look at us now.'

5

The Disappearing Act

Yeltsin would later admit it himself. Of all the mistakes of his rule, his failure to consolidate his victory after the coup was the gravest of all. For the last four months of 1991 there were two Presidents in the Kremlin, but neither of them was really in charge. As the economy deteriorated further, the hardliners began to regroup.

Some of Yeltsin's advisers urged him to call elections at every level, from the smallest district upwards. A constituent assembly could prepare a new basic law that would replace a constitution that dated back to Brezhnev's time and was wholly unsuitable for the task at hand. But Yeltsin had little reason to distrust his parliament or to feel threatened by any opposition from within Russia itself. As for the other leading politicians, Khasbulatov had been one of his staunchest allies in the White House during the coup, while Rutskoy had emerged with honour after coordinating the military defence of the building.

Yeltsin was tired. As soon as he had put Gorbachev in his place and secured top jobs for his own placemen, he disappeared off to Sochi to rest and write his memoirs. He thought he could leave his lieutenants to themselves.

The problems began at once. An atmosphere of gloom and dire foreboding had once again enveloped Moscow. A leaked KGB report warned of civil war, a loss of central control of nuclear weapons as the republics went their own way, and the onset of fascism. Its alarmist tone was interpreted as perhaps an attempt to prepare the ground for another coup.

Khasbulatov and Rutskoy were worried. They tried to get hold of Yeltsin. They reported back to parliament that they had tried more than a dozen times to get through to him at his holiday home but had failed. They inadvertently touched off a new round of speculation about the President's health. Had Yeltsin suffered the same fate as Gorbachev? Had his communications also been cut off? The confusion increased when Tass, the official news agency, issued a dispatch entitled 'Yeltsin back at work', only to withdraw it and report that the President was due back later in the day. Just before departing for his holiday, Yeltsin had cancelled several appointments after suffering a recurrence of heart trouble.

The rules, according to Voshchanov, who by now was Yeltsin's press secretary, were simple. Yeltsin was to be disturbed on holiday only *in extremis.* 'The phone is always answered by the head security man. If he thinks you're enough of an insider and serious enough to warrant it, he'll put you through to Korzhakov, who's always around him. And after that it depends on Korzhakov and what he thinks is the mood of the President.' Khasbulatov and Rutskoy did not merit attention. The only person who got through was Burbulis.

After more than two weeks away, Yeltsin finally returned to the capital to find his staff in turmoil. Burbulis likened it to a minefield. Rutskoy had always been suspicious of Burbulis. By the autumn they couldn't bear to look at each other. Each believed he was Yeltsin's number two. Rutskoy felt he should have been running the show in Yeltsin's absence. Annoyed that he had been overlooked for the presidential campaign, Burbulis was determined to ensure that the Vice-Presidency would be a purely ceremonial job, perhaps to receive the credentials of foreign ambassadors, represent the President on uncontroversial foreign trips or open hospitals. At most its powers could correspond to those of the American Vice-President. Yeltsin agreed with Burbulis. Rutskoy, he believed, should be thankful for being plucked out of obscurity.

Sensitivity was not Yeltsin's strong point. According to Poltoranin, the President was fully aware of Rutskoy's wounded pride but nevertheless would have underlings inform Rutskoy of a particular decision on his behalf. Most would go and see Rutskoy in his office along the corridor. Burbulis would bark orders down the phone.

Voshchanov recalled that it was not difficult to know where the balance of power between Yeltsin's team and Gorbachev's lay.

> With each day that passed it became clearer that we were really the inheritors of power. You could sense it from the attitude of the Kremlin guards. They're the kind of people who react quite differently to their masters. When I first started coming to the Kremlin they'd scrutinize my pass very carefully, but as time passed they started smiling, greeting me by name.

There was a complication. Often when Gorbachev wanted to use a particular hall in the Kremlin, he would find out that Yeltsin was already using it.

Gorbachev's rapid descent from power was watched with alarm in many of the republics, which were wary of the increasingly nationalist tone emanating from the Yeltsin camp. By mid-September all the republics had declared some form of independence from Moscow. The Baltics had already extricated themselves from the fold, while some of the fiefdoms of Central Asia saw separation as the only means of avoiding the multi-party Western models of government towards which the Russians were leaning.

The first challenge from outside to Yeltsin's inexperienced leadership came from the unlikeliest of quarters. It was from Number One Shakespeare Street, a bungalow surrounded by armed hoodlums and roaming goats, that a certain General Dzhokhar Dudayev took on the Kremlin. A former commander of a bomber squadron in Estonia, Dudayev had declared his small republic of Chechnya, population 1.3 million, independent. It was not even the future of the Soviet Union that was at stake, but that of Yeltsin's Russian Federation. The capital of Chechnya bore an appropriate name: Grozny translates as Terrible or Formidable. Young men sold Kalashnikovs on street corners. Imported Mercedes with Jordanian number plates outnumbered Ladas. Everyone, it seemed, belonged to the mafia.

The General received me in the kitchen of his latest hideout. It was not the most awe-inspiring location for the leader of a new state. The whirring of the fridge behind didn't add to the aura of authority. But Dudayev was nothing if not determined. 'I will restore my people's pride after our enslavement by the Russians. The Russians will soon learn that they will never have peace as long as the Chechens are angry.' He was referring to the deportation of the Chechens, and other ethnic groups, from the northern Caucasus by Stalin during the war. Dudayev said talk of his republic's mafia links was Communist propaganda. 'They are trying to neutralize me and my guards. That is why I cannot sleep in the same bed on successive nights. We must be alert.' Dudayev said the Russians were doing all they could to destabilize his young regime. He was preparing to 'legitimize' his rule with elections, but made clear none of his opponents would be allowed to come to power. 'Some are puppets of Russia. Some are clansmen, some are psychologically ill.'

When the crisis broke out, Yeltsin left its resolution to others. Rutskoy and Burbulis tried to negotiate with Dudayev, even sending delegations down to Grozny. They were given short shrift. The defiance was infuriating. Rutskoy urged Yeltsin to act tough and send in the Interior Ministry troops. No sooner had the 700 men arrived at the Khankala military airbase than they were surrounded by Chechnya's rag-tag but fearsome National Guard. Within hours the frightened Russians had been escorted out of the city by bus, leaving many of their weapons behind. Locals lined the path in celebration, waving the green flag of Islam. Mighty Russia had been outsmarted by a little tinpot dictatorship.

Parliament was furious that it had not been consulted over the deployment of troops. A chastened Yeltsin was forced to apologize. For Rutskoy, the military man, the loss of face was harder to bear. He had been countermanded by the Interior Ministry and left in the lurch by Yeltsin. He would not forget it.

Yeltsin needed a Prime Minister. From the moment of his election as President, he had entrusted Burbulis with the task of finding one. There was no shortage of candidates; Yeltsin had considered, and rejected, several figures from the Gorbachev era, such as Yavlinsky, the economist, and Svyatoslav Fyodorov, the eye surgeon. Burbulis persuaded him that if he were serious about radical reform he needed an untried figure, one with fresh ideas. He urged him to see Yegor Gaidar.

The meeting was planned for 19 August, the first day of the coup. It would be more than a week after that date before Yeltsin could finally hear what Gaidar had to say. He was impressed by his intellect. Gaidar started off in academia with six years' research at the economics faculty of Moscow State University. There he developed close links with two of Gorbachev's most trusted economists, Stanislav Shatalin and Nikolai Petrakov. He was also a junior member of a state commission for economic reform set up during the time of Yuri Andropov in 1983. He was a model of the Party establishment. Gaidar's father, Timur, was a naval commander, while his grandfather, Arkady, had commanded a Red Army regiment before achieving fame in Stalin's time as a writer of children's fables. During Gorbachev's time, Gaidar was economics editor at the journal *Kommunist*, which was anything but radical. He moved on to the top economics job at *Pravda*. His career pattern stuck firmly to the straight and narrow, but from the mid-1980s he came into contact with an entirely new generation of economists, no longer content to discuss reform from within the confines of Gorbachev's 'socialist choice'.

Andrei Illarionov was part of the Leningrad set, one of two circles of young economic brains that had been gathering to discuss new theories and swap texts since the early 1980s. The Moscow one was led by Gaidar and Pyotr Aven, who then went off to work in the Soviet mission in Vienna; the Leningrad one was headed by Sergei Vasilyev and Anatoly Chubais. Illarionov remembers how they devoured their first Western textbooks, how soon the ideas of their mentors, elder figures such as Shatalin and Petrakov, looked tired and jaded. 'From 1987 we could just about do what we liked,' recalled Illarionov. 'It was a rapid-fire education. We had a lot of catching up to do.'

Yeltsin appointed Gaidar one of his State Counsellors with the task of drawing up an entirely new economic programme for the Russian government. His brief was simple: to do something *radically different*. He looked far and wide for people to help him. Illarionov was a postgraduate student on secondment to Birmingham University when he received the call-up. 'There was a general mobilization of everyone who had any understanding of economics. Russia may be a big country, but there were only a few people who have any *real* education in economics,' he said.

The young economists summoned to their government's aid converged on Moscow at the end of September. For a month they were holed up at government *dacha* number six in Arkhangelskoye. It was an ivory tower of sorts. 'Number six was quite well known because in general everything that's been written there has been put into practice,' said Illarionov. 'It was more modest than some of the others. We all lived, worked and slept there.' Burbulis would come from time to time. Another to join the group was Alexander Shokhin, a more experienced figure, who had been personal adviser to Shevardnadze.

Their conclusions were revolutionary. Many of them were based on the Polish experience. Under its Finance Minister, Leszek Balcerowicz, the first post-Communist government in Warsaw carried through a dramatic transformation in the financial health and competitive strength of the Polish economy. The Poles were proud to call their work 'shock therapy'. Gaidar wondered whether it could be applied directly in the Russian context. He argued that the 'classical reform sequence', as he called it – macro-economic stabilization followed by privatization and then price liberalization – was not suited to the Russian economy. The main stumbling block to any form of progress in Russia was the system of fixed prices. Artificially low prices had strangled the consumer sector, destroyed the basic laws of supply and demand. Once those had been re-established, everything else would fall into place.

Yeltsin's more circumspect aides persuaded him that Gaidar would be too much of a gamble as a figurehead. A scheme was devised whereby Yeltsin would assume the formal role of Prime Minister, Burbulis would take operational control as First Deputy Prime Minister, chairing most of the cabinet meetings, while Gaidar would be left the job of driving the reform programme from the relatively safe position of Deputy Prime Minister, the number three.

'There was a great deal of hesitation at first. I knew I was being considered, but when my appointment to the government came, it was news to me,' said Gaidar. He went off immediately to see Yeltsin, to accept the offer. 'Yeltsin was very keen to understand the limits of what was possible. He asked me questions about a separate currency, land reform, monetary policy, privatization. It was obvious from the questions that he had consulted with a lot of people. He didn't try to disguise the fact that he was not a professional economist, but he had a good basic grasp and energetic approach,' Gaidar said.

That first cabinet was a golden period, the stuff of nostalgia for the reformers. Alexei Golovkov was chief aide to Burbulis. 'Everyone said this was a kamikaze government, it wouldn't last more than three months. All we wanted to do was take the first and most important step,' he said.

'It was like jumping out of an airplane with a parachute that you weren't sure would open. But everyone was already so exhausted, working around the clock for weeks, that we didn't fully appreciate the implications of what we were doing,' said Illarionov.

Khasbulatov was upset. He had wanted the post of Prime Minister for himself. He too was an economics professor, he reminded Yeltsin. The

President assured him he still had a vital role to play, but he needed him to remain as Chairman of Parliament, to keep the flag flying in the legislature, keep the hardliners at bay. He meant it sincerely. Khasbulatov was still an asset.

A Congress was called to enshrine the economic revolution. Yeltsin's keynote address that October was one of his most convincing. He extolled the virtues of the free market with the fervour of the recently converted. Without mentioning Gorbachev, he said: 'In recent years everyone understood this but no-one had the courage to take this drastic step. Hence the endless compromises which have prepared the way for economic chaos.' He asked Congress to grant him special powers, promising them he would make himself personally responsible for his government and for the welfare of his citizens. Only a handful of the thousand deputies railed against the proposed reforms, warning of social strife in their wake.

After several days' debate, Yeltsin was granted the powers he wanted. They were vast; never again would he have it so easy. Congress approved three motions: proposals to introduce a free market based on privatization and free prices; measures that would allow Yeltsin to take control for one year of all layers of government, and ban elections at all levels; and the authority for him to issue decrees at will.

Time was pressing. Talk of price liberalization added to the despair on the streets. Popov, the Moscow Mayor, said food ration coupons would be issued for basic provisions such as bread, sausage, butter and eggs in an attempt to get supplies back on to the shelves. The fewer the goods, the more people were prepared to pay on the black market. The rouble was losing its value by the day. Yeltsin was already speaking of 100 million people below the poverty line: two-thirds of the population. It was an arbitrary figure but it spoke volumes for the depth of the crisis.

For the first time since the coup, Communist diehards paraded on the streets. The crowd on Red Square marking Revolution Day, 7 November, was not large, but the red flags and the posters of Lenin and Stalin were back. The protesters denounced Gorbachev as a traitor and Popov as a 'miserable Jew' (he was of Greek origin). Yeltsin himself was still untouchable; his role in the coup had assured that he would remain beyond criticism for some time.

The big day was set for 16 December. The government had less than two months to prepare for it. Leaders of the neighbouring republics frantically tried to contact Gaidar and Burbulis to urge them to delay price liberalization, fearing the knock-on effect of Russians pouring over the borders in search of cheaper food. The ministers agreed to put the date back to 2 January 1992.

Yeltsin often said he could not reform what he did not control. Many of the basic economic levers were still nominally in Gorbachev's hands.

Yeltsin acted quickly, assuming jurisdiction over the Soviet Union's reserves of precious metals. The Central Bank and Foreign Trade Ministry were the next to be seized.

Rutskoy, meanwhile, had had enough. He had gathered around him a large entourage of advisers and officials, taken from good Party stock. Andrei Fyodorov had worked briefly as number two to Russia's Foreign Minister, Andrei Kozyrev, but he had grown disillusioned with Kozyrev's love affair with the West. Fyodorov had made his career as Chairman of KMO, the Komsomol's foreign wing, and the training had left its mark. Also prominent in the team were Valery Krasnov and Nikolai Kosov, two former diplomats in the KGB-dominated Soviet Embassy in London.

Then there was Gulbinsky, the man I was so shocked to see at Yakubovsky's. Gulbinsky came from more humble beginnings as a Spanish interpreter for the Central Committee's Academy of Social Sciences. He would translate material of writers considered to be anti-Communist, to enable the Party in Moscow to keep tabs on 'political developments' in the Spanish-speaking world. It was one of those pointless jobs that kept thousands in work and kept the wheels of paranoia turning. By the late 1980s, Gulbinsky had become the mildest type of reformer; wary of upsetting his employers by joining Democratic Russia, he opted for Rutskoy's newly formed group, Communists for Democracy. From there it was a short step to recommendation for a good position in his office. No sooner had Rutskoy made him his press secretary than Gulbinsky was having to fend off a barrage of enquiries about the Chechen débâcle.

The most influential member of Rutskoy's kitchen cabinet was General Alexander Sterligov, a veteran of twenty years' service with the KGB and an unashamed nationalist. He had earlier been a member of the first prominent far-right and anti-semitic group *Pamyat*, Memory. Sterligov had as little time for Communism's ideologues as for capitalism's young Turks. 'People like Gaidar and Yavlinsky have one thing in common with Marx and Engels,' Sterligov said. 'None of them have ever done anything practical, just sitting there in libraries all their lives.'

As Yeltsin and Gaidar were preparing the reforms, Rutskoy decided it was time to go back on the road, to meet the people. He made a brief swing through southern Russia and Siberia. Each speech was more vituperative than the last. The cabinet, he said, was made up of pampered little rich kids who knew nothing about real life. These 'boys in pink trousers' were now at the helm of a sinking Russia.

'I didn't write the speeches,' said Gulbinsky.

I was as surprised by them as everyone else was. We knew Rutskoy had his doubts about Gaidar, but he seemed to have been getting along all right with him. Not that they had much in common, a fighter pilot and an academic. On the flight home I wrote Rutskoy a note saying he mustn't behave like that. Whatever he thought of the government, and I had plenty of misgivings myself, it would create a very bad impression throughout the civilized world if a Vice-President started speaking out in public against his own President. And speaking against the government was tantamount to speaking against the President, I told him. Tsaregorodtsev appended to my note a list of words Rutskoy should avoid using in public – scum, faggots, dregs, mongrels. Rutskoy took it all reasonably well, but nothing really changed. He gave more interviews, bad-mouthing the government each time.

News of the speech was slow to reach Moscow. There were more pressing problems for the President and government. Most ministers brushed it off. 'People laughed,' Illarionov said. 'We were almost flattered by the attention.'

But Burbulis would not let it rest there. He ordered that the television footage of the Novosibirsk meeting be sent to Moscow. He summoned Rutskoy. It was a good opportunity to pull rank, to make him feel small. In front of Gaidar, he asked him to explain his speech. Rutskoy became confused, blushed and mumbled: 'I didn't really mean the government.'

Round one was won by Burbulis. But Rutskoy's injured pride would make him all the more tough an adversary in the years to come.

6
The Secret Deal

T hey met close to the Polish border so that if anything happened they could always seek asylum abroad. Or so their detractors would say. Yeltsin, the Ukrainian leader Leonid Kravchuk, and Stanislav Shushkevich of Belarus gathered together in a hunting lodge deep inside the Belarussian forest. The Belovezhskaya forest was renowned for its boar hunting.

They had come on the first Saturday in December to bury the old Soviet Union in one weekend. Yeltsin and Shushkevich met first in Minsk. Kravchuk joined them. Out of the blue, they decided to travel on, westwards, into the forest. Their aides followed. They spent the first day sitting by an open fire going through the various options. First they considered the possibility of keeping Gorbachev on as some form of central figurehead. Their deliberations on this point did not take too long. Every step Gorbachev had taken since the coup had been too little, too late. His latest plan was a development on the Union Treaty that would have been signed had it not been for the coup. He was now trying to sell the idea of a 'democratic confederation', to be called the Union of Sovereign States. Yeltsin had agreed, reluctantly; Kravchuk had refused, point-blank. Everything had to be put on hold, Kravchuk had told Gorbachev, until after the Ukrainians voted. Gorbachev was crestfallen.

Radicalism was the last thing on the minds of most Ukrainians when they went to the polls on 1 December. They had two votes: in a referendum on independence from the Soviet Union, and in the election of their own President. The two main candidates for the presidency could not have been more of a contrast: Kravchuk, formerly the Ukrainian Party's head of ideology, and Vyacheslav Chornovil, leader of the Rukh independence movement and a former dissident who had spent fifteen years in jail for 'anti-Soviet activities'. Like all of Ukraine's Communist elite, Kravchuk scoffed at the idea of independence in the old days. But by the time he was elected Chairman of the Ukrainian Parliament in July 1990 the situation had changed. Kravchuk adroitly turned himself into an ardent nationalist, stealing the carpet from under the feet of Rukh's radical activists. It was not for nothing that he was called 'the wily fox'.

Kravchuk was seen as a steady hand on the tiller. Many voters considered his Party past as a sign of a responsibility, denoting a man of experience and integrity. I asked one middle-aged woman leaving her polling station in Podol, a district of Kiev, why she had opted for him and not Chornovil. She replied: 'How could you possibly trust a former prisoner?' Such remarks were not heard very often any more in Moscow and St Petersburg. It contributed to a sense that any hopes Ukrainians might have harboured of transforming Kiev from a provincial outpost of the Soviet Union to a world capital would take a long time.

Kravchuk's conversion might not have been sincere, but he took it seriously. As usual, Gorbachev failed to see the warning signs. In July 1991 he made a rare sortie out of Russia into another republic. His talks at the country residence of Ukraine's Communist leaders of old, just outside Kiev, were not with Kravchuk, as would have been expected, but with Germany's Chancellor Kohl – a Soviet–German summit, and not a mention of Ukraine. Gorbachev was booed as he drove down Kiev's main street, Kreshchatik. Even after that episode, the reality had still not sunk in among world leaders. A few weeks later it was Bush's turn to visit Ukraine, on his way home from a summit in Moscow. With Gorbachev's sermon about the evils of independence ringing in his ears, Bush chastised his Ukrainian hosts for undermining the Soviet leader with their 'nationalist extremism'.

Life beyond Moscow's remit had its appeal. Even to the millions of ethnic Russians living in the industrial cities in the east of the republic, it had its positive sides. Smaller would surely be more beautiful? Ukraine, the second largest of the Soviet republics with a temperate climate and a population of more than 50 million, was potentially prosperous. It had avoided much of the turbulence of Russia. Independence was worth a try. Nobody had really thought the idea through – a fully independent country, with a different language, different currency, full passport and customs controls, its own armed forces? The history was fuzzy. The word Ukraine derives from 'on the edge', part of a unified Slav empire. In the view of most Russians, Yeltsin and company included, ancient Russia began in Kiev. The USSR might have been an aggressive empire based on a moribund ideology; the annexation of the Baltics might have been unfair; the Georgians and the Armenians would be far happier if left alone. But Ukraine was part of the motherland.

There was no love lost between Yeltsin and Kravchuk. The Ukrainian leader had not distinguished himself during the coup, when he ingratiated himself with Varennikov, one of the conspirators. As the putsch collapsed, Kravchuk, like the other republican bosses, sang from a different songsheet. Days after the failure of the coup, Ukraine was one of the first republics to declare its independence – pending the results of the referendum.

Yeltsin, like Gorbachev, feared the devolutionary process was taking place too quickly that autumn. He wanted to counter the tough talking coming from Kiev and the other republican capitals, to frighten them a little. He summoned Voshchanov, his spokesman, to his office and asked him to put together a statement. The text they came up with was uncompromising. Russia warned its neighbours that if any of them violated the provisions of Gorbachev's Union Treaty, Russia would reserve the right to reopen discussion about borders and disputed territory. This, it was stressed, did not apply to the Baltic states, whose independence had been recognized around the world. Still, it was a dramatic announcement, calling into question the Helsinki Final Act that had enshrined the inviolability of national frontiers as a central tenet of international diplomacy. Voshchanov insisted Yeltsin and his aides knew what they were doing. He claimed he had phoned Yeltsin, who was in his limousine on his way to a meeting, read him the text, and received approval. Voshchanov and his staff of two were inundated, on their two city phone lines, with requests for clarification. He tried to set the matter straight, but managed only to dig himself deeper into a hole. Moscow, he added, had territorial claims against republics such as Kazakhstan and Ukraine: 'Russia will hardly agree to give away these territories just like that.'

Nazarbayev and Kravchuk were furious with Yeltsin. Yeltsin was furious with Voshchanov. 'You have made a grave error,' he said to him, his gravelly voice punctuated by long silences. Top-level delegations led by Rutskoy and Stankevich were dispatched to Kiev and Alma Ata. The row was defused. For the next few months Yeltsin eschewed such rhetoric. He decided it would be more propitious to act as an intermediary between an embittered Gorbachev and a recalcitrant Kravchuk. He was playing a double game, trying to prevent an outright break-up of the Union while doing everything he could to usurp Gorbachev.

Yeltsin knew that whatever he did, without Ukrainian agreement Gorbachev's hopes of preserving any sort of Union were finished. Less than a week after the Ukrainian elections, Yeltsin realized it was time to pre-empt the inevitable, to work out an entirely new arrangement between the republics. He told Gorbachev he was off to meet his Slav colleagues, but gave no hint of his plan. He promised only to brief the Soviet President and Nazarbayev back in Moscow on the following Monday. In fact, Yeltsin was on his way to address parliament in Minsk and sign an economic agreement with Shushkevich. The two of them would then sit down with Kravchuk to discuss the way ahead. Yeltsin told Gorbachev he would not sign any deal that would commit Ukraine to being part of another country, and that there was no point in being part of any new arrangement if Ukraine wasn't. It was all very vague, very cryptic. Gorbachev didn't read much into the remarks.

Starovoitova, the Russian President's adviser on nationalities, was asked by Yeltsin ten days before the Ukrainian referendum to make a prediction.

She told him at least 75 per cent would vote for independence. 'He was shocked. "It can't be that many," he said.'

Gorbachev was at a loss. He broadcast two rambling, impassioned, televised appeals on successive nights, warning Ukrainians that independence would be a catastrophe. Even Jesus Christ could not untie the bonds linking the peoples of the Soviet Union, he said. In spite of – perhaps because of – his threats, Ukrainians voted overwhelmingly to go their own way. They also gave Kravchuk the mandate he needed. Gorbachev's reaction to the results was even more frantic. It convinced Yeltsin's team that Gorbachev himself was at the core of the problem, that nothing could be solved as long as he remained in office. The thinkers behind the Belovezhskaya agreement were Burbulis, Kozyrev and Sergei Shakhrai, an ambitious lawyer who would become a prominent figure in the new establishment.

On day one they put paid to Gorbachev. They celebrated their achievement over a large dinner, laced with vodka and champagne. On day two they came up with the Commonwealth of Independent States.

The announcement was sudden. As the leaders left for their respective capitals on Sunday night, their aides agreed the final wording of a brief communiqué, to be issued by Shushkevich's office. 'We, the republics of Belarus, the Russian Federation and Ukraine, note that the Union of Soviet Socialist Republics as a subject of international law and a geopolitical reality ceases its existence.' The fine detail would be left for another time.

Yeltsin didn't bother to inform Gorbachev. He left it to Shushkevich and instead telephoned Bush as he flew back to Moscow that Sunday night. Nazarbayev had just landed on his way to his scheduled talks the following morning with Gorbachev. Yeltsin broke the news to him at Vnukovo airport. He was speechless.

Starovoitova believes Yeltsin had been influenced by Alexander Solzhenitsyn, whose long essay 'How Do We Rebuild Russia?' had been published in two Soviet papers in 1990. Solzhenitsyn was seeking to redefine what 'Russianness' entailed. On one point he was adamant:

> The way things are moving in our country, the 'Soviet Socialist Union' will break up whatever we do: we have no real choice, there is nothing to ponder, and it remains only to bestir ourselves in order to forestall greater misfortunes and to assure that the separation proceeds without needless human suffering and only in those cases where it is truly unavoidable.

Moldova could go off to Romania for all he cared, the Baltics, the three republics of the Caucasus and the four in Central Asia could go their own way. That left White Russia (Belarus), Little Russia (Ukraine) and Great

Russia, which would merge into 'an entity that might be called *Rus*, as it was designated in olden times'. Kazakhstan fell into none of these categories. Solzhenitsyn reminded his readers that Kazakhstan had been considered part of Russia until 1936, and that the majority of its inhabitants came from Russia proper. Let the Kazakhs slice off a chunk of their vast country for themselves, and Russia should subsume the rest.

'I'm not exactly sure why Yeltsin didn't want Nazarbayev to participate,' Starovoitova said. 'I believe he thought the idea would be more popular if the Commonwealth were perceived as a Slav entity. When Solzhenitsyn wrote his article he also claimed that we should start by unifying the Slavs. I think that had some influence on Yeltsin's thinking. Intuitively, almost subconsciously, he was thinking in terms of a Slavonic entity.'

Nazarbayev was as upset as Gorbachev. Anything that smacked of a pan-Slavic revival was a 'throwback to the Middle Ages', he said. He would never quite forgive Yeltsin, especially as Nazarbayev had, as early as the start of 1991, been one of the first public proponents of a complete break with the USSR and of a new arrangement that would include the four major republics.

After a frosty meeting with Yeltsin, Gorbachev insisted he was still in power. He called an emergency session of the Soviet parliament, but it had long since stopped functioning as a serious body. A small group of hardliners demanded urgent measures 'to restore constitutional order and work out radical and political solutions to prevent chaos, anarchy and civil war'. The appeals fell on deaf ears. According to Yeltsin's office, Soviet institutions no longer existed. But they continued to work for several weeks as if nothing had happened. Officials were petrified of losing their jobs. The smartest had transferred themselves over to the Russian authorities a long time ago. The advice for the rest was 'keep your head down, say little, but if forced to, pledge allegiance to Yeltsin'. Foreign diplomats were in a similar quandary. Were they accredited to Gorbachev's Soviet Union or Yeltsin's Russian Federation? 'Not sure,' one ambassador replied. 'Probably both.' It would not be long before the problem was settled. The Russian parliament announced it was taking over all the property of the Soviet one, including its holiday homes, sanatoria, rouble and hard currency bank accounts, and business interests. Soviet institutions were picked off one by one – the ministries, the KGB, the Kremlin grounds themselves.

It then came to the question of ratifying the Belovezhskaya agreement. Yeltsin presented the facts before parliament: that the collapse of the USSR had been made inevitable by the Ukrainian referendum, that the CIS was the least painful solution to the many problems. Several deputies expressed reservations, but Yeltsin was given a very easy ride. The motion was passed overwhelmingly.

Rutskoy had heard about the Belovezhskaya agreement only on the television news. He understood and appreciated the independence aspirations that followed the August 1991 putsch, but he had no idea Yeltsin and the other leaders were planning to sign an agreement behind the back of Gorbachev and the Russian parliament. Once again Rutskoy felt snubbed. He wanted to issue a declaration denouncing it, but was talked out of it by his aides.

The hardliners would come to regret their pliancy that December. 'There was an atmosphere of fear all around,' said Vladimir Isakov, one of Yeltsin's toughest foes. 'People were afraid that if they didn't support Yeltsin they'd be sacked. Nobody was going to risk their necks for Gorbachev, and at a national, Soviet, level there was no leader worthy of respect. So we waved the Belovzhskaya decision through.' Isakov's interpretation was true only in part. There was an element of fear that autumn, there were some denunciations, but Yeltsin's mistake was the weakness of his purge rather than a surfeit of zeal.

The other republics jealously guarded their newly won independence, but were very anxious about being left out in the cold. Kozyrev mooted the idea that 'Armenia and some other republics' might want to join the Slav club – as well as, perhaps, former Warsaw Pact allies such as Romania and Bulgaria. The original declaration had held open the prospect of Commonwealth membership for all former Soviet republics, as well as any other state that shared 'the aims and principles' of its founders. The aims and principles were a matter of guesswork.

The Central Asians met in the Turkmen capital of Ashkhabad to coordinate policy. On 21 December 1991, in Alma Ata's House of Friendship, eleven of the fifteen republics (Georgia and the three Baltic states were absent) sealed Gorbachev's fate. A Commonwealth that went beyond *Rus* had been formed. The leaders sent a message to Gorbachev informing him that the Soviet Union and his post had ceased to exist. Yeltsin boomed: 'It is no more.'

They drank to the future, but the displays of harmony were illusory. The arguments began immediately. Russia proclaimed itself the legal successor to the Soviet Union, responsible for all its agreements and obligations under international law, including its large debt commitment. It took over all Soviet embassies abroad and the Soviet seat at the UN Security Council. Everything was up for grabs, from air traffic control and Aeroflot to the railways, banking system, television and the space programme. The CIS was to have a coordinating headquarters in Minsk, but this was not to be a capital, as the CIS was not a state. There would be no flag, no emblem, no anthem. The Winter Olympics were to take place within weeks in Albertville, France, and nobody knew what to do about the Soviet athletes. Eventually it was decided they would compete under the title Combined Team, march under the Olympic flag and stand before the Olympic anthem. The arrangement proved unsatisfactory for all, and for future international events the individual member states went their own ways. Even then, with nationalities so mixed, many sportsmen and women didn't know which country they would rather represent.

The most pressing issue was the military, and specifically the control of the Soviet Union's arsenal of 30,000 nuclear warheads. Kravchuk announced that he had appointed himself commander-in-chief of all non-strategic forces on Ukrainian territory. Soviet battlefield and tactical weapons had been moved out of the more turbulent regions such as the Caucasus and Moldova long before. But both short-range and strategic forces remained based in the four most powerful republics – Russia, Ukraine, Belarus and Kazakhstan. Despite official assurances, nobody knew who was in charge of conventional forces those confusing days in December, let alone nuclear ones. Burbulis said it was Marshal Shaposhnikov, who had become Soviet Defence Minister after the coup. Burbulis was asked whether Gorbachev was still Commander-in-Chief. He paused, licked his lips, gave a wry smile, and said: 'This is something that can be dealt with in the next few days.' At that very moment Yeltsin was meeting the army top brass and promising them an immediate 90 per cent pay rise. 'I am told they were very satisfied,' Yeltsin said afterwards.

Both in Alma Ata, and in a meeting in Minsk a week later, the leaders fudged the issue. They spoke of joint overall control, but with day-to-day operational command in Yeltsin's hands. Yeltsin would have the authority to launch a nuclear strike only in consultation with the three other nuclear leaders. A process would be established whereby the warheads in the other republics would over a period of years be transferred to Russia. Azerbaijan and Moldova joined Ukraine in announcing they would form non-nuclear armed forces of their own. The West was extremely worried, but apart from seeking assurances from the various leaders could only sit back and hope.

Yeltsin's idea was to build a cohesive Commonwealth, with Russia setting the agenda but letting the others have their say. Nazarbayev had his own interpretation. 'Russia must not be our Big Brother,' he said. But with one eye on the impending price liberalization, he added: 'There is no way around a single economy.' Kravchuk was suspicious and thought it best for Ukraine to keep its distance. 'We must wait and see what kind of Commonwealth it is and only then talk about signing any joint charter.'

For a man of Gorbachev's international stature, it was an undignified exit. He said he would go only after meeting James Baker, the US Secretary of State, who was despatched hurriedly by Bush to talk to the leaders of the newly independent states. The speed of the collapse of the USSR had wrong-footed the West. The Americans drew up a pecking order in the way the newly independent states should be treated, based on their interpretation of each country's human rights record and commitment to Western democracy. Gorbachev cut a lonesome figure, with little to do but reflect. His last few days in office were taken up with valedictory phone calls from his friends in Western capitals. He would meet just about anyone who would meet him. One afternoon he invited a visiting German heavy metal band, the Scorpions, to come and see him.

Yeltsin and Gorbachev met in the latter's office for one final time. After sorting out the remaining details, Gorbachev was supposed to announce to the world that he would be resigning. The order went out to the state television studios to have a team on stand-by for the Kremlin. The two of them talked for seven hours, then Gorbachev went home. He left it to his close confidant, Alexander Yakovlev, to sort out the rest. The speech which his aides had begun writing was cancelled. On Tuesday morning he took his leave of his 200 advisers and army of back-up staff. 'They have poisoned the air. They have humiliated me,' Gorbachev said. His resignation speech, timed to coincide with Christmas morning across the Atlantic, was solemn and devoid of his characteristic preaching. He ended it with the bathetic line: 'I wish everyone all the best.' He remained in his seat, waiting for the live television cameras to cut away. The delay lasted no more than a second, but it seemed painfully long. He then gave an interview to CNN and waited for Yeltsin.

At 7.35 p.m. on Christmas Day the hammer and sickle was lowered from the main Kremlin flagstaff and the white, blue and red tricolor was raised. No sooner was the artificial wind machine switched on again than the workmen realized they had put the flag up upside down. They rectified their mistake instantaneously, hoping nobody had noticed. The main evening news at 9 p.m. relayed Gorbachev's speech in full and dwelt briefly on his achievements. Then it was on to the violence in Georgia. That was that.

Boris Grishchenko, lobby correspondent for the Interfax news agency, was leaving the Kremlin that evening after watching the speech go out when he bumped into Shaposhnikov, who was accompanied by three men in civilian clothes as he left Gorbachev's office and hurried towards the lift. Shaposhnikov was carrying a black attaché case. Grishchenko asked him what was inside. 'What is needed,' he replied, before his guards pressed the lift door shut. Yeltsin had not bothered to turn up for the nuclear handover. Gorbachev was forced to give Shaposhnikov the command codes in Yeltsin's absence.

Gorbachev had been promised a day to clear his desk. As he arrived at the Kremlin on the morning of the twenty-sixth to do so, he found his office occupied by a new boss. Overnight the head of the Kremlin guard, General Mikhail Barsukov, had gone around the corridors removing name plates. The one at the entrance to Gorbachev's office read Yeltsin B. N., President of the Russian Federation. Gorbachev walked to the floor below and took a chair in the office of his former chief aide, Grigory Revenko.

Soon the Yeltsin entourage arrived. The most important question was who should sit where in the Senate building. Everyone wanted to be as close to the boss as possible and to get a big office. It was Ilyushin and Korzhakov who decided. The guards watched closely. The nearer the office was situated to the President, the more polite they would be to its occupier. Yeltsin was on the third floor, but he, like Gorbachev, had a separate entrance. He could come and go without the advisers knowing. Guards stood between his section and the rest of the building. Korzhakov was naturally close by the President, as were Sukhanov and Voshchanov, who was given Yakovlev's room. At one point in history it had been the office of Lavrenti Beria, Stalin's chief killer. Ilyushin put himself on the second floor together with Petrov, possibly to keep an eye on the Rutskoy camp. Rutskoy was assigned Yanayev's old office – appropriately enough, some would say later.

The treatment of Gorbachev that day was shabby. But by the standards of Russian leaders gone by, the indignity was minor. Gorbachev had not been shot or imprisoned. He was allowed to keep a state *dacha*, albeit not the one in Barvikha, a city flat, and a staff of twenty including bodyguards and secretaries. His mansion at Foros was taken over by the Ukrainian government. His official monthly salary was set at 4,000 roubles, more than twenty times the average pension but still worth just over £20. Nobody expected him to live on his state income, though. Between lucrative lecture tours to the West, he was to concentrate most of his time at the think-tank he had established the previous August. The Gorbachev Foundation had been given offices stretching two blocks along the Leningradsky Prospekt, in the north of the city on the road to the international airport. The building used to house the Central Committee's Institute for Social Sciences, an innocuous name for a dubious organization. There young Communists, mainly from the Third World, would be trained in the art of agitation – a finishing school, Marxist-Leninist style. It seemed fitting for Gorbachev that for his first trip to the USA following his downfall, he was flown courtesy of the publisher Malcolm Forbes on the American's private jet, Capitalist Tool.

7

Monumental Madness

L ev Kerbel was born on 7 November 1917, the day of the Bolshevik revolution. He was proud of the coincidence. He owed much to Lenin and spent most of his life repaying the debt. One of the Soviet Union's most decorated sculptors, Kerbel was responsible for bringing Marx, Lenin and every other conceivable Communist 'hero' to the high street in Moscow, Omsk, East Berlin or Havana.

I first met him in the autumn of 1985, days before his last great offering to the people of Moscow was unveiled. The marble and granite monument to Lenin dominated October (now Kaluga) Square, a collection of ugly, grandiose grey buildings. The statue itself, with a strident Lenin surrounded by a united proletariat – sailors, workers, mothers and young pioneers – was one of the more impressive examples of giganticism that the capital had to offer. The mid-1980s marked the high point in Kerbel's life. He showed me photographs of himself surrounded by Gorbachev and the Politburo, of himself shaking hands with Yeltsin ('even he was a Communist once,' he said ruefully), Erich Honecker, Fidel Castro. There were many other cherished moments.

The old system treated him royally. Kerbel's studio occupied the ground floor of his two-storey detached house – itself a rare privilege indeed in a city of deathly high-rise blocks and acute housing shortage. The studio was a Madame Tussaud's of the Soviet state. Every inch of floor space was taken up by Lenins, Marxes, a Stalin lying in state, Italian Communists, Bashkirian poets, composers, soldiers, female collective farm workers with their headscarves signifying youthful purpose, coalminers, their lamps shining the way towards a triumphant future. The wall in his kitchen became a visitors' book. Messages of greeting from Yeltsin, American historians, Spanish painters, British Communists were scrawled on it. There was mine, and a few months later, Yeltsin had put his own alongside.

As Communism retreated, the work dried up for Kerbel. In the late 1980s he received only one major state commission: a Lenin in the Arctic port of Arkhangelsk. The world was collapsing around him. Worse, after the coup came the anti-Communist backlash. When the people took to the streets at the end of August to celebrate their victory, they vented their wrath on statues. The first to go in Moscow was the memorial to

Felix Dzerzhinsky, the founder of Lenin's secret police, which was taken down from its plinth in the square outside KGB headquarters. Within hours other monuments had tumbled, and Kerbel's huge bust of Marx opposite the Bolshoi Theatre was daubed with graffiti. 'It was sheer hooliganism,' Kerbel said. 'Let them set up a commission to decide which of these monuments does not make the grade artistically. We're talking about art here, about history.' The city authorities could have cleaned up Marx if they had wanted to. 'I would jump into the car straight away and remove the paint if only they would let me.'

Kerbel continued to espouse faith in the party, months after it had been suspended by Yeltsin. He was no political dinosaur. He knew things had to change and respected Yeltsin's courage. He didn't go to demonstrations and had little time for the hotheads waving the flags and chanting the slogans for one ideology or the other. All he wanted was for some of the familiarity of the old order to be re-established. He was passionate about monuments. The closure of the Lenin Museum and the removal of the mausoleum from Red Square would be acts of 'cultural vandalism', he said. 'Whatever your political line, you have to concede that Lenin was a truly brilliant figure.'

It seemed appropriate that on the day the Soviet Union died, I should go and see Kerbel. Christmas Day on the Western calendar was an ordinary working day for Russians. It was late in the evening, and Kerbel was hunched in the kitchen watching television on his small flickery screen. He made tea, poured some brandy, and tried to make sense of it all. 'We fought fascism, we fought for the Soviet Union, and now we are told it's no longer there,' he said, looking up for some form of explanation. I suggested that maybe things wouldn't be that bad, that it was a political sleight of hand by Yeltsin to get rid of Gorbachev and surely there was nothing wrong in that ('Of course not,' he replied), that there would be no problems travelling to the various republics. He listened, but didn't really take it in. What about the other worry, he asked, 'this price liberalization thing'? Prices, I replied, would go up several times, but then, with competition, they would settle down.

For all his allegiance to the old era, Kerbel made a valiant attempt at adapting. The possessor of the Order of Lenin and Hero of Socialist Labour medals, he swallowed his pride and took on any commission that came his way. He made mistakes at first. He had no idea what to charge, sometimes giving his works away at a snip. He couldn't get his mind around currencies. He would miscalculate the dollar–rouble exchange rate and end up out of pocket. Entrepreneurs, the dodgy and the less dodgy, came to him with orders for busts of themselves or members of their families for their grand entrance halls. A Chechen businessman asked if he would do a statue of his wife, who had just died of cancer. The man produced a blurred photograph. Kerbel said he needed more than that to go on. The man insisted, implored him. 'I'll pay you whatever it takes,' he said, as he rummaged in his wallet through his wad of large dollar bills to prove his worth. The man didn't leave a phone number and never came back to collect the piece. Kerbel forgot to take a deposit and lodged the bust at the back of a basement shelf. He was devastated because, for the first time in his life, after decades of state sanction during which lorries, architects, builders and tonnes of stone were ready at the end of the telephone, he was having to pay world prices for scarce materials. Sometimes Kerbel would work without commissions, chancing his arm, as he ventured into a strange world of selling, marketing, hustling. His first piece was on the Holocaust, a theme that the former Communists glossed over. He was not sure if anyone would want it. It was the only time he would give any expression to his Jewishness, something that was not talked about by aspiring Party members.

Kerbel did begin to make money, and just as he adapted to the new, so the new let him be. Marx was returned to his former glory outside the Bolshoi, Lenin remained in pride of place on October Square. His studio was given over to him personally, his *dacha* in Razdory, not far from Yeltsin's, became his own. His neighbours in the country were flashy surgeons and lawyers, their status-symbol Mercedes parked teasingly in the driveways. He was content with a swing chair in the garden where his daughters would visit. He was intensely proud of them. One was a reporter on the evening news on Moscow's local channel, the other was still at school but was soon to go on an exchange to Albuquerque, New Mexico. They were both gregarious and good linguists, at home with the opportunities to travel and mix freely that had been denied even him.

In the old days retirement would have brought Kerbel laudatories, moderate comforts by Soviet standards, but few challenges. Now he felt obliged to work, but didn't seem the worse for it, despite his arthritis. He was invited to exhibit his works in major galleries and to lecture at an art college. Yet for all his flexibility and willingness to start afresh, he could still not come to terms with the collapse of the USSR more than two years on. He provided a home of sorts to a Georgian friend who had been forced by the fighting there to flee his home town of Poti. To Kerbel, and others of his generation, commercialism had its limits. He would help out friends in need, and receive it back from them. When, early in 1994, his drive had been blocked by a heavy snowfall, he telephoned an old comrade, the head of the local naval academy, who sent out a dozen cadets, shovels in hand.

The last time I saw Kerbel, to pick up works I had commissioned from him, he had just come back from a week's package holiday in the Canary Islands with one of his daughters. 'It was fun,' he said, 'but not a patch on the Georgian coast. If only we could still go there to the sea.'

8

The Shock of Therapy

─────────

For the 'boys in pink trousers' the new economic programme was a journey into the unknown. Subsidies that had accompanied Russians from the cradle to the grave were about to be withdrawn. Many warned of social strife. It was not just Rutskoy who was raising the alarm. Nikolai Shmelyov, an economist of the Gorbachev era, likened Yeltsin and Gaidar to surgeons in the Crimean War, amputating a soldier's arm without anaesthetic. 'The patient's hands are not tied. What if he takes a knife and attacks the surgeon instead?' he asked. Pessimists predicted tenfold price rises. The reality would be considerably worse.

The state, still the main employer by a long way, sought to soften the blow by raising incomes. But it could not keep up with the increasing cost of living, and only contributed to the inflationary spiral. The hoarding and the panic reached a peak in the week before New Year, traditionally a time when Russians stock up for the long holiday, when the shelves in the shops are even emptier, the service surlier, the floors muddier and the tempers shorter than usual. But the last days of 1991 marked a new low in the humiliation of the Russian consumer. Local councils in Moscow and other cities had talked of reintroducing ration cards for some produce, so low were the stocks.

The problem, according to Golovkov, Burbulis's assistant, had been exacerbated by Yeltsin's keynote speech to Congress two months earlier. 'He started speaking off the cuff. He spoke of price liberalization, which was fine, but then, totally out of the blue, he said it would take place before the end of the year. We had wanted to introduce it suddenly.' As the big day approached, collective farm managers and other producers simply stopped supplying the shops. What was the point of distributing their goods if the decimal place on the price was about to change? The queues lengthened. The more intrepid would be first in line at 5 a.m. at the butchers and the bakers. Days were taken up in unseemly jostles in the slush outside the stores. For those with deep freezes, a small but slowly growing number, the problems were not so bad. For the rest, it was a matter of using up every square inch of the ledge outside the window, and hoping there would be no thaw.

From government headquarters in Old Square ministers watched the first days of the economic revolution with a mixture of terror and exuberance. One joked about being sent to the Gulags in Siberia if the experiment failed. It was not entirely clear whether he meant the remark in jest. They sat together late into the evening, with sandwiches and coffee being produced from time to time. Each movement in prices was closely monitored. The process started in confusion. On 2 January, the first day of the experiment, shopkeepers had no idea what to charge. In some cases prices would double overnight, in others they would not. The producers and middlemen were equally in the dark.

The government was relying on producers bringing food back into the market quickly. It was also counting on Western food aid to have an effect. With fuller shelves and the beginnings of competition, prices might begin to fall steadily and tempers would be calmed. That was the theory. But with both sides of the food chain still in the hands of monopolies, the improvements took a long time to filter through. Prices went down for a few days, and that was all. Then they rose again sharply. To make matters worse, much of the aid which was supposed to go directly to the needy fell into the hands of speculators. European Community intervention butter found its way to commercial shops. Tins of ham were sold at street kiosks. Other items went missing. The fiasco prompted the EC Commission hurriedly to send a delegation to Russia to find out what to do. They returned none the wiser, but put on a brave face. It was not politic in those days to cast doubt on the value of Western aid. Many Russians were less gullible. One comparatively well-to-do Moscow family giggled when I tucked into the chicken they had served up for dinner. 'Bush's legs,' said Dmitry. American food aid was being sold in ordinary shops at a price lower than home-produced poultry, providing the middlemen with a handsome profit. 'Market economics, I think you call it,' he added.

For the first time in their lives, millions of Russians went to their local shops and found that they could not afford to buy items they had taken for granted. It mattered little that people at the middle and top end of the scale could find six different types of salami and twenty different types of beer. Dietitians warned that the nutritional balance was getting worse. It had never been very good. Fruit and vegetables had almost always been *defitsitni* – unavailable. The nearest approximation to them in state shops was pickled cabbage in grimy tins. Chickens would be delivered from Hungary on a good day. On entering the butcher's, the customer would ask for 'meat'. Nobody would dream of finding out whether it was beef or pork before joining the queue. Anything would do. Household goods were in desperately short supply – bath plugs, light bulbs, sugar from time to time. Other products had simply never been seen, such as television sets that didn't blow up or even tampons.

I remembered once, back in 1985, being invited for dinner by a friend. She was more perky than I had seen her for some time. She told me she had been around all the markets in Moscow looking for the herbs she needed to cook that evening's delicious stew. She was happy because she had got hold of them. Russians did not speak of buying things, but getting hold of them. When they did, no matter what the effort, it was cause for celebration. And when they did, they bought as many as their string bags would allow, for someone who they knew would need them. Money was no object, because goods had no value, and there was little to spend money on anyway.

Everyone knew about the special shops for Party officials and the *beriozki*, the hard-currency shops for foreigners. To set foot in any of these stores without permission was to ask for trouble. They were well guarded. This was economic apartheid. The dollar had a mythical quality. Muscovites would stand and stare at us as we walked out, laden with plastic bags. Behind the frosted glass and the curtains they imagined a cornucopia of luxury. By their standards there was; by Western standards the merchandise was perfectly ordinary. There seemed no limit to the humiliation the rulers were content to inflict on the people.

In the first months of price liberalization, Russians had to come to terms with entirely different emotions. Many of them simply could no longer afford to buy even those goods that were in the shops. Pensioners were being forced to live on bread and potatoes. As the prices increased with each day, there seemed little end to the misery.

It was easy to stir up envy. *Sovietskaya Rossiya* asked its readers how they would see in the New Year. It advised them what was on offer at one of the five-star hotels: 'Blinis with black caviar, smoked salmon in a marinated pumpkin sauce, sturgeon soup with dumplings stuffed with crab, breast of pheasant, fillet of beef in red wine, followed by pears with chocolate mousse. The price? The most reasonable compared with other establishments – only $85, the equivalent of 10,370 roubles.' That was twenty months' average salary at the time. The same newspaper published an open letter, signed by four members of parliament, entitled 'Stop this experiment against the people'. They demanded that the government be replaced by an administration of national accord. Many of those who had carried the tricolor of the pro-Yeltsin demonstrations had swapped their flags for the hammer and sickle. The opposition played to the fears of the downtrodden. The first demonstration, the March of the Hungry Queues, passed off peacefully. Others would not. Already banners were being waved aloft calling for Yeltsin to be put on trial and for the Soviet Union to be restored.

Whatever their economic qualifications, the 'boys' often lacked political deftness. Sometimes they seemed to get carried away, as Gaidar demonstrated when he boasted at a public dinner that he would slash state orders to military factories by 85 per cent and make 'very drastic reductions in military expenditure'. He acknowledged the dramatic consequences for unemployment, social stability and discontent in the military such a measure would have, but left it at that. He was soon persuaded to temper his appetite for cutbacks.

The government established a Working Centre for Economic Reforms, which advised it on macro-economic policy. It was headed by Sergei Vasilyev and Illarionov, with input from Western academics, notably Professor Richard Layard of the London School of Economics. The West's most vigorous proponents of the radical line were Jeffrey Sachs and Anders Aslund. Theirs would be frequent faces in government corridors as a small army of Western experts descended on Moscow as honoured guests, granted meetings with top officials on request. 'It's quite remarkable what they have achieved,' said Sachs, two months into the experiment.

The *rynok*, the market, was the holy grail. The official line was that anything Western had to be good, and civilized. On television the same reporters who a few years earlier would have dwelt at length on beggars scavenging for food in New York rubbish bins, or Yorkshire miners battling with police, were now explaining how cash machines and dishwashers made life so easy for everyone. The viewers never believed the older reports but wanted to believe the newer ones.

The former enemy was portrayed as the new saviour. Having refused to bail out Gorbachev, because of the half-heartedness of his commitment to economic reform, the West, it was assumed, would open up its pockets to the new Russia. The mystical figure that was mentioned was $24 billion, a sum that emerged from the totting up of all the various credits, loans and reschedulings of earlier debts. It sounded a huge amount, but much of it was never delivered. In any case, it all seemed a little pointless considering the flight of capital out of Russia in the hands of the new rich – tens of billions of dollars, far in excess of the amount being invested in it. At one point Russia was losing $1 billion a month. For all their outpourings of support for the process of reform, in Western capitals the mood was always circumspect. Gaidar and his ministers could hardly be criticized in the open for carrying out policy that had been advocated by the Group of Seven and the IMF. But there was a fear that these young men, for all their bravery, for all the macro-economic wisdom, might be getting carried away. 'We wondered out loud whether they might not let up a little. It was they who, after all, were urging conditionality for aid with more vigour than we were,' said one G7 ambassador.

The 'do-gooders' and advisers, great and small, flocked to Russia. International financial organizations took over suites in hotels, flying their executives in and out at huge expense, as part of their mission to explain and guide reform. They concentrated their efforts on Moscow and St Petersburg, taking in the odd 'model' town in the provinces. Often they appeared in competition with each other. Much of the technical assistance was beneficial, but the mood in which it was handed down was all wrong. Russians would never accept the role of supplicant. Some schemes were criticized less than others. One of the better ones was the British Know How Fund, which was established in Eastern Europe in 1989 and spread to the former USSR. The money involved was peanuts – £78 million spread over twenty-four countries – but working on the principle of 'small is beautiful' it had positive benefits on the ground, partly because it knew its limitations and worked with clearly defined goals. One Moscow-based project, to overhaul production and distribution of bread, the most vital of foods for Russians, also enjoyed some success. The British consultants found out to their dismay that the average shelf life of a loaf was twelve hours and that officials in charge of factories and shops had never met each other before. For every problem solved, another was discovered.

Moscow suddenly became *the* destination for the more adventurous Western companies. Word went around: quick money could be made and a good lifestyle could be had. Very often it was businessmen who had not made it back in Basingstoke who would go off to Novosibirsk to lecture the locals or stitch up a deal. Many of them didn't speak a word of the language and had only a passing knowledge of Russian culture and history. They showed little desire to learn, only to teach. Banter at many a Western dinner party would revolve around mockery of local work habits, dress sense and other 'oddities'.

It was a dispiriting experience for Russians to come back from the West with good qualifications such as a Master of Business Administration degree, only to be offered a salary with a Western firm a tenth of that of the less qualified Westerner sitting opposite. One of my friends, a senior Ukrainian economist, was delegated by her employer, a major Western financial institution, to supervise the horse-riding classes of the boss's wife. Behaviour was often worse than patronising. Robert Strauss, the US Ambassador, a millionaire businessman and no softy himself, was often incensed with the bearing of the burgeoning Western community. Once he threw an American oilman and a Russian associate out of his office. 'It's like the old Texas oil-boom towns, a constant parade of con men, promoters and shady customers,' Strauss said, 'the greatest collection of sleaze bags in the world.'

Throughout the winter and spring, as he held his breath for the anticipated upheavals, Yeltsin resolutely defended his young ministers and their Western advisers. Evoking memories of his Moscow Party days, he made a couple of celebrated, and televised, 'spontaneous appearances' at shops, where he was shocked at the prices and the lack of good-quality products. He would blame the 'mafia', who, he said, were undermining the move to the market. At every opportunity Yeltsin pledged to continue the reforms, but by the late spring he was already talking of 'corrections'. In parliament they were less sure, and as the next Congress convened, he knew he had a battle on his hands persuading deputies to stay faithful to the government. He realized that Burbulis had become part of the problem, and hoped that by removing him from the government he would take some of the sting out of the accusations. Nobody was fooled, however, when he created a new title for his right-hand man, State Secretary.

From the opening minutes of the session it was clear the reformist streak the parliament had shown the previous autumn, when it granted Yeltsin extra powers, had been lost. One deputy demanded to know why a statue of Lenin had been removed from behind the speaker's chair. Others complained bitterly about reviving Leningrad's pre-revolutionary name, St Petersburg. It took three votes for that decision to be ratified. During each debate Yeltsin looked on from his raised podium, poker-faced, trying hard to conceal his contempt for what he called this 'pseudo-democratic ritual'.

The ritual disintegrated into circus. Congress ordered Yeltsin to present a draft law on government and a new list of ministers within three months. Then, just when it seemed he was most needed, Yeltsin disappeared. The idea had been to show himself above the fray, a 'menacing absence' as his close aides would later describe it. But many of his supporters were decidedly twitchy. 'He's always resting at the wrong time,' muttered Viktor Sheinis, an elderly liberal. Two scenarios were offered. Yeltsin had invited Sergei Krikalyov, a cosmonaut who had set off into space when the Soviet Union was around, and returned to earth, to a new country. The two men could be drinking together, deputies wondered aloud. Or maybe Yeltsin was playing tennis. Or both.

Burbulis decided to go for broke. He and Gaidar led an orchestrated walk-out from the chamber. The ministers threatened to resign *en masse*. In a fit of pique Khasbulatov shouted: 'the little boys have lost their heads'. In the lobby outside nobody dared predict the next step. Gaidar did his best to sound tough: 'The government is not an assembly of naughty boys and girls,' he declared. On the next day Yeltsin sprang back. He took to the rostrum first thing and presented a draft law – as he had been commanded; only this draft law was pointing in the opposite direction. It would reinforce his control over the government for the next six months until his extra powers came up for renewal. 'The time of puppet governments is gone,' he said. 'Without strong executive authority there will be neither reforms, nor order, nor statehood, nor a dignified Russia.' Congress was cowed. The first battles had been won. The hyperbole of the previous winter, the talk of 'civil war', 'famine', 'economic genocide' was looking a trifle foolhardy. Complain the people did, but most were making ends meet. 'We survived the blockade in the war, we can certainly survive this,' some would say. They were still prepared to give the *rynok* the benefit of the doubt.

9

Reds and Browns

The 'extraordinary sixth Congress of People's Deputies of the USSR' slithered and died in the mud of a dairy farm outside Moscow. Two months after the dismantling of the Soviet Union, and two months into the economic revolution, a group of stalwarts declared they would reconvene Gorbachev's old parliament. So worried was Yeltsin that he ordered the new Mayor of Moscow, Yuri Luzhkov, to deny them access to all public buildings within the city limits. The police were told to deal firmly with trouble-makers. We were told to gather early in the morning in the lobby of the Hotel Moskva, where many of the deputies still retained rooms. About 200 of them showed up – less than a tenth of the old contingent but an impressive total given the pressure they were under. After much whispering and huddling, the gang charged out of the hotel and into waiting buses.

We headed south, a calvacade of rickety Soviet buses and the ubiquitous Volvos of foreign correspondents, stretching as far as the eye could see. Everyone followed everyone else in a farcical forty-mile chase down country roads. Inevitably traffic lights got in the way and we headed off in clusters in different directions. One of the buses ended up in a field. Out stepped Baburin. He grinned broadly. He and his comrades helped the bus driver to reverse back on to the road. We headed into the suburban town of Podolsk. Perhaps, we thought, the local council had agreed to host the meeting. But the boss there had no idea and we trudged back to our cars. Eventually we caught up with the rest of the troupe. They had reached the House of Culture of the collective farm in the village of Voronovo. The council officials up the road were not so innocent after all. They had heeded the order from Moscow and switched off the electricity in the farm meeting hall.

Aided by the lights of Western television cameras and a few candles of their own, the deputies began to contemplate the affairs of state. The concrete shack bore little resemblance to the Kremlin Palace of Congresses where they had last met, in September 1991. Undeterred, they passed a series of motions which, just as in the good old days before Gorbachev, were passed unanimously by show of hands. They condemned Yeltsin's 'government of occupation' and its controllers, the Western intelligence services. They went on to elect the new leaders for the Soviet

August 1991: a soldier with a picture of Boris Yeltsin on his tank. (*Jeremy Nicholl*)

Yeltsin points his finger at Gorbachev during the Soviet President's only appearance at the White House, days after the defeat of the coup leaders in August 1991. Many would criticise Yeltsin for humiliating Gorbachev that day. Khasbulatov is on the right. (*Roberto Koch*)

Yeltsin and admirer during a visit to Gorky Park in 1992. (*Jeremy Nicholl*)

Celebrating the failure of the August 1991 coup. (*Jeremy Nicholl*)

Rutskoy and Khasbulatov confer in August 1993 during a ceremony marking the 1943 tank battle between the Nazis and the Red Army at Kursk. (*Jeremy Nicholl*)

Sergei Baburin, one of the more charismatic hardline members of parliament. (*Yuri Kozyrev*)

Vladimir Zhirinovsky at his fiery best during the opening session of the State Duma, January 1994. (*Jeremy Nicholl*)

Gennady Burbulis, Yeltsin's long-time right-hand man dubbed 'The Grey Cardinal' by the opposition. (*Jeremy Nicholl*)

Mikhail Kalashnikov, inventor of the automatic rifle that bears his name, out hunting for elk near his home town of Izhevsk in mid-winter. (*Jeremy Nicholl*)

Yegor Gaidar at the inaugural conference of Russia's Choice in November 1993. (*Jeremy Nicholl*)

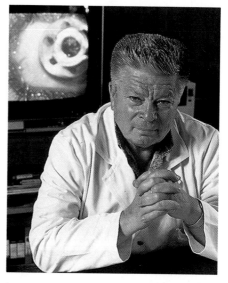

Svyatoslav Fyodorov, multi-millionaire eye surgeon and once touted as possible Prime Minister, in his office with banks of television screens behind him monitoring operations. (*Robert Wallis*)

Pavel Belenko, the President's image-maker, standing on the street with a cardboard cut-out of Yeltsin. (*Jeremy Nicholl*)

Woman at rally in support of Communists and nationalists carrying a poster that reads: 'A president so well catered for is not a president'. Yeltsin, who is wearing a skull cap, is shown raising his head out of a bottle of alcohol with a prostitute fawning herself over him. (*Peter Blakely*)

Yeltsin with President Clinton at their Vancouver summit, April 1993.
(*Bayne Stanley*)

nation. Chairwoman was Sazhi Umalaitova, a peroxide blonde firebrand from Chechnya. Also appointed to the presidium was Viktor Alksnis, the 'Black Colonel' of Latvian extraction whose rabid calls for a strong union had brought him to the fore during Gorbachev's last years. Another prominent figure was General Albert Makashov, the retired commander of the Urals–Volga Military District who been one of the candidates in the 1991 presidential elections. Alongside him was Roy Medvedev, a dissident in the old era, a learned man who had never flinched from attacking the Communist Party which he believed had sullied the good name of socialism. Seeing Medvedev with this group of intolerant, often anti-semitic and rabidly nationalist diehards was one of the sorrier sights of the political transformation.

Job well done, they returned to Moscow at a more sedate pace to hold a demonstration in Manezh Square. They called it a *veche*, invoking the term used for political rallies of the pre-revolutionary period. Several thousand supporters, mainly the elderly, joined them, waving their banners and cheering the speeches about solidarity and the victory of the proletariat. But they were a poor spectacle. Their country would not return, no mattered how loudly they shouted. Yet on seeing Alksnis I couldn't but remember something he had said just after the August 1991 coup, when everyone else was running scared: 'We have suffered a defeat. But I am an optimist. The idea of a great state, which has been created over a thousand years, will win out. The new democracy is doomed. I think there's no point in doing anything, just sit and wait for it to collapse.'

Despite that first débâcle, it did not take long for the opposition to Yeltsin to summon its strength. Initially it was not a cohesive force but a collection of splinter groups. On the surface they had little in common. The proponents of orthodox Marxism–Leninism mixed uncomfortably, often on the same platform, with those who harked back to the days of the Tsars and those who espoused the fascism against which Soviet patriots had fought. Some of those who became 'national-patriots' had throughout the Gorbachev era considered themselves allies of Yeltsin's, men such as Mikhail Astafyev, Viktor Aksyuchits, Ilya Konstantinov and Baburin. Some had been members of Democratic Russia. A few were dissidents, such as Aksyuchits, who was thrown out of the Communist Party in 1979 for reading emigré literature. During 1991 several of them had reservations about Yeltsin. Yet at least he was strong. They were attracted by his call to arms against the discredited establishment, his promise, after all Gorbachev's procrastination, to tackle the economic malaise. Many were with him inside the White House, fighting against the elderly adventurists. What appealed most were the calls for a Great Russia, to rise out of the ashes of the dying Soviet state. Nobody quite thought through what would happen and they most certainly did not believe the republics would all go their own ways. The consensus was broken by the secret deal at Belovezhskaya.

The Baburin–Konstantinov group became the most numerous faction in parliament. Initially they saw Khasbulatov as a toady of Yeltsin's, but the embittered speaker steadily came round to their views. They also resented Rutskoy's initial support of Yeltsin in 1991, but forgave him as the fight against the President intensified. It was this group, whose forces steadily grew during 1992 and 1993, that posed the main political threat to Yeltsin. Back in 1990, when it elected its chairman, the Russian parliament was split evenly between Yeltsin's supporters and opponents. He won only by the narrowest of margins. By 1993 the outright opposition had grown to almost two-thirds, with many more sitting on the fence.

Of those groups which disavowed the parliamentary process, the most prominent and vocal was Working Russia. Whenever there was a demonstration or a picket, this band of thugs would be there. The group consisted almost entirely of the underclass of Russian society, men with bloodshot eyes, desperate pensioners with nothing to lose, manual labourers who had lost their jobs. They did not bother with ideology, confining themselves to expressions of hatred for those responsible for the state of affairs – foreigners, the mafia, the rich, and, of course, *zhidi*, yids. The group's heyday was the summer of 1992 when it picketed the Ostankino television studios to demand air time, creating mayhem for weeks. The leader of Working Russia knew his media well. Viktor Anpilov had been a correspondent for the state broadcasting organization in Nicaragua and was enraged at American support for the Contra rebels and at Gorbachev's disowning of Castro. He refused to toe the Gorbachev line and was withdrawn back to Moscow. He was elected a member of Moscow city council in 1990 but never got into the national parliament.

Working Russia was behind particularly bloody scenes at a May Day march in 1993 when one policeman was killed. Anpilov was called in for questioning by the Moscow Prosecutor's office, whereupon he was 'kidnapped' for two days, beaten 'cruelly and professionally' and abandoned in a hut in woods. He was hailed by his followers as Russia's own Che Guevara. While wary of his antics, the more astute members of the parliamentary opposition were happy to play on the hysteria he would whip up. The government had little reason to fear Anpilov. In some respects he helped them because his antics would be broadcast on television and could be used to depict the entire opposition as rabble.

Far more dangerous was the Officers' Union of Lt-Col. Stanislav Terekhov. Established in January 1992 to coordinate the anti-Yeltsin camp in the army, 'to assist in the cohesion of officers on state patriotic ideas', its role was not as small as the authorities suggested. Its influence was mainly among decommissioned officers, but within the serving ranks it was always probing away. Terekhov boasted he could have as many as

25,000 men under arms within hours. His followers fought openly in the wars in Abkhazia, Nagorno Karabakh, as well as in Serbia. What the Officers' Union was doing for malcontents in the army, the Russian National Assembly sought to do for disgruntled KGB officers. The idea belonged to General Sterligov, who formed his group after splitting from Rutskoy. He had little difficulty attracting money from KGB insiders and the Communist Party. His group was also one of the first to attract prominent entrepreneurs to the anti-Yeltsin cause.

Many of these individuals had started out together in Pamyat, which began innocuously enough in the early 1980s as a lobby group aimed at preserving Russia's heritage but developed into a rabidly anti-semitic group, encouraging desecration of graves, spitting, anything that would encourage Jews to flee to Israel. One of Yeltsin's most lamented mistakes was his agreement to receive a delegation from Pamyat in the mid-1980s while he was Moscow Party boss. The meeting was used by his opponents to demonstrate that he was a closet nationalist. He argued in defence that he had wanted to seek out a broad range of non-conformist views and did not know the extent of the hideousness of Pamyat. Riven by in-fighting, Pamyat split into several factions, but several of these proved even more influential. By mid-1992 many of the views originally propagated by Pamyat had been brought from the fringes into the heart of the body politic.

Still, for many of these nationalists, the notion of fascism posed a dilemma. How could they espouse an ideology practised by the enemies of the Red Army and responsible for the sufferings of millions of Soviet people during the Great Patriotic War? The victory over Nazism had been the single greatest sacrifice of the Soviet state, commemorated every year with much pomp and emotion by the entire nation. According to Yuri Belyayev, the answer lay not in the ideology that Hitler had espoused but in his 'tactical error' in invading the USSR. I met Belyayev in his basement office in a northern district of St Petersburg. Those who believed his cause had no backing from influential circles needed to look no further than his headquarters. He and his leather-jacketed thugs shared the same guards with a major private company, which supposedly was dealing in 'the travel business and exports'. We went upstairs for coffee to a very pleasant bar with cable television, a good selection of drinks and posters of American heavy metal bands on the wall. 'It's becoming quite a popular place to be seen,' Belyayev said.

A former criminal investigator in the local police, with a rank of senior lieutenant, he had few noticeable political affiliations when elected to St Petersburg City Council. Belyayev suddenly 'went brown', as he likes to say (a reference to Hitler's brownshirts), shortly after the Gaidar team came to power. He wrote a series of articles in the local press under the title 'Does criminality have national characteristics?' He argued that it was not Russians who were dragging the country into the mire of violence and lawlessness, but people from the Caucasus like Georgians and Chechens, and, naturally, Jews. His was one of the first groups to rally to the cause of the Serbs. He established training centres in Moscow and St Petersburg, with firing ranges and political 'discussions'. When I saw him he had just returned from commanding another group of mercenaries to Belgrade and Pale, the headquarters of the Bosnian Serbs. 'I know there are enough people behind me,' he said. 'In St Petersburg it's been easier to get the message across. It's a purer Russian city.' He was hoping to lobby parliament to enact a law setting limits on the number of 'non-Russians' holding high office. Non-Russian was a euphemism for Jew, and anyone whom the hardliners disliked was included in this conspiracy. Thus Kozyrev, the Foreign Minister, was renamed Kozenstein. Anyone with aspirations to high power but the remotest trace of Jewish blood, such as Yavlinsky, knew he was labouring under a handicap.

When Sobchak took over the city, David Raskin dared to hope that the fascist element, which had always been underground, would be rooted out. The opposite was the case. Raskin worked in an institute from where he compiled a newsletter on the fascist threat. 'We are not talking about a spontaneous movement,' he said. 'They have support among former KGB officers, in the police and elsewhere, among people who don't like the way the country is trying to move West.' Outside Gostinyi Dvor, the main department store in the heart of St Petersburg, newspapers carrying Nazi emblems and articles about the 'yid-masonic conspiracy' were sold. While Belyayev contributed the brawn, one of the 'brains' behind the extremist upsurge in the city on the Neva was Viktor Bezverkhy. In February 1993 a St Petersburg district court acquitted the 62-year-old businessman turned cooperative owner on charges of inciting racial hatred. He won the case by claiming that his company's printing and distribution of *Mein Kampf* had been dictated by commercial considerations alone, and was not connected with its ideology. From time to time the authorities in St Petersburg tried to clamp down on the likes of Belyayev and Bezverkhy; but the pressures against conviction were too strong. Many on the city council were reluctant to suspend Belyayev's immunity from prosecution.

Another example of official support for these causes was the success of the *Military-Historical Journal*. Once an obscure monthly, its fortunes were transformed by the appointment of Major-General Viktor Filatov as its editor in 1988. Thanks to the publication of excerpts of *Mein Kampf*, which would have landed Filatov in jail had he not been a friend of Yazov's, circulation jumped from 27,000 to 377,000. Among its other 'contributions' was a revival of the infamous anti-semitic forgery, *The Protocols of the Elders of Zion*, which had been used as a pretext for pogroms against Jews before the 1917 revolution.

It took a karate expert and car mechanic with a Hitler lookalike moustache to bring fascism back to the centre of Moscow's agenda – not Zhirinovsky, but Alexander Barkashov. Throughout this period Zhirinovsky was a bit-part player. At the hardliners' rallies he would be shunned as a maverick. Deprived of the right to speak on the podium, he and his merry band would walk around the fringes of meetings, in Manezh Square or Gorky Park, loudhailers in hand. Zhirinovsky was desperate for publicity and would do whatever was necessary to gain it. In January 1993 he despatched ten volunteer paramilitaries to Iraq to help out his friend Saddam Hussein. The spectacle, for which journalists had been notified in advance, took place in front of astonished onlookers at the Sheremetyevo international airport. 'You are going to defend Iraq, a victim of reckless aggression by America and Israel,' Zhirinovsky told his unarmed, uniformed heroes. 'I wish you a safe return though some of you may die there. You should know you will die for a noble cause.' Another piece of clowning, people thought.

Barkashov started out in Pamyat in 1985, as bodyguard for its leader Dmitry Vasilyev. He organized Pamyat's thugs, its 'fighting force', but gradually fell out with his boss, whom he accused of inactivity. Barkashov formed his own group, Russian National Unity, which made a name with its open calls for a violent seizure of power. He set up his office in two grubby rooms in a building down the road from the headquarters of the criminal police on Petrovka Street. The commercial banks and other companies in the buildings seemed to have no problems about sharing their premises with him and his henchmen, who would parade their armbands, bearing a modern-day variant of the swastika, with pride. The Barkashovtsis' newspaper was entitled *Russian Order*, a flysheet that called for the arrest of Gorbachev and Yeltsin and the flushing out of *zhidi* from public office. Barkashov represented rebellion against the new capitalist establishment. The young fascists saw themselves as simply taking over where the radical anti-Communists had left off with Yeltsin's election as President.

Even though it was Yeltsin's signature on the document, it was Gorbachev who was invariably blamed for the disintegration of the USSR. It was he, many said, who destroyed the Party and the motherland; Yeltsin merely took advantage of it. The denunciations were usually confined to hysterical banners at demonstrations. Occasionally they went further. In a council hall near Moscow's northern port in September 1992 a small group of extremists played out their fantasy. A 'people's court' was convened to try the ex-Soviet President for treason. Sitting in front of a Soviet flag, the panel of nine judges and three prosecutors called witnesses to testify against him. Some members of parliament took part, while several military officers were happy to be seen at the kangaroo court. The district council had no qualms about giving over its conference room to the proceedings. The only trouble was that Gorbachev didn't show up. Still, the exercise was not altogether pointless. To loud cheers, the judges sentenced Gorbachev to prison *in absentia*. The man in charge of proceedings was a certain Viktor Ilyukhin, once a top official at the public prosecutor's office. In December 1993 Ilyukhin was elected to the Duma and given charge of its Security Committee.

For the great mass of voters at the time, the ideas espoused by these various extremist groups were anathema. That is not to say that they didn't have misgivings about what was going on in the country. The sense of disorientation ran deep, and anxieties grew about the cost of living and about crime. The fears existed, but they lacked focus. For those who were old enough to remember, one man would have sorted out the mess: Yuri Andropov, the man who briefly succeeded Brezhnev before dying in office. Andropov was remembered with affection for how he clamped down on idlers and crooks. On sunny summer days he would send the police around to the city's outdoor swimming pools and ponds to demand of bathers their ID cards (which they rarely took with them on such mini-excursions). They would want to know why people were not at work; unemployment officially did not exist and everyone of working age was required to have a job. 'If only Yeltsin's lot did the same,' some would say. 'Get people back to work.' If only Russia could *produce* more, everything would be all right. The logic was flawed, but the message was compelling.

For the President's more serious opponents, the main task through 1992 was to develop an organization that could bind them together in the battle for the soul. That they succeeded testified to their discipline, a discipline that was reminiscent of the radical reformers in 1990 and 1991, who had managed to paper over their differences in pursuit of their goal. The banner they found was 'national-patriotism'.

The founding conference of the National Salvation Front, one Saturday morning in October, presented a frightening scene. The Communist diehards had come to recognize their joint endeavour with the nationalists. The hammer and sickle was borne proudly alongside the black, gold and silver flag of the Tsarist empire. The third group in this unholy trinity was also represented – on stage, by jackbooted guards in black uniforms and black berets, with leather straps across their chests.

The Front's main coordinator was Alexander Prokhanov, who belonged to the school of *derevenshchiki*, village writers, that also included Valentin Rasputin and Vasily Belov. Prokhanov shot to fame with his romanticized tales of the heroism of Soviet soldiers in Afghanistan. His novel *The Tree in the Centre of Kabul* won him among the military the label the 'Soviet Kipling'. He would not be the only member of the cultural world to ride to fame on the backs of the exploited conscripts. Prokhanov certainly had talent. His weekly newspaper *Dyen*, Day, was one of the best popular newspapers in the country. Perhaps its only rival in the industry for turning out outrageous and entertaining articles, with scant concern for fact, was *Moskovsky Komsomolets*, on the opposite end of the spectrum. *Dyen*, the Newspaper of the Spiritual Opposition, as it called itself, boasted some genuine scoops, including some from inside the presidential administration, supplied by a sympathetic telephone operator. *Dyen* would accuse government ministers of the most heinous of crimes, with always just a hint that their blood might not be truly Russian. But Prokhanov's people got away with it all, because they had managed to make their message fashionable for many of the young. Veneration of the West had become distinctly *passé* in many circles.

The hall of the Parliamentary Centre was packed. Delegates spilled over into the aisles and hundreds of sympathizers stood in the street outside listening to proceedings broadcast by loudspeaker. The National Salvation Front was indeed a broad church, united in its strivings for a Great Russia and its distrust of all manifestations of Western life, especially of the hedonism and *laissez-faire* described by Solzhenitsyn as the 'liquid manure which seeped under the Iron Curtain'.

Yeltsin tried to have the Front banned. His decree was first ignored, then overturned by the Constitutional Court. To some, the court's decision was a demonstration of the strengthening of Russia's democratic institutions in the development of the division of powers. To others it was a sign that the supporters of the forces of reaction had, after a year of lying relatively low, finally regrouped. The Communists and the fascists had found common cause, just as Hitler and Stalin did at the start of the Second World War. Once again the enemy was Western-style democracy.

Valery Zorkin, diminutive, mild-mannered and with a propensity to whine, was not the sort of man who would naturally engender fear. Yet the Chairman of Russia's first Constitutional Court would become the scourge of Yeltsin and the government. He didn't seem to fit the role model of a man with a historical mission, to act as arbiter in Russia's shaky experiment with democracy, its transition to a law-based state. During sessions of the Constitutional Court, Zorkin rarely looked the part. His designer robes – the creation of Slava Zaitsev, the couturier to the court of Gorbachev – seemed to hang limply over his shoulders. His meteoric rise, and his nomination by parliament, were due at least in part to his associations with Rutskoy's party. A professorship at the Interior Ministry's high school of law was not the most distinguished of pedigrees.

The case against the Communist Party of the Soviet Union opened on 7 July 1992. The radicals had wanted another Nuremberg. They had wanted to see those in the Central Committee and KGB who had hounded dissidents, stashed away public money and humiliated millions of ordinary citizens with the arrogance of Communist rule *punished*. They were not sure how they could do it, or under whose laws. The Soviet constitution and criminal codes weren't much to go on, and there was little chance of securing some form of international tribunal. It was a highly sensitive and complicated task for even the most learned of judges. Hardliners had brought a case against Yeltsin, declaring that he had exceeded his powers by banning the Party. Yeltsin's supporters in parliament, fifty-two of them, filed a counter-claim, arguing that the Party had violated the Soviet constitution and the norms of international law. It had never been a party in the truest sense of the word but a state within a state, a 'special mechanism for the creation and realization of political power'. Zorkin decided to hear the two suits simultaneously, a decision which aroused no objection.

Police were out in force that day. As Yeltsin's men arrived, hundreds of demonstrators shouted 'fascists' at them as they waved their red flags and their small portraits of Stalin. The court had been assigned a wing in the complex of buildings that had housed the Central Committee. The irony was lost on no one. The room itself was a a poky, remodelled conference room, with not enough seats for the army of party loyalists who had arrived to lend their support. They would stay, day after day, week after week, through the summer and autumn, a veritable *Who's Who* of the old world. There was Yegor Ligachev, the ideology chief in the Politburo who had been instrumental in Yeltsin's downfall in 1987, and Ryzhkov. But no Gorbachev. The judges sat on a curved dais, with the Russian tricolor behind them. All but one of them had been members of the Party to the very last.

So determined was he to win that Yeltsin sent his top guns: Shakhrai, his personal legal adviser, who had been responsible for many of his decrees; Mikhail Fedotov, another respected lawyer; and the controversial Makarov. To oversee them, and the court, he asked Burbulis to go there from time to time. The team spent hours poring over documents that had been hidden in Party, presidential and KGB archives over the years. No innocents themselves, even they were shocked at much of the material they saw – the extent of the KGB's eavesdropping, the number of *stukachi*, informers, the dirty financial dealings. They had a wealth of documents proving Party involvement in the August coup, money laundering and sponsorship of terrorism. Their problem was to make the evidence conform to the narrow legal confines of the case, to prove the technical *unconstitutionality* of the Party, as opposed to its *immorality and criminality*. After all, parliament in those days consisted only of Party placemen and it was they who laid down the constitution, including the infamous article six which defined the Party's 'leading role' in society.

The Party's case was presented with greater verve, by men who seemed in a permanent historical trance. Sometimes they got carried away, as on the first day when one parliamentary deputy warned that if the case went against them and the government remained in office he and his comrades would feel 'obliged to seize power'. He was rapped on the knuckles by Zorkin. It was like the good old days for the Party men. The court laid on Volga cars to bring them in, the buffet was good and cheap. One of the ever-present observers was Mike Davidow, a veteran American Communist who had moved to Moscow to join in the proletarian struggle decades earlier. Even in Gorbachev's time I remember him being singled out at official press conferences to plant easy questions. Davidow believed what he said with a passion.

Ligachev's testimony was a *tour de force*. He apologized for nothing, denied any wrongdoing and argued that if the Party had only been left alone, it would have transformed society along democratic lines. 'The Party was not a Robinson Crusoe organization. We were not out on our own, but with the people. Most of us were committed to reforming the system, but from within the existing structures,' he said. Yakovlev, effectively Ligachev's successor, begged to differ. He reminded the court of Stalin's purges and the Party's other crimes over its seventy years. His only regret, he said, was that it had not been destroyed earlier.

The answers to many of the questions lay with Gorbachev, especially concerning the coup. He was politely *invited* to appear as a witness in September. He refused, describing the proceedings as a 'show trial and political farce'. This was followed by a summons which drew an even more acerbic response. He would not attend 'this shitty trial even if they dragged me there in handcuffs'.

Others with less than clean histories had testified, and been left in peace. As head of the Central Committee's International Department, Valentin Falin knew as much as anyone about the Party's money and its sponsorship of unsavoury groups abroad. It came as no surprise when he resisted the court's demands, pleading a weak heart and a lecture engagement in Hamburg. Only after receiving a guarantee of immunity from prosecution did he appear. He said little, was thanked for his efforts, and was sent back at Russian government expense to Germany where he was a contributor to a German newspaper.

Gorbachev's truculence reinforced the suspicion that he had something to hide. He became convinced that Yeltsin's people were seeking any pretext to have him arrested. Relations between the two men had plunged to rock bottom. Yeltsin had already downgraded Gorbachev's limousine from a Zil to a humble Volga and taken away some of his other privileges. During a CIS summit in May, Yeltsin completely lost his cool when asked to comment on another of Gorbachev's ritual criticisms of his administration. Yeltsin said he had been given an assurance by his predecessor that he would stay out of politics. What had particularly irked Yeltsin was that Gorbachev continued to bad-mouth him in the West. He could not understand why in foreign capitals they continued to worship

Gorbachev and regard him as a major player in Russian politics. His resentment was thoroughly understandable, but his reaction to Gorbachev's meddling did nothing to further his cause abroad.

Early one morning three busloads of militia, supervised personally by Murashev, the head of Moscow police, appeared at Gorbachev's Foundation. The building was sealed. A presidential decree said the building would be given over to a training organization for financial experts. The Foundation could rent a few rooms if it paid for them. Gorbachev was apopleptic when he arrived at the scene. 'The police have blocked the building as if it were a nest of spies. This is all happening in a country its leaders call democratic.' The man who opened up the Soviet Union to the outside world, and dramatically changed its attitude to human rights, was then prevented from leaving the country. It was not clear under what law the travel ban was imposed, but it produced a furious reaction in the West. Gorbachev was supposed to have gone to South Korea later that week, and on to Italy and Latin America. He likened himself to a 'political refusenik', using the word coined by those refused permission to leave in the old days. Yeltsin backed down. Gorbachev was fined 100 roubles (about 20p) by the court for his refusal to testify.

After five months of deliberations, it was left to Zorkin to read out the judgment. The court declared that Yeltsin had exceeded his powers in disbanding local Communist groups, but had been right to dissolve central Party structures in the aftermath of the coup. The clumsy compromise provided hardliners with a morale boost, allowing them to organize again at the grass roots and giving them a theoretical legal base on which to impeach Yeltsin. The Communists were jubilant. They and their fellow-travellers praised the court for demonstrating its independence. Some, especially the young, couldn't care less either way. But many saw the judgement as a missed opportunity to tackle the past head-on. The oppressors and the oppressed had been lumped in the same category. That was that. Russians were never going to be forced to confront their history. A second Nuremberg did not come to pass.

10

Class Act

───────────

The half-chewed piece of salami dangled from his mouth. Viktor Khrolenko gulped down another glass of vodka. 'You little islanders with all your poncy ideas. You're finished. Your time's up. We'll buy you out, including your filthy little newspaper.' Khrolenko, a Siberian businessman making serious money in America, had not finished. 'Look at my watch,' he screamed, pointing at a huge gold timepiece Liberace would have been proud to wear. 'That cost $17,000, more than you're ever likely to earn.'

I had been invited by an old friend, Artyom Troitsky, a rock journalist whom I got to know in 1985, and his wife, Svetlana Kunitsina, for dinner at the Aragvi, a Georgian restaurant in the heart of Moscow. It was one of those very Soviet places, where good old-fashioned 'atmosphere' – the surly man at the door and the bribe to the waiter to get you dishes that were not on the menu – was prized above the quality of the food. I had been in one of those 'things are changing for the better' moods. New shops, restaurants and services were opening all over. Moscow was looking more and more *normal*.

It was Khrolenko's birthday. He was enjoying his drink and his diatribe. I had never met him before. I learnt how proud he was to show his *Soviet* passport when travelling abroad and how the rouble would one day outstrip the dollar and how Russia's rich would lead the way. I sat there expressionless for a good while, but finally, after yet more insults, I couldn't help but walk out. His friends rushed out, apologized and asked me back. I declined the offer. Instantly I regretted my reaction. There they were for all to see, the stereotypes: the haughty Englishman, the boorish Russian. I reassured myself with the thought that I was unlikely to see him again and it didn't matter much anyway. After all, I said to myself, every country had its unpleasant pursuers of the big buck. I was in for a shock.

A week later I was in the dining room of the Savoy Hotel, a somewhat more elegant setting, lunching with the newly appointed presidential spokesman, Vyacheslav Kostikov, discussing the finer points of Yeltsin's Kremlin. Waiters hovered discreetly as Kostikov demonstrated the *penchant* for finer French wines acquired during his years in the West. Suddenly, to my horror, Khrolenko marched up to our table. I was praying he wouldn't create a scene, not in front of Kostikov. He ignored me completely and gave Kostikov a bear hug. I had no idea whether he recognized me or not. The two went off for a discreet little chat in the corner. When Kostikov returned, I enquired, in all innocence, who the man was. 'You should know him,' he said: 'He's very influential'.

Khrolenko was another of the children of the Gorbachev years. He started doing business in the mid-1980s, taking *matryoshka* dolls and other souvenirs over to America and bringing back American goods to Russia. His company, Belka Trading, diversified. One of the more lucrative areas was importing vodka into Russia – American vodka. Taking coals to Newcastle; but if the market dictated it, then so be it. He fell in love with Americana and with an American. They married and bought a house in New Jersey. Such was the fascination with the USSR in the late 1980s, it seemed any Russian would be warmly received in the USA. Khrolenko encouraged Boris Grebenshikov, one of the country's top rock stars, to try his luck over there. The venture did not work out. By the early 1990s, Khrolenko was feeling a little homesick. Life in the West was pleasant, but essentially dull. In any case, it was much easier to be known in Moscow. It hurt people like Khrolenko to know that money was not the key to acceptance in Western society. In the new Russia nobody lost too much sleep over quaint issues such as social justice and egalitarianism.

In the midst of the new Russian craze for expensive cars, over at the British Embassy they were phasing out the ambassadorial Rolls Royce. The official reason was the escalating cost of maintenance just at a time when Whitehall was calling for financial prudence. Unofficially, concern was expressed at the display of 'unnecessary opulence' at a time when many Russians were suffering. Russia's seriously rich felt no qualms about splashing out more than £100,000 for the ultimate status symbol on wheels. 'Our businessmen began with Mercedes, but now that they all have the latest top-of-the-range models, they want to move on,' said Peter Terian, an American of Russian extraction and owner of what promised to be one of the motoring world's most lucrative dealerships. The Rolls Royce showroom, only five minutes' drive from Red Square, had for years been a demolition site. The inauguration ceremony was a curious cocktail of uncomfortable-looking British diplomats, international businessmen and shady-looking types in dark glasses. Nothing dampened the thirst for the big motor – not the pot-holed streets, not the anarchic driving habits, the gridlock, the pollution, the cold winter temperatures or the crime rate. Mercedes and BMW reported more sales of top-of-the-range models in Moscow than in any other European capital.

What went for cars applied even more to property. It was a risky but lucrative business. One Frenchman made a fortune selling Russians penthouse suites in Monaco and chateaux in Provence, but he felt the need to bring over a couple of French bodyguards *en tout cas*. Property was a huge money-spinner. Russians were buying second or third homes in Europe, America and beyond. Only the best areas of London would do: Chelsea, Kensington, Hampstead. I came across the phenomenon, inadvertently, during a brief trip back to Britain. An estate agent I had arranged to see on my own private business arrived an hour late. 'Very sorry,' he said, 'You'll never believe what happened to me. This man, this man with a strange accent walked into my office, and asked to buy a house. Anywhere in London, but big, he said. I told him that was no problem, I'd put him on the mailing list. "You don't understand me," he said. "I need it now." He proceeded to open his attaché case and produce £300,000 in cash.' That was back in 1992, when such an incident was a novelty. A year or two later it had become a commonplace, and the amounts involved had risen sharply. The Russians continued where the Saudi Arabians had left off in the late 1970s.

Britain, in the eyes of many Russians, was the land of Dickens, Sherlock Holmes and Jack London. The 'foggy albion' was the home of tradition and old-fashioned values. After buying their house, the next step was to send their children to an English boarding school. Heads of preparatory and public schools quickly caught on to the trend, some travelling to Moscow to promote their product. The first such advertising conference at a five-star Moscow hotel was mobbed by upwardly mobile Russians, who thought nothing of spending $100 just for a look.

Another good way to throw money around was to go on holiday to the sun. In the old days, the choice was confined to the 'Soviet Riviera' – the Crimean peninsula, which had suddenly become 'foreign', Ukrainian territory, and the Black Sea coast, much of which was now inaccessible because of the war in Georgia. By 1991, as foreign travel restrictions were eased, thousands of Russians were flocking to Cyprus, Crete, Malta and other relatively inexpensive destinations, especially those that didn't demand visas. Some countries were visited almost exclusively for business. At one end of the scale, the mass-market end, hordes of Russians flocked over the border to Poland, Turkey or further afield to the Arab Emirates and Pakistan, where they would buy up cheap or duty-free electronics or linen and sell them for more back home. Entrepreneurs would charter planes for groups of 100 or so from a particular provincial town for these *shopturi*, shopping tours. The very rich had different destinations. A glance at the Aeroflot timetable offered some clues. New scheduled flights were laid on to Hawaii, Thailand, the Caribbean.

Understatement was an alien concept, especially at night when the rich came out to play. Within a few years Moscow must have built more casinos and more lurid nightclubs than any other city. A few gambling dens had always existed in the main Western hotels, but soon, it seemed, everyone was at it. The trend began somewhat demurely with the opening in 1990 of the Casino Royale at the Hippodrome racetrack. The building had served as the royal entrance and private grandstand for Tsar Nicholas I and his friends. The money came from Fyodorov, the eye surgeon, and German partners. Their idea was to try to recreate a semblance of Tsarist opulence, but almost exclusively for foreigners. The house language was English and the currency dollars. Gamblers had to show their passports on entering. Soon that changed. The many microcosms of financial apartheid were demolished. In any case, few Westerners would be able to flash wads of hundred-dollar bills as wealthy Russians now did. Far less salubrious casinos appeared all over town. Huge complexes were built. They were not for the faint-hearted. The abiding philosophy was that women were there to entertain men, as whores, strippers or simply dancers. The Red Zone was a popular haunt, where young girls in lycra would dance in cages. A favoured mafia hangout was the Turgenev café, where naked girls would perform pelvic thrusts by your plate. The audience loved it. The place was always packed. The girls were followed on stage, incongruously, by an elderly male jazz band.

In the daytime some of the girls were university students. They saw nothing wrong, nothing demeaning about their work. Prostitution had for many years been seen as a laudable vocation. It was one of the few that presented women with the chance of financial independence from their husbands. The plight of women under both Communism and crude capitalism was equally miserable. In the old days women would work as long and as physically exhausting days as men, but were also expected to do all the housework in the evening and at weekends. Men would lift a finger on one day a year, 8 March, International Women's Day, when they would fete their wives with flowers and endearing attempts at making the dinner. Russia epitomized the very worst aspects of traditional relationships between the sexes – a point not lost on many Westerners, especially Americans, who saw in it a temporary escape from the straitjacket of political correctness. They packed the clubs.

Not everything about the Moscow night life was sleazy. Predictions that the free market would destroy high culture proved unfounded. The Bolshoi Ballet went thoroughly commercial, with tickets set at exorbitant prices and the troupe spending long periods abroad. Most theatres, helped by some subsidies from the city council and sponsorship deals with businesses, managed to survive, even to thrive. The film industry was the exception. Cinemas, which had fallen into the hands of the Azeri mafia, pandered to the very lowest in taste, putting on the latest violent American trash and confining Russian directors to showing their works at festivals or at the couple of more up-market cinema clubs.

The imaginative and *outré* set were in St Petersburg. Well-heeled but not necessarily monied, they built a nocturnal world that rivalled anything the globe over. *Tusovkas*, happenings, had existed since the 1950s for young Russians, who would make up their own fashions by improvisation and a vague guess at what was going on in the West. They had their own gang loyalties and rivalries. To be a *stiliaga*, a local equivalent of a New Romantic, was to ask for trouble from the *rokeri*. By the early 1990s fashionable Russians knew everything they needed to know about the West, but were doing their own thing with at least as much style. The trend setter in St Petersburg was Alyosha Haas. In early 1991 Haas established his first club in a disused nobleman's house overlooking the Fontanka river. The club outgrew itself and Haas sought fresh fields, in New York. He came back to St Petersburg, bringing his experience of the West with him, pledging to turn his city into Europe's night-life capital. The next winter came the Polaris Crystal party, a rave on ice. This he followed up with a party on the roof of a palace. The only disappointment was a last-minute change of heart by the local Air Force commander, who had agreed to have helicopters fly overhead to provide extra lighting, only to change his mind. A little while later the city authorities gave Haas permission to use the grounds of the Armoury, now a museum of military history, for another party. Such was its build-up that that groups came from Britain and America just for the chance to dance atop a T-80 tank or an SS-20 missile.

A fixture at all these parties was Vladik Mamyshev. As a teenager, Mamyshev couldn't stop dressing up. He got severely reprimanded at school for turning up one day as Hitler. During his military service he became Marilyn Monroe, padded bra, wig, make-up, high heels and all. He was sent to a psychiatric hospital, because nobody would believe he was doing it just for effect. His mother, a prominent member of the district Communist Party, got into hot water about her errant son. On his release, Vladik would soon be featuring on the covers of glossy magazines the world over. One of my more precious memories is the sight of Monroe, née Vladik, at a reception held by a German magazine at Moscow's Hotel Metropol, being chatted up by some of those very same censorious and lecherous elderly Party hacks.

Perhaps Haas's most successful venture of all was one of his first, in the Cosmos Pavilion at the Exhibition of Economic Achievements in Moscow: the capital's first acid house party. Gagarin One was part sacrilege, part brilliance. The hall had been built as a monument to the first man in space, the ultimate hero. In the days of Soviet delusions of grandeur, the park was a mecca to which visitors were taken to learn the marvels of electrification, industrialization and the happiness that only Communism could bring. The space programme topped it all. With its giant picture of the man himself, in his spacesuit, and models of Soyuz spacecraft hanging from the ceiling – perfect objects for lasers – the Cosmos was the ultimate venue. The party was the talk of the town. Some of New York's and London's hippest disc jockeys had come for it. And this in December 1991 when nobody knew who was in charge of the country or indeed what the country was called.

The good ideas were invariably hijacked by the mob. Haas started his own full-time club in St Petersburg, called the Tunnel. Modelled on a similar club in New York, it was housed inside a narrow bunker dug in the 1960s to save the city's elite from nuclear attack. He had to agree to various conditions with the landlords, the Ministry of Defence. One of them stipulated that the premises must be vacated within six hours in the event of war being declared. Trouble arrived within a month of the opening. It was nearly 3 a.m. and the party-goers were milling about outside on the street. They were prevented from going down the steps by a group of armed *byky*, bulls or hoodlums. They had come to demand protection money from Haas. He already paid one group for protection; these were either cowards or in league with the others. 'I knew this would happen,' he said as he took two of the *byky* into his tiny office. They emerged satisfied; an arrangement had been made.

It was a familiar story. At the Hermitage Club in Moscow, Sveta Vickers and Dima Petrov passed on a fifth of their entrance fees to the man at the door in the leather jacket. A uniformed policeman sat next to him, but his job was quite different. He was there to ensure there were no fights. For many organizations paying the *krysha*, their protectors, was financially preferable to giving money to the state. With VAT, income tax, profit tax, tax on staff salaries, municipal transport tax, export and import tax, use of minerals tax, even a tax on the use of the word 'Russian' in a name or title, nobody could afford to pay them all. A token was usually offered by the organization, and the mobs would fob off the taxman with a sizeable cut. Sometimes, just to make more money, the firemen would appear and warn that they would have to close the place down because safety regulations were not being followed. Usually the safety regulations didn't exist. If payment wasn't made, the owners were told, the building could suddenly catch fire. Sometimes it did.

The police also liked to know what was going on. One night at Art Pictures, a club established by the sons of the film-makers Nikita Mikhailkov and Sergei Bondarchuk, the paramilitaries carried out a raid, forcing everyone against the wall and smashing a few heads before leaving. They said they were looking for drugs. Funny things did happen at that club. One night a selection of eighteenth-century tapestries were sold at an impromptu auction. Nobody asked how they had come to be there.

Of all the clubs, the White Cockroach was *the* most fashionable place to be seen. It broke new ground in that it went out of its way not to be opulent. It resembled a central London basement wine bar with low beams, candles and wooden benches. Members, including a smaller proportion of the criminal world than was usual elsewhere, could bring their guests to eat and drink quietly until the early hours, far away from the sleaze of elsewhere. Their idyll was smashed one New Year's Eve when a drunken member of the local police branch who had managed to make his way in drank too much and became a little too intimate with the girlfriend of a renowned mafia boss. A fight broke out, the policeman radioed for reinforcements, and a small gun battle ensued. The altercation made one paragraph in one newspaper. The guests stayed away for a couple of nights, a metal door was built and a couple of new guards employed, then it was back to business as usual. No investigation. No explanation.

One evening, having discovered that my car had been broken into again, I was standing outside my apartment block, flagging down cars, as was the custom when seeking taxis, when a police car screeched to a halt. 'What's the problem?' I enquired. 'Nothing. Hop in. We'll take you wherever you want. Only three dollars,' the officers said. After polite haggling we compromised at two and set for off for the other side of town. Sasha and Pavel were in their mid-twenties, married and extremely disillusioned. They should have been dealing with urgent calls in a rapid squad that responds to emergency 02 calls. So long was the response time, and so great the demand, that the authorities would later appeal to the public not to call the emergency services. For a meagre sum by Western standards, Sasha and Pavel drove me around and were all too ready to open their hearts, describing the dozens of grisly crimes they had to deal with each week for miserable pay, and the corruption of their superiors. Most, they said, were in league with criminals. The two men, I thought, epitomized the new Russia. They showed considerable resourcefulness in making ends meet, within or without the law. They had long ago lost respect for their employers and their leaders. They had no nostalgia for the past, but little hope in the future either. For them, dog eats dog. It was the same for the GAI, the traffic cops, who would always be ready to come to an arrangement. It was a matter of negotiating, and smiling.

I soon understood why the police's clear-up rate was so low. I had to go along one morning to my local station to report that my flat had been broken into. The detective was sitting at a desk, one of its corners propped up by bricks. She sat in her overcoat, with a small bar fire from a highly unsafe socket providing the only heating. The pipes had burst long ago and nobody had come to repair them. The room looked as if it had never been cleaned. The detective was extremely polite and concerned as she asked me to list the items stolen and their true value. I wasn't sure whether to cry or scream as I rattled off a pair of shoes, fifty dollars, leather jacket, five hundred dollars. This woman earned as much in a month as the replacement value of one of my shirts. She winced occasionally as I mentioned a figure, and fiddled with the ribbon she had been using on her clapped-out typewriter several weeks after the end of its natural life. Her pen ran out and I lent her my plastic biro. As I left she asked me if she could keep it.

The only serious investigations were being carried out by private detective agencies run by former KGB officers, many of whom retained good links with their former employers. The police had neither the incentive nor the money to tackle the mobsters. There were never enough fast patrol cars, flak jackets, handcuffs – or typewriter ribbons – to go round. Radio equipment was so antediluvian that officers sometimes had to rely on telephone booths, most of which didn't work themselves. Manpower was not the problem; the size of the Interior Ministry, into whose remit the police fell, was put at more than two million. In Moscow alone there were said to be at least 120,000 police employees, three times more per head of population than in New York. Nobody in their right mind and of above average intelligence would dream of joining the Russian police. Many of the ordinary officers were *limitchiki* – desperate workers from beyond the city limits who would do any job, however miserable, just to gain a Moscow residence permit. They could be likened to the Mexicans who stream over the border into California.

It was no wonder the police were easy prey for the mafia and their bribes. All the major cities had been carved up between the groups into a series of wedge shapes, points towards the city centre, fanning outwards, giving each group a slice of the Western hotels. Many in the police had a visceral hatred for 'blacks' – by which they meant anyone who hailed from the Caucasus or Central Asia. They were only reflecting prejudices that were prevalent across society. The crime figures encouraged such views. In Moscow alone there were said to be 3,000 Chechens working in gangs. Their speciality was stealing cars and reselling them in Europe or the Caucasus. They then diversified into counterfeiting money. The Azeris ran the farmers' markets, where they ensured that nobody undercut the high prices. If anyone tried, he would be kneecapped. This group also dealt with drugs and flowers (the latter an extremely lucrative business), as well as the film industry. The Georgians took an interest in the casinos, while Dagestanis were left with the muggings. This 'racial interpretation' did not always, as Soviet newspapers would have readers believe, correspond to the truth.

There was another kind of market, too: the *tolkuchka*. All around Moscow, on virtually every street corner, lines of men and women, young and old, would form, each person holding an offering – a piece of salami, a pair of plastic shoes made in China, some crystal glass from Bohemia. The ignominy was overwhelming. These people were desperate, but not down-and-outs. Some were trying to eke out a living by buying food in shops and selling it at a small mark-up. Some were selling their heirlooms. Others had come from even greater misery in the provinces to try their luck in the capital.

Even in Soviet times, railway stations were miserable sinks of poverty and iniquity. In the new era they had descended to a different level of human life. The Kursk station, which served all points to the Caucasus, was home to some of the most pitiful itinerant wretches. On each of the three floors of the terminus, an anonymous modern structure, the human mass seemed to wander aimlessly. Some people inched their way forward in the long line for tickets, some loitered at the sex-book stalls in the basement floor, others queued for soggy sausages or a bottle of vodka at the buffet. With airports cancelling flights because of lack of fuel and spare parts, and few guesthouses to cater for them, there was not a free seat to be had.

It was there that I met Andrei. He was swaggering with the confidence of one who controls his patch. He brushed past two old women lying crumpled on the muddy floor, their coats tattered, their eyes staring blankly at the weary travellers. 'Young man, give me cigarette, just a drag, please,' one of them wailed. Andrei swung round and bawled: 'Fuck off, granny.' The more she beseeched him, the more he and his friends laughed, their chortles turning into a roar when he threw his empty box of matches in her face. 'Go die, old bag,' he said, beckoning his entourage to move on. Andrei was twelve, the 1990s Russian version of the Dickensian artful dodger. He smoked, took drugs when he could get them, drank and robbed. He was the new type of *bomzh*, the Russian acronym for 'person with no fixed abode'. Andrei had a round boxer's face and a crew cut. He couldn't help scratching his armpit inside his torn shirt for fleas. He was one of dozens of children, some as young as eight, who had made the station their home. Their job was to steal. Behind the chaos there was order. A hierarchy existed and discipline was meted out to those who broke the rules. At the head was the Chechen mafia. Under them were 'commandos', who operated small areas, 'running' the children.

Andrei was in a good mood. He had just lifted a plastic waist belt from a passenger. He went off to a side room on the first floor to do the books. He was quite a dab hand at maths. He reckoned he would have to give away 4,000 of the 17,000 roubles to commandoes and 4,000 to the police. 'If I didn't cough up,' he said, 'they'd haul me away.'

11
The Boys are Expelled

As he embarked on his political rehabilitation in the late 1980s, Yeltsin consulted a professional image-maker. Pavel Belenko tried to work at the President's posture: 'It was as if Yeltsin was made of rock – immobile, with his shoulders, head and neck all tense.' In short, he looked too much like an old Communist in a grey suit. 'He goes down better with the people when he's more alive and begins to move, because left to himself he is a charming man.' Belenko was convinced that a consultant would have done Gorbachev's career no harm. For a start, he would have told him not to pontificate and harangue the viewers on television. Belenko told Yeltsin not to feel so self-conscious about showing his left hand, which had been missing two fingers since a boyhood escapade. When he was eleven and the war was on, Yeltsin and a few friends broke into an arms depot in a local church. They climbed through three layers of barbed wire and stole a couple of hand grenades. Yeltsin took charge. Without removing the fuses he tried to open the grenades with a hammer. The explosion mangled the thumb and forefinger on his left hand and when gangrene set in the fingers had to be amputated.

Shortly after the coup, it dawned on the old-timers who surrounded Yeltsin that it was about time they learnt the art of the sound bite. They discovered to their amazement that public relations meant *talking to people*, explaining policies. The younger radicals had acquired the knack. So why couldn't they? Starovoitova was touched one day when Petrov and Ilyushin, who were senior to her in the Kremlin hierarchy and were anything but her political bedfellows, came up to her with a surprising request. This was early in 1992.

They asked me: 'Galina Sergeyevna, why does everyone hate us so much? Why is everyone so rude about us all the time?' I told them: 'Because no-one knows what you really do. If you were more open with people, told them what your work involves, perhaps they'd respect you more.' So they invited in some journalists and gave them a couple of interviews, but they came over so stilted that I think they made matters even worse.

Both returned to type and shunned most enquiries.

Of all the 1,400 *apparatchiks* in Yeltsin's administration, Ilyushin was about the only one who throughout the years did not attract serious criticism. This respect was due in part to the distance he kept from the others, as he acknowledged in one of his rare public statements: 'From the time I began to work with Yeltsin I have become, as it has turned out, an invisible person, and I reckon that this is normal. I know of practically every document that gets to the President.' According to Voshchanov, Ilyushin's lack of political passion was one of his strengths. 'He functions more or less like his notebook or computer. His liking for a particular policy document is based more on his feelings for the individual presenting it than the argument actually expressed. He's a man who is simply concerned with preserving stability and with keeping power in the hands of the President.'

Only two people had direct access to Yeltsin during his first years as President. One was Ilyushin; the other was Korzhakov, his bodyguard. They were the only ones who could walk past the secretaries in Yeltsin's ante-room (the secretaries were always male, so they could double up as yet another line of bodyguards) and into his office, or to his resting-room just behind it where the President would eat his lunch, usually alone, or have a nap. Yeltsin did not appreciate overbearing personalities, or professional colleagues who assumed too much personal contact. He would use the polite mode of address *vy* instead of the casual *ty* with which Gorbachev preferred to patronize people. Yet Yeltsin often took his formality to extreme lengths. He and Petrov, his chief of staff, were good friends. They spent a lot of time together, hunting and walking. But when it came to seeing the President at work, Petrov had to sit in the waiting room until the secretaries allowed him to go in.

For all the denunciations of Communism and declarations of imminent change, Yeltsin's Kremlin returned to the old secretive ways. The *propusk*, the permit, maintained its exalted position. Without it, it was physically impossible to get into most buildings. The archives became harder to get at, journalists would be told to submit written questions when requesting interviews, and telephone calls were not returned. There were, however, notable exceptions. Many of the offices of the 'boys' in government were keen to demonstrate their Western ways. To hear for the first time: 'Gaidar's office, what can I do for you?' was enough to bring tears of joy. But gaining access to reliable information became harder. More and more meetings would be held in closed session. Usually one of the participants could be prevailed upon to leak the contents, but usually he did so from a particular standpoint. Often a more straightforward brief for the press would have saved the leadership considerable trouble.

Yet for a few months after the coup it seemed as if all the doors had been opened. I conducted an experiment of my own on the most furtive of all the institutions – the KGB. I went in search of my file. I arrived a few minutes early at the Lubyanka and stood outside, shuffling my feet and gazing at the Russian flag and the graffiti – all that remained of Dzerzhinsky's statue. The public relations office said it would be all too happy to invite me for a get-acquainted session. My point of contact had just been promoted. I had always been curious about the KGB, and I assumed the interest was mutual. I tried my opening shot: 'What have you done with files you've amassed on foreign correspondents?' 'What files?' my host replied. 'How could we have kept files on all of you? There have always been far too many of you and far too few of us.' 'How many of us merited being observed?' I asked. 'I would say considerably fewer than half,' he replied. 'Those whom we suspected of black marketeering or having contacts with dissidents, especially Sakharov, or doing anything else that was considered criminal at the time.' But any correspondent worth his salt had met dissidents, supposedly clandestinely in parks, taking slips of paper from them on which the evidence of human rights abuses was scribbled. As to the existence of my own file, they would not say. 'Our journalists, when they return from England, tell stories of being followed by your British agents. But everyone likes to feel important, don't they?'

There was something touching in the insouciance. I recalled several incidents during my assignment in the mid-1980s. There was the time they slashed my car tyres after I had reported on an illegal demonstration, another when they tampered with the brakes. Their imagination seemed to know no bounds, as when they replaced an Elvis Costello album in my collection in my flat with a record of Red Army marching songs, leaving it slightly askew and returning the original a week later. What about the men with the black briefcases who would take the lift to the eighth floor of our foreigners-only block and then walk up and unlock a door on the ninth? What were they all doing now?

Yeltsin made several attempts to clip the wings of the KGB. After everything it had done in the past, he knew it was part of Russia's problem, not the cure, and that failure to change the institution could lead to his downfall. Yeltsin never shook off his distrust of the KGB. On his visit to London in November 1992, he admitted that he had chosen to stay at a hotel because he did not trust the communications inside the Russian Embassy, a traditional centre for KGB operations in the West. Yet he was persuaded to tread gently. Both Bakatin, who was Gorbachev's appointee, and Ivanenko, whose information was invaluable during the coup, were dropped. Bakatin was roundly denounced for handing the US Ambassador details of the bugging system that had been built into every brick of the new American compound. Barannikov was Yeltsin's new choice, a man who had made his career in the Interior Ministry, and thus a relative outsider, but no liberal. As a first step, foreign intelligence was hived off from the rest of the operation, under the leadership of Yevgeny Primakov, an old-timer who under Gorbachev came to prominence on his shuttle missions to Saddam Hussein just before the Gulf War. The Ninth Directorate, which looked after the safety of top politicians, was transformed into the President's own 5,000-strong Kremlin Regiment. The remaining parts were reconstituted under the title of Security Ministry, which was told to concentrate on the fight against international terrorism and other aspects of organized crime. Foreign intelligence, especially in the Third World, was scaled down. Initially, counter-intelligence was downplayed.

Ministry officials had their own interpretation of free-market principles. Information was declassified, at a price. Lee Harvey Oswald, Wallenberg – the great mysteries were there for the buying. Retired agents were free to supplement their income. When I went to see Leonid Shebarshin, head of foreign intelligence until the coup, he initially asked for money. Courteous, cultured, but icily committed to a peculiar brand of *Soviet* patriotism, Shebarshin was happy to expound on the evils of Gorbachev and Bakatin and the West's duplicity. The compleat KGB insider, he spent much of his career abroad under diplomatic cover in Pakistan, India and as KGB 'resident' in Iran at the time of the downfall of the Shah. Ayatollah Khomeini was, to him, 'a brilliant man'. Gorbachev, Shebarshin said, had thrown the leaders of Eastern Europe to the wolves. 'He and his friends lived in a world of self-delusion.' The West was having a heyday. 'They are determined to see no resurrection of Russia as a great power, to ensure that Russia never again becomes a rival.' He then checked himself. 'You must observe, I'm trying hard not to slip into paranoia.'

Shebarshin went into private business. He set up his own security agency, but struggled to make inroads in an area where competition had set in. His office, in a stand at the Dynamo sports club, was shabby. But Shebarshin's old KGB friends never stopped coming to see him. More than once during the various attempted shake-ups his name was touted as a possible Security Minister or foreign intelligence chief.

It took eighteen years for Rufina Philby to come out of the shadows. I first met her through Yuri Shekochikhin, an investigative journalist from *Literaturnaya Gazeta*. We were to meet several times, in my flat and in her own, just behind McDonalds on Pushkin Square. She was Kim's fourth wife, and was thirty-three when they met. He was twenty-five years older and had drowned his frustrations at the Brezhnev regime in drink. 'He felt superfluous and it hurt him desperately,' she recalled. 'It was awful to see how an intelligent man could lose his senses before your own eyes. I fear that without me he would have drunk himself to death.' Rufina kept his library of books intact, his photographs on the mantlepiece. She felt no nostalgia for Communism, enjoyed her recent trips to England, but saw no reason to reassess her husband's defection. She, too, tried to make a go of the market, selling some of her late husband's memorabilia to auction houses and writing her own memoirs.

Each time she contacted a publisher or an agent she felt they were out to deceive her. 'People are put in touch with me sporadically,' she said. 'I think "what a polite young man or woman," and then they go behind my back just to get my material on the sly.'

By 1993 the Security Ministry was back to many of its old ways, filtering information selectively to the President. Many politicians wanted to believe, and have the people believe, that someone else was responsible for Russia's misfortunes. Yeltsin was given 'evidence' that the West had exploited the turmoil in the former USSR to strengthen its own espionage foothold. The Baltics and Eastern Europe had become major centres for the CIA, he was told. As the atmosphere changed, few of the promised changes were carried through at the ministry. The total number of staff was reduced, but only slightly. Yeltsin learnt to his dismay that Barannikov was almost as unreliable as Kryuchkov had been to Gorbachev. The Security Ministry continued to operate as a law unto itself.

Yeltsin's personal guards were convinced that he was the constant target of assassination plots. Barsukov, the Commandant of the Kremlin Regiment, said his men had investigated more than 100 terrorist 'signals' against the President from telephone taps and intercepted letters. The most publicized assassination attempt involved a disillusioned army major from the Russian Far East. In December 1992 Ivan Kislov absconded from his regimental headquarters in Khabarovsk and made his way to Moscow. He slept rough on railway station floors by night and walked the streets by day. The next stage was to slip past the guards and into government headquarters in Old Square and, with everyone away over the New Year holiday, hide himself in the attic. But his plans went awry when he discovered that the home-made explosives he hoped to use had been soaked by rain, forcing him to arm himself with a penknife. He was found in the building before he had time to carry out his mission. He claimed he was a street sweeper but did not resist when arrested. He later told interrogators that killing Yeltsin was his 'civic duty'. He was diagnosed as schizophrenic.

The dangers, perceived and real, enabled the entourage to maintain a wall of secrecy around the President. Yeltsin seemed to have learnt little from his inaccessibility in the autumn of 1991. The man with the sole charge of Russia would sometimes simply not turn up to meetings, and very few people were told where he was. Nicholas Brady, the US Treasury Secretary, suffered this fate, as did a top-level Japanese delegation. For snubs, nothing beat the experience of Juan Antonio Samaranch, President of the International Olympic Committee, in January 1992. It was a Friday afternoon, and Samaranch was already on his way to Moscow on an important mission to discuss what to do with the old Soviet Olympic structure following the collapse of the USSR. He was due to meet Yeltsin the next morning in the Kremlin. A hapless aide was given the job of phoning Samaranch on his plane and telling him that Yeltsin was not available that day and that a meeting with Burbulis had been arranged instead. Samaranch ordered the plane to turn around and went back. Yeltsin had been relaxing at his *dacha* in Zavidovo. When he found out on the Monday morning how miffed Samaranch had been, he angrily demanded to know which of his officials had been responsible for cancelling the trip.

When he did apply his mind to a subject, Yeltsin was not ashamed to defer to his many aides. He had several expert groups as well as the Presidential Council that dealt with broad strategy and the Security Council that looked after defence and security matters. One long-time adviser said Yeltsin was a particularly good listener, unlike Gorbachev.

> There's no comparison. Yeltsin almost never interrupted. Only if he thought it really necessary would he raise an objection. Gorbachev would do all the talking himself. It was hard for anyone else to get a word in. If someone went to see him he would hold forth himself and then at the end say: 'So, we're agreed on everything then. Off you go and get on with your work.' They would leave with no idea of what to do because they hadn't managed to tell him what they came to say.

In theory, Yeltsin's week was organized. Nobody would get to see the President, no document would reach his desk, without Ilyushin's say-so. Every minute of every day was meticulously organized, well in advance. As Yeltsin himself revealed, his working week adhered to a strict routine: on Monday, reports from his 'power ministers'; Tuesday mornings, meeting with Prime Minister; Tuesday afternoons, meetings with advisers; Wednesday, Security Council; Thursday, regular cabinet meeting; Friday, 'presidential services'; Saturday, reports from analysts and selected members of the press, as well as meetings with regional leaders or leaders from the CIS. Tuesday and Saturday, he claimed, were also 'sports days' when he would swim or play tennis in the evenings.

Everything depended on Yeltsin. Whenever rumours of bad health circulated, a sense of panic was never far from the surface. There was no obvious successor, but no shortage of people vying for his ear. The Kremlin became a Byzantine court of intrigue, with political allies spreading malicious gossip about each other in order to climb a few rungs on the ladder of access to the President. *Dyen*, the extreme nationalist newspaper, called it the Collective Rasputin. The description was characteristically over the top, but it was pointing in the right direction. At one point *Dyen* received a series of sensitive leaks that so obviously came from the Kremlin that they were not too difficult to trace. One was a transcript of an alleged conversation between Yeltsin and Bush, in which Yeltsin said he had decided to keep Kozyrev in his post in deference to the American President: 'I have fulfilled your request.'

Politicians of all hues were prisoners of their secretariats. There were so many papers to be signed, so much bureaucracy to get through in the day-to-day routine that it was hardly surprising documents were signed without being read. Yeltsin was no exception. Sometimes, after he signed a decree, his staff would go off and secretly make alterations to it. Poltoranin was in the thick of the in-fighting. The situation, he said, would not improve in the back rooms until civil servants were properly trained – and paid. 'We need a training establishment to educate public officials for the needs of the new regime, people who would be less bureaucratic, less inclined to take bribes. There are still leftovers from the Gorbachev and Brezhnev periods, even some who served under Stalin.'

Yeltsin did little to discourage the rivalries. It was as if he enjoyed playing the disinterested mediator, the king who could bestow gifts or take them away. Yavlinsky likened the President to an actor who did not know his lines. 'The worst thing is that there are several prompt boxes and each prompter has his own text.' For Yeltsin, personal loyalty was paramount. He started to consult Korzhakov, his bodyguard, in setting political strategy. For the experts in the camp, it was galling to see Korzhakov's earthy advice taking precedence.

Gaidar was never part of Yeltsin's inner circle, excluded by his age and background. Their meetings were formal. Gaidar tried to keep out of the intrigues, and to confine himself to economics. Before cabinet sessions, he told his ministers not to burden the President with long presentations studded with statistics. As he said to one of his ministers: 'Keep it slow, keep it simple. That's the way Yeltsin likes it.' Yeltsin had stood staunchly by Gaidar during the April Congress. He gave him the benefit of the doubt, promoting him to the post of Acting Prime Minister, but by the late summer of 1992 he was becoming distinctly edgy. Industrial production was plummeting, inflation had not been brought under control, mass unemployment was looming. Workers were not being paid because of a shortage of cash, even though printing presses were working flat out. Many families had been unable to take a summer holiday, a relief that was eagerly anticipated every year after the interminably long winters.

Yeltsin was encouraged by his advisers to dilute Gaidar's influence by appointing some of the old industrialist generation to senior positions. These were people who liked to think of themselves as experienced in 'real life', the nuts and bolts of running factories and local regions. First came Viktor Gerashchenko, who had been Chairman of the Soviet Central Bank in Gorbachev's day. Gerashchenko was the epitome of the late 1980s Soviet bureaucrat, smug and cynical, but efficient at his job in the narrowest sense of the word. Gerashchenko had little time for the 'boys' and their monetarist schooling. He saw the Bank's task as being the purveyor of gifts for his friends in industry. Nevertheless, it was Gaidar who proposed him as chief of the Russian Central Bank that July. Gaidar knew he would be difficult to work with, but believed his appointment would help take some of the sting out of the opposition's attacks on the government. The only other candidate under serious consideration was Boris Fyodorov, Russia's representative at the World Bank in Washington at the time, and before that at the European Bank for Reconstruction and Development in London. Fyodorov was a confident, abrasive monetarist who pulled no punches. Gaidar denied that he had passed over Fyodorov for fear that he would become a rival for the mantle of 'chief reformer'.

By now the radicals were in a state of alarm. They spoke of a 'creeping coup' masterminded by the likes of Petrov and Skokov, the increasingly influential head of the Security Council. The 'corrections' to economic policy called for by Yeltsin and implemented by Gerashchenko had an immediate and devastating effect. Inflation, which had been brought almost under control, soared as Gerashchenko handed out credits to all-comers. In one week alone prices rose by 5 per cent. Hyperinflation loomed.

When Yeltsin lost faith in a particular aide, he would rarely confront him. He didn't enjoy arguments. He simply let it be known that he wanted to see less of that individual. The *vertushka*, the internal Kremlin line, would ring less often, and eventually the decree would be issued announcing the appropriate change in personnel. The victim would rarely learn about the sacking from the horse's mouth. Usually he or she would find out from the newspapers. Starovoitova was one of those to suffer. She was one of the last figures from Democratic Russia still in the administration. Throughout all the early election and parliamentary battles, Starovoitova had been a close ally of Yeltsin's. In the heat of the moment after the coup she had even been mooted as a potential Defence Minister, an astonishing proposal even in those few months when anything seemed possible. In Yeltsin's early months in power, Starovoitova could see him almost whenever she wanted; by the summer of 1992 she had to make a formal application and was received far less frequently. She was sacked not long after, when the leader of one of the Communist fiefdoms of the northern Caucasus, North Ossetia, complained about her views on the ethnic conflicts in the region. Yeltsin, she said, did not seek her side of the story before ordering that a decree be drawn up. As with so many dismissals, the recipient read the bad news in the papers.

Her face and her ideas simply no longer fitted. 'It happened gradually,' she said.

Yeltsin started to combine a variety of people from different backgrounds in his staff. It was true that many democrats didn't know anything about administration or organizational work. Because they were dissidents and weren't part of the Communist machine they were never able to get the necessary experience of running things. Yeltsin came to see that the people from the old *apparat* understood about administration, so he chose them instead. They started holding on to information and using it to their advantage, while supplying the democrats, and Yeltsin, with disinformation.

During the 1991 presidential election campaign, Yeltsin had walked arm-in-arm down Tverskaya Street in Moscow with Father Gleb Yakunin – a former Politburo member with a priest who had spent eight years in labour camps for 'anti-Soviet agitation', Soviet-speak for human rights work. The two shared much in common in their determination to challenge the status quo. Yakunin was a thorn in the side of the Orthodox Church establishment. He drew attention to the seamier side of its recent past, its collusion with the KGB and the Party, and its persecution of radicals in its ranks. Once in power, Yeltsin realized he needed the Church to reinforce his authority, so he distanced himself from the likes of Yakunin. The Patriarch was happy to lend the President his support. While extreme nationalists such as the head of the St Petersburg diocese were allowed to propagate their views freely, Yakunin was defrocked. The official reason was that he had indulged in politics. Despite the lack of support from his former ally, Yakunin was reluctant to criticize Yeltsin personally. But he saw in his acquiescence an unwillingness to delve any further into the Party's past. 'If democracy really came into force and all the archives on the Church were opened, many in the Church leadership would be forced to quit their positions, because there are such disgraceful episodes in their biographies. People wouldn't stand for it, so they are at pains to cover it up.'

The President was becoming more circumspect towards the radicals in general. He believed Gaidar had let him down on one crucial point. As the reforms were being planned at the end of 1991, Gaidar told him the drop in living standards would bottom out within nine months. Yeltsin believed him and passed the message on to the people during a televised address at New Year used to explain why the tough medicine was unavoidable. Illarionov explained: 'Yeltsin didn't understand that it was the opponents of shock therapy who undermined our stabilization programme. He equated Gaidar with the reforms, and as it became clear that they weren't going the way he had hoped, he felt let down.'

Yeltsin had not lost faith in reform itself. He appreciated many of the positive aspects of the changes. The first stage of privatization had been a success. The consumer sector had been revolutionized. The queues that had dictated the daily routine in previous years had disappeared, except in those few areas where prices were still controlled. New, brightly lit and well-stocked privately owned shops replaced the dirty, miserable, grey state stores of old. GUM, the department store opposite the Kremlin, offered a glittering array of Western names: Galeries Lafayette and Christian Dior from France, Benetton from Italy, and many more.

Much depended on the second stage, when thousands of medium-sized and large enterprises were to be sold off. The programme was coordinated by Deputy Prime Minister Anatoly Chubais and the State Property Agency, with advice from the International Finance Corporation. The idea was simple. Every member of every Russian family, including children, would be given a multi-coloured cheque with a nominal value of 10,000 roubles. This corresponded to £24 at the time. These vouchers, or cheques, bearing a picture of the Kremlin, could either be sold for cash, given over to an investment fund, or swapped for shares in a company, either at a public auction or in a management–worker buy-out.

The opposition denounced the plan before implementation even began. *Pravda*, the master of the tabloid headline in its latter years, contrived a neat little play of words. For *privatisatsiya* read *prikhvatisatsiya*, snatch and grab. Yeltsin appeared on television on the eve of the inauguration to urge the nation's support. Instead of lining the pockets of the rich, he told them, this was a laudable egalitarian measure: 'We need millions of property owners, not a small bunch of millionaires.' The public was also sceptical at first. When Gaidar went to Nizhni Novgorod, a town to the east of Moscow that had established itself as a paradigm of economic reform, he was heckled as he launched the first privatization auction. The first day of the national campaign was an anti-climax. Few savings banks were prepared, and few citizens seemed to know where to go, or what to do, to register for their vouchers. The idea quickly caught on, however, and the agenda moved from the merits of privatization *per se* to the different ways of implementing it. The results were mixed, but Chubais pursued his goal with steely determination. Such was the pressure from the directors' lobby that Chubais was forced to amend the law to give the combined workforce and management of any company the option of taking a controlling 51 per cent share. Many firms took up the offer, but overall the spread of ownership was impressive.

Despite the start of privatization, the fashionable concept that autumn was 'centrism'. A new group was formed, Civic Union, led by Arkady Volsky. Yeltsin made overtures towards them in the hope of broadening his administration's appeal. Volsky began as an engineer at the Zil car factory, became head of the Party organization there, and made his way up through the Moscow Party hierarchy to become a senior figure in the offices of Gorbachev's predecessors, Andropov and Chernenko. His power base was the Department of Machine Building of the Party's Central Committee, whose unglamorous title belied its influence. After two years as Gorbachev's special envoy in Nagorno Karabakh, the region over which Armenia and Azerbaijan were at war, Volsky returned to Moscow to form the Scientific and Industrial Union in 1990. Caution was his watchword. He saw the Belovezhskaya agreement as inevitable, but said Yeltsin should have held off radical reform for at least a couple of months, until the dust had settled. 'I talked to everyone. You name him, I talked to him. Yeltsin had other problems on his mind,' he said. They listened to Volsky but rejected his entreaties. His argument, in any case, was specious. Once price liberalization had been announced at the end of October, any delay would have led to even more panic.

Volsky maintained an entire office building just off Old Square, even though he wasn't in government. To keep up with the times, he renamed his organization The Russian Union of Industrialists and Entrepreneurs. He and the other 'red barons', as they were known, never tired of advising from the wings. 'The reason Russia is not like Japan,' Volsky would tell his visitors, with consummate charm, 'Is because we don't have enough Japanese.' Russia would follow the Russian model, whatever that meant. He also liked to praise China's move to the 'controlled market'.

Volsky and Rutskoy compiled lists of ministers they wanted sacked. Their scheming led four prominent radicals – Burbulis, Kozyrev, Poltoranin and Chubais – to claim that another coup attempt was underway. Burbulis was obsessed with plots. His think tank prepared position papers for Yeltsin with a heavy emphasis on hyperbole. One of its studies carried the absurd title: 'Revenge of the *Nomenklatura* as a Threat to Mankind'. He was not alone in this tendency; dozens of politicians on all sides seemed, like Burbulis, to take a visceral pleasure in talking up crises. Rarely a week had gone by since 1990 in which a major figure, a Shevardnadze, a Kozyrev or a Sobchak, had not warned of a coup in the making or accused an opponent of committing genocide, only to be seen at a cocktail party with him the same evening. So febrile was the atmosphere, however, that the threats could never be dismissed out of hand, no matter out outlandish they might appear. On the odd occasion, they turned out to be right.

Izvestia was one of those newspapers that tried to keep its passions in check, even though it made no secret of its support for Yeltsin and the government. It was by far the most authoritative paper. If anybody else had written about parliament's own army, accountable not to Yeltsin, the Commander-in-Chief, but to Khasbulatov, it would have had trouble sounding convincing. On the face of it, the existence of the Guards Department for the Protection of High State Institutions had always been a matter of public record. Somehow it had slipped everyone's notice. A detachment of 5,000 troops, which until the August 1991 coup had fallen under the jurisdiction of the Interior Ministry, had covertly been transferred to the presidium of parliament. It was only when *Izvestia* reported that one man had been killed and another injured in a shoot-out between guardsmen and unnamed gunmen one lunchtime in a Moscow café that the department hit the headlines. Its remit, the journalists found out, stretched to seventy-five buildings in the capital. The men wore exactly the same uniform as normal police but served completely different masters. The revelation was embarrassing for both Yeltsin and his opponents. The President decreed the Guard illegal and ordered that its functions be taken over by the Interior and Security ministries within ten days. Khasbulatov was at his flamboyant best. 'I will die a violent death,' he told reporters. 'I am being followed and my telephone is being bugged. Parliament is the only guarantor of democracy.' The guards said they knew nothing about Yeltsin's move. One of its commanders, who was protecting the Constitutional Court, ordered his men to use force to protect their positions and relented only when the Alpha Group was deployed. The other units were transferred back to government control with less brinkmanship.

The next round of the Congress circus was due in December. It would have to decide on whether to extend Yeltsin's special powers, and almost no one was betting that it would. Yeltsin sought extra time. He urged Congress to postpone its work until the spring. Parliament refused. Yeltsin's backroom team was fighting among itself. They discussed imposing emergency rule. Would this involve the dissolving of parliament? Would the military back it? Would the Constitutional Court quash it? The Burbulis clan argued that there was no other way. 'We told him if he gives in to the conservatives this time he'll lose everything,' recalled one. Khasbulatov heard about the discussions – obviously an informant was in the midst of the President's inner circle. He frantically telephoned Pavel Grachev, the Defence Minister, who denied all knowledge. Yeltsin's instinct was to heed the advice of the moderates, and wait.

Congress began in familiar style, with calls for Yeltsin's impeachment and denunciations of the 'government of national occupation'. It was Gaidar who went for broke. Smacking his lips, and wiping the sweat off his round, balding head, Gaidar heaped scorn on his critics. His style was didactic, as if designed to annoy the deputies even more. The hunger and riots they had predicted with such relish had not taken place, he reminded them, because the government had stuck to its guns. His arms laid carelessly on the lectern, his voice shriller than usual, Gaidar made a mockery of Khasbulatov's claim to economic prowess. It was the most belligerent speech of his brief career so far, but in the short term it would finish him off.

Khasbulatov liked to emphasize that he had been a professor of economics, at the Plekhanov Institute of Economic Management, no less. The trouble, however, with all economic qualifications achieved under Communism was that the smarter academics were having to 'unlearn' their theories as quickly as they had acquired them. Khasbulatov was finding it hard. In his keynote speech on the opening day of Congress, he dwelt at length on the merits of a Scandinavian-style 'socially oriented' market economy, and the defects of the more monetarist Anglo-Saxon approach. Khasbulatov's speech, as Gaidar told the chamber, was not a bad little lecture on differing philosophies. 'Unfortunately, the real dilemma facing our society is far more dramatic than a choice between those models.' The choice, he said, was either his monetarist recipe, or 'the chronic poverty and political instability, the populist politicians and dictators so common to Third World states'.

Gaidar sat down, puffy of cheek, in the front row. The heckles and jeers resounded across the cavernous hall. He had forced the President into a corner. His emergency powers at an end, Yeltsin was being forced to seek parliamentary approval for his premier. The chances of securing that post for Gaidar were now perilously thin. Tension was high. With so much at stake, both sides suspected the other of trying to rig the vote. When Khasbulatov declared the voting should take place in polling booths, several radicals marched towards his podium accusing him of constitutional skulduggery. 'Protect me against these insults,' Khasbulatov yelled. Several hardliners came to his rescue. The country's first televised political brawl did little to improve the reputation of its leaders, already at a dreadfully low ebb. A disgusted Yeltsin stomped out of the hall.

Yeltsin believed that by offering concessions he might be able to secure a truce. He proposed making the heads of the four 'power ministries' fully accountable to parliament. The President would retain full control only over economic matters. The wolves ate up the offer, but then went for more. Yeltsin thought he had done enough to keep Gaidar. He was wrong. 'What they failed to do in August 1991 they have decided to do now by way of a creeping coup,' he declared. Again he stormed out; but again the Yeltsin entourage had got its tactics wrong. It had hoped to stage a mass exodus from Congress, but failed to tell many in its ranks. As a result only a fifth of the members followed the President out.

Burbulis came up with the next plan. The old Yeltsin would be re-created. He would do what he used to do best – rally the crowds. After some frantic calling around to friendly factory directors, Yeltsin's entourage sped to the southern outskirts of the city. First stop was the assembly line at the Automobile Factory of the Lenin Komsomol, where the Moskvich car was made. The machines were switched off minutes before his arrival. The workers stood around in their blue overalls, disconcerted by the sudden interest about to be taken in them. Yeltsin climbed on to the foreman's rostrum, surrounded by Korzhakov, Burbulis and the managers. Gaidar, he told the workers, may not be perfect, but he was the best around. 'I cannot possibly entrust the government to anyone but him.' They listened intently but, unlike in the old days, the fiery talk left most of the workers cold. The intrigues in parliament no longer concerned them. One woman muttered 'tut-tut' as Yeltsin spoke, another shouted 'rubblish'. One young convener reminded him that a few years ago he drove to debates in parliament in his Moskvich and that was why he became so popular.

Yeltsin, forlorn, returned to the Kremlin. The perennial question was haunting him. Was he the leader of the radical reformist caucus, a modern version of the Democratic Russia that had brought him to power? Or was he above party politics, the President of all Russians? He never resolved the dilemma. He could have continued with Gaidar in an interim capacity, at least until the following April, and bitten his lip. But something snapped. He sat up until the early morning alone with Burbulis, who told him to go for broke. At 10 a.m., after a sleepless night and having failed to consult Gaidar or the government, Yeltsin went for the deputies' throats. Even by his pugnacious standards, his speech was staggering. 'The walls of this hall have blushed from the endless insults, from the vulgar abuse against specific people, from the malice, rudeness and disrespect, from the dirt which the Congress is filled with, from the sick ambition of failed politicians,' he told them. He announced he was appealing directly to the people. A referendum would be called in January on who rules Russia. Luzhkov, the loyal mayor, brought out his big guns. A long cavalcade of lorries, headlights on full and with the lead bus displaying a banner announcing 'We support Yeltsin', drove around the Kremlin several times. Bus drivers joined in half-heartedly, many complaining they had been ordered to do so by their management. The rival groups of protesters gathered below St Basil's Cathedral, close to the gate through which the deputies entered the Kremlin grounds. The chants of 'Russia, Yeltsin, Democracy' drowned out the rival chants of 'Yeltsin – Judas', but only just.

Many democrats were anxious. Yeltsin, they feared, had gone too far once too often. The do-or-die stunt had been Burbulis's idea and at first glance it had backfired. Yeltsin had been given an unrealistic assessment of his support in Congress. Rutskoy declared that criminal proceedings should be started against the radicals in Yeltsin's entourage. Some deputies called for Burbulis and Kozyrev to have their passports confiscated pending investigation. Travkin had become a strong but independent critic of Yeltsin. His assessment was bleak. 'For the last five or six months, the President has not been running the country, he has been passively reigning. I think the President himself would be glad to call it a day, but his entourage won't let him. Today we have been witness to the first signs that Yeltsin's potential has been exhausted.'

The deputies struck back by banning all referenda. The country had reached deadlock. They could not force a new Prime Minister on Yeltsin, but they could block Yeltsin's attempt to break the constitutional impasse. By his inconsistency, by blowing hot and cold, by his displays of belligerence and weakness, Yeltsin had brought the battle to the fore. That is not to say that he created it. The deputies' destructive powers were immense, and most of them were determined to use them. It was left to the Constitutional Court to seek a way out. After extensive talks in the Kremlin chaired by Zorkin, it looked as if Yeltsin and Khasbulatov might have found a compromise. On a full reading of the text it became clear that Yeltsin had done most of the retreating. He agreed to a vote on a new Prime Minister and to withdraw his demand for a referendum on public confidence in parliament. In return, parliament agreed to withdraw its constitutional amendments of the previous week and to organize a referendum on the main points of a new constitution.

Seventeen candidates for the premiership were put forward. In the lead was Skokov, followed close behind by Viktor Chernomyrdin. Yeltsin had become suspicious of Skokov's intentions, so he opted for Chernomyrdin, who he hoped would be easier to deal with. Gaidar was out. The remaining radicals threatened to resign. Russia's reform programme, they said, was dead.

Yeltsin had not been so humiliated since his dressing down by the party back in 1988. He demanded a shake-up of his staff. He needed sacrifices. First to go was Petrov. But Yeltsin reserved most of his ire for Burbulis, who had, he felt, led him up the garden path. He abolished his job as State Secretary; yet within days, Burbulis had persuaded the President to create a new post for him. This time he was to become Chairman of a new Presidential Advisory Council. It involved nothing and everything, just as before.

Some of those who had dealt with Chernomyrdin during his days in charge of the energy sector were much more sanguine. He was seen to be a good manager and possessed of a clear head. He was nothing if not experienced, and his experience had been gained the hard way. Born in 1938 in a village in the Orenburg region, in the south of the country, he first worked as a compressor operator and then graduated from a technical institute through correspondence courses. He joined the Party in 1961, working his way up through the ranks to join the industry department of the Central Committee. He worked in the Tyumen oil and gas fields in 1983 as a deputy minister and took over the whole of the gas industry two years later. It was one of the few areas of the Soviet economy that was doing comparatively well. When the ministry was reorganized in 1989 into the state-owned gas company Gazprom, Chernomyrdin became its chief. There were few more powerful jobs in industry than his. He was brought into the Gaidar cabinet in May 1992 as a Deputy Prime Minister in charge of the energy sector, to broaden the government's base. It was not a meeting of minds, but he was seen as a good operator.

Unlike the 'boys', the podgy, bald new premier had no public relations skills. His first press conference, a day after his appointment, was a disaster. Asked by one reporter how he intended both to support ailing industry and to prevent hyperinflation, he paused, apparently at a loss, and replied: 'Let's think about it.' He tried to laugh off his difficulties. 'I'm more used to hard work than speaking into microphones. But I'll have to get used to them.' Chernomyrdin had only a vague idea what he wanted, to tone down the reforms and create some sort of 'social market' managed by the state sector. He was adamant, though, about what he didn't want. 'A country like ours, with a powerful infrastructure and such riches and resources, should not turn into a country of street vendors. I am for a market economy, for reforms, but not for a bazaar.'

They hated Kozyrev already. They would come to hate him even more. Everything about him was anathema to the nationalists. He was suave, young (in his thirties), a good linguist who felt just as much at home at a function in London or New York as in Moscow. He was born with a silver spoon in his mouth, in Brussels to a diplomat father. He walked into the Foreign Ministry at a young age and became a senior adviser to Shevardnadze. He was one of Yeltsin's first appointees. He became Foreign Minister of the Russian Federation in October 1990 at a time when nobody knew what the point of the job was. Shevardnadze, the *Soviet* Foreign Minister, did all the travelling and all the decision-making. It was a masterful piece of judgement, or luck, by Kozyrev. Within just over a year he was the top dog, sitting in Shevardnadze's old chair, with the entire diplomatic corps of the former USSR answerable to him. Kozyrev was one of the more outspoken radicals, warning consistently of coups and civil wars which would make Yugoslavia 'seem like a kindergarten' and blaming the Russian military for stoking ethnic unrest in Russia's peripheries.

On 14 December 1992, Kozyrev travelled to Stockholm for a meeting of the Conference on Security and Cooperation in Europe. The foreign ministers of all fifty-two participant states had been invited, ostensibly to discuss a new American plan for ending the war in the former Yugoslavia. When it was Kozyrev's turn to speak, nobody expected anything out of the ordinary. This is what he said.

I have to introduce corrections in the conception of Russian foreign policy, and wish to inform you briefly about the part relating to CSCE problems.

First: while maintaining a general policy of entry into Europe, we are clearly conscious that our traditions to a great extent, if not fundamentally, are in Asia, and this sets limits to our *rapprochement* with Western Europe. We see that the goals of NATO and the Western European Union are essentially unchanged. They are working out plans to strengthen their military presence in the Baltic States and other regions of the territory of the former Soviet Union, and to interfere in Bosnia and in the internal affairs of Yugoslavia. This course evidently dictated the sanctions against Yugoslavia. We demand their removal, and if this does not happen we assume the right to undertake necessary unilateral measures to defend our interests, all the more since they are causing us economic harm. In its struggle, the present government of Serbia can count on the support of great Russia.

Second: the space of the former Soviet Union cannot be considered a zone of full application of CSCE norms. It is essentially a post-imperial space, where Russia has to defend its interests by all available means, including military and economic ones. We will firmly insist that the former republics of the USSR immediately enter a new federation or confederation and there will be a tough discussion about this.

Third: all those who consider that they need not reckon with these particularities and interests, and that the fate of the Soviet Union is in store for Russia, must not forget that this is a state capable of looking after itself and its friends. Of course we are ready to participate constructively in the work of the CSCE council, although we will take a cautious attitude to ideas leading to interference in internal affairs.

The speech met with stunned silence. The acting American Secretary of State stared at Kozyrev in disbelief. How could a man considered an ambassador of reform threaten international policy on Yugoslavia, threaten Russia's CIS neighbours and warn the West that Moscow no longer needed its friendship? Members of Kozyrev's own delegation also had no idea what was going on. Had something dramatic happened in the Kremlin? Another coup perhaps? Forty-five minutes later, Kozyrev returned to the rostrum. He told the other delegates:

> I wish to assure you that neither President Yeltsin, who remains the leader and guarantor of Russian internal and foreign policy, nor I as Minister for Foreign Affairs, will ever agree to what I read out in my previous speech. I wish to thank you and all those present for the opportunity to employ this rhetorical device, but I did it for the most serious reasons, so that you should all be aware of the real threats on our road to a post-Communist Europe. The text I read out earlier is a fairly accurate compilation of the demands of what is by no means the most extreme opposition in Russia.

He called it his own version of shock therapy. 'Our experience in Stockholm shows that our partners in the West have to be woken up from time to time.'

So taken aback were my own editors that they asked me to do a doomsday variant of my own. The article, 'If the bear awakes', was published in the following issue of the *Sunday Telegraph*. I toyed with doing an outlandish version, but decided I would stick to a more plausible scenario. The scene was April 1993, five months hence. Yeltsin's promised referendum had been delayed, the President had retreated even further into the background. The eighth Congress began. Yeltsin took to the podium with a sensational announcement. His decrees, he said, were being systematically ignored, his position had become untenable. Rutskoy and Khasbulatov had completed their constitutional coup. 'Constitutionally my hands are tied. I considered taking more drastic action, but I desisted so as not to inflame the situation in the country.' Yeltsin, pale and drained of energy, said he was resigning with immediate effect. According to the constitution, the Vice-President would take charge for three months to allow for new elections to be held.

Rutskoy began his speech by thanking Yeltsin: 'The Russian people will always hold you dear to their hearts for beginning the long process of reviving our great fatherland.' The disingenuousness was painful. He went on to outline a fundamental reverse of economic and foreign policy. 'Esteemed deputies, we are not and never have been against reform. We are not against close economic cooperation with our partners in East and West. We do not want a return to the Communist command system that for seventy years instilled fear and stifled enterprise. But nor do we want a return to the equally criminal year of 1992 when the mafia, the criminals and their friends in the Gaidar government held sway.' He spoke of strengthening the CIS along the lines of a confederation, but warned Russia's neighbours not to go too far. Unspecified measures would be taken to bring Ukraine to heel on the nuclear issue and the troop withdrawals from the Baltic states would be suspended in protest at the violation of the human rights of ethnic Russians. The West, he said, had taken advantage of Russia's weaknesses. 'The CIA has amassed such a network of agents, especially among our so-called "democratic" politicians, that our security has been endangered. After two years of negligence, some would say betrayal, our Foreign Ministry has only now begun to represent our interests. We are showing at the United Nations that no longer will we raise our hands in obeisance at each American initiative.'

A few days later *Pravda* reproduced the article in full (with an accurate translation), accompanied by a commentary about how I should feel ashamed at spreading lies and distortions and a reminder to its readers that the aim of Western journalists was to plant disinformation. Later that week, the British Ambassador to Moscow was summoned to the Kremlin by Rutskoy's chief of staff to explain why some of *his* journalists were putting out lies. Rutskoy, he was told, would *never* have held such reactionary views and would *never* have done anything to undermine the President's position.

Part III

12

Suitcases and Briefcases

Yeltsin stopped pretending. He had begun to enjoy the luxuries that came with the job. 'Some changes have taken place within me,' he said in a television interview. 'I'm more relaxed in my moral attitude towards privilege.' Not for him any more the trip on the trolleybus – not that he'd ever really done it seriously.

The outrage expressed by millions, and harnessed by Yeltsin, over the indulgences of the Communist elite in the late 1980s now seemed quaint. In *Against the Grain* he described how the old system worked.

> Obsequiousness and obedience are rewarded in turn by privilege: special hospitals; special sanatoria; the excellent Central Committee canteen; the equally excellent service for home delivery of groceries and other goods; the Kremlin line closed telephone system; the free transportation. The higher one climbs up the professional ladder, the more there are comforts that surround one, and the harder and more painful it is to lose them.

He described the opulent lives led behind the high green fences.

> Even at my level as a candidate member of the Politburo, my domestic staff consisted of three cooks, three waitresses, a housemaid and a gardener with his own team of under-gardeners. My wife, my family and I, long accustomed to doing everything with our own hands, simply didn't know what to do with ourselves.

Why had Gorbachev failed to change the system, he asked himself? 'I believe the fault lies in his basic cast of character. He likes to live well, in comfort and luxury. In this he is helped by his wife.'

Arkady Vaksberg, an investigative journalist on *Literaturnaya Gazeta*, chronicled the corruption of the Communists in his book *The Soviet Mafia*. It came out in 1991, at the peak of public anger over privilege. 'Every government official – literally each one – was using his position to take bribes for providing any service,' he wrote. 'This ubiquitous corruption seemed to the public to take only one form, namely the obtaining of money or valuable gifts. There was only one kind of difference between members of the high oligarchy – some took more and some took less.'

Solzhenitsyn put it more forcefully: 'The corrupt ruling class – the many millions of men in the Party–State *nomenklatura* – is not capable of voluntarily renouncing any of the privileges they have seized. They have lived shamelessly for decades at the people's expense – and would like to continue doing so.' He called the new breed of Russian businessmen 'sharks bred in the murky waters of the Soviet underground'.

When it came to investigations, *glasnost* had its limits. A television interview with Galina Brezhneva, the drunken, dissolute daughter of the corrupt geriatric in the Kremlin, was banned because she alleged she had received presents from Raisa Gorbacheva in an attempt to curry favour on her husband's behalf. There was nothing surprising or iniquitous about that. It was the done thing for provincial leaders such as Gorbachev, the Party chief in Stavropol at the time, to bestow gifts after being promoted and transferred to Moscow.

Gorbachev was, however, more than happy for the unsavoury practices of others to be revealed. Prompted by radicals, a Soviet parliamentary committee uncovered a scam in 1991 in which ministers and army chiefs bought their *dachas* and their contents at rock-bottom prices. Gorbachev's military adviser was said to have paid 215 roubles, five times below the official price, for three refrigerators. Ryzhkov was forced to give back a *dacha* he had bought at a snip, 35,000 roubles. It was priced at 78,000 a month later. The episode caused a furore at the time. These were the first publicized cases of the privatization of privilege. Overnight the new owner would be several thousand dollars richer. The army was a keen player, but every institution would take its slice. For those involved in the handing out of property it too became a lucrative business.

The sums involved initially were risible. The privilege to which Party members and hangers-on were accustomed was a very Soviet phenomenon. They were set apart not so much by wealth as by freedom from the miserable grind to which their countrymen were subjected. Their flats were comfortable, but nothing special by Western standards. As the system collapsed, however, Communists and self-declared anti-Communists began fighting over much bigger spoils. Hundreds of millions of dollars were up for grabs. It was called *nomenklatura privatization*. It was the biggest give-away of state assets in world history, a bargain basement sale of an entire country.

Instead of fighting it, Yeltsin realized that to win his political battles he would have to play the game. He needed allies. His aides concluded after the débâcle of the last Congress that working with parliament had become impossible. Instead they would try to neutralize it by depriving it of its more talented and cooperative figures. These individuals would be wooed into the government or the presidential office, with considerable attention paid to their financial well-being. The first big catch was Sergei Filatov, who had been Khasbulatov's number two. He was made Yeltsin's Chief of Staff in December 1992.

The prize for the most unctuous defection went to Nikolai Ryabov. Ryabov was an interesting case, a lecturer at an agricultural college and a latecomer to the Communist Party. He joined the growing anti-Yeltsin bandwagon and, as another of Khasbulatov's assistants, launched some of the fiercest attacks on the President in Congress. Then, suddenly, Ryabov jumped ship in May 1993. He became a leading figure in the President's Constitutional Assembly, and was appointed to the highly influential position of Chairman of the Central Election Commission. A few months later he was followed by several other important figures, including the head of parliament's committees on defence and security, and the budget. This left parliament dominated by the bilious folk from the National Salvation Front.

Relations with parliament might not have deteriorated so far and so quickly as they did if Yeltsin had pandered more to the egos of its members. Many of the 200 full-timers did develop an element of professionalism. The same could not be said for the Congress. Like thick grey treacle, the 1,000 deputies would seep through the Kremlin corridors twice or three times a year. The sluggish flow would come to a stop at the the *bufet*, with its long queues for subsidized chocolate, caviar sandwiches and cabbage pies. Some took time out to collect their complimentary theatre tickets. The trips from the provinces provided a welcome opportunity to live it up for a few days. Plane tickets were always found, again at subsidized rates, to bring them to the capital. The more acrimonious the debates, the more time they could spend in Moscow. The members of the Supreme Soviet were given comfortable three-roomed flats in Krylatskoye, a district with excellent views of the city and (by Moscow standards) clean air. A car pool was readily on hand to drive them into the centre.

Khasbulatov had more ambitious designs. Among his many perks that went unchecked, he would call upon the air force to assign him planes to take him on official trips. While holidaying in Sochi he thought nothing of giving his extended family guided aerial tours of the Black Sea coast, courtesy of the Russian military. Yeltsin clamped down at one point, but his egalitarian fervour was highly selective and his motives for exercising it purely political. He signed a decree prohibiting the assignment of state aircraft for people's deputies. But apart from the odd instance of car- or *dacha*-snatching, he didn't go very far. It would serve little purpose.

Shekochikhin invited me one day to one of the round table meetings his newspaper put on with prominent politicians. These meetings were supposed to be polite exchanges of opinion. Shekochikhin had other ideas. The previous weekend we had met in the countryside. He took me to a spot at the end of a friend's garden where, through a hole in the fence, we could see *dachas* being built for Filatov, Barannikov and other members of the elite. The red-brick detached houses looked not unlike an English suburban estate, except that they were closed off to the public. We now had a good opportunity to confront Filatov head-on. We asked him why the government needed sixty aeroplanes of its own, how an aide to the Prime Minister could afford to spend $200,000 on an apartment in central Moscow and how he himself had acquired his new property. Embarrassed glances were exchanged all round. Filatov choked a little, before waffling on about bank loans and rental systems. He thought quickly on his feet. The money, he said, would be recouped from the sale of his garage. It was an intriguing idea. 'Must be one hell of a garage,' muttered one journalist out loud.

That was only the start of the construction boom. Just inside the city limits, workmen were finishing off a building with a very atypical industriousness. The reason was simple. The owners of this new block of flats were anything but ordinary. The five-storey brick structure, with its uninviting high walls protecting it from the main road, was not everyone's idea of the most aesthetic piece of real estate. But it was not lacking for amenities. Each flat had an average of fifteen rooms, with bullet-proof glass windows, huge fireplaces and balconies of carved oak off each master bedroom. Downstairs were a swimming pool, two saunas, a tennis court and an underground car park. The penthouse flat had been reserved for the Yeltsin family. Other portions were given over to his friends – Korzhakov, Barsukov, Gaidar, Luzhkov and others.

Yeltsin's favourite spot was Zavidovo, a hunting reserve north-west of Moscow created for Brezhnev and his cronies. Over an area of 125,000 hectares elk, wild boar, roe deer and several bird species were raised. Siberian stags and spotted deer were introduced at vast expense. In Brezhnev's time there were several hundred workers there, some of whom had the task of laying traps or doping up the beasts so that they would stroll right into the line of the doddery General Secretary. Even he usually hit one or two. Yeltsin preferred to stroll in the thick pine forests collecting mushrooms.

The most lavish of all the *dachas* was the Foros mansion, which had taken six years to build for Gorbachev at a cost of $20 million. The main house had rooms on three stories, an indoor swimming pool and a lift to a private beach directly below on the Black Sea, guarded by the navy. The grounds also contained a guesthouse that could sleep thirty and special quarters for staff and security. So much for the man who sought to break the mould. Gorbachev never went back to Foros after his fall from power. Following independence it was confiscated by the Ukrainian government, which harboured plans of turning it into a money-spinning luxury beach resort for Japanese and German visitors.

One of the best ways for politicians to earn a fast buck without any hassle was to give interviews. Gorbachev's aides were the first to cash in, with lucrative appearances before superpower summits or major trips. The main customers were Japanese television and the American networks. Under Yeltsin there was even an attempt to give the practice a gloss of respectability. A firm called Alen, set up by a husband and wife team, was given the go-ahead to sell photo opportunities of filming sessions with the President, playing tennis or down at the beach, at his desk in the Kremlin or at home. For this privilege, several thousand dollars would be paid into the company's foreign bank account. Everyone was doing it – the Prosecutor's office, the Defence Ministry, the intelligence services.

Throughout the business world graft was widespread. Any foreign company that said it was not greasing the palm of its opposite partners was either being liberal with the truth or presumably missing out on the major contracts. The Italians had the fewest qualms, one of its firms sending a million dollars to one prominent politician to lobby for it to win a major contract for installing new technology. In the early years they didn't bother to hide their activities. One minister brought back dozens of boxes of gifts provided by an American company in the cargo hold of a government plane which was carrying several of his colleagues. Nothing, of course, was ever done; reaction amounted only to a few sniggers all around.

It was not a matter of whether Chernomyrdin or Gaidar was in charge. Neither would have been able to stop the process, even if he had wanted to. The wheels of the bureaucracy rolled inexorably.

Illarionov was one of the few members of the Gaidar team to be retained by Chernomyrdin. He knew many in the new administration were on the make, but said he was only once witness to a bribe offer.

I was shocked it was done so openly. The man offered me $50,000. He wanted me to help him obtain an export licence. He phoned up, I had at least twenty visitors a day so I thought nothing of it. We had met a couple of times before, very briefly. He came into my office and after a few pleasantries got to the point. He explained which documents he needed. 'It won't remain without thanks,' he said. I thought what kind of profits he must have been making to be offering that kind of sweetener. I told him I wasn't in a position to help but was grateful for the offer. We left it there and he left without acrimony. I'm not sure I could have done anything. The deal must have been worth millions. You need to be fairly influential, you need to understand how documents are processed so the whole thing can be done in such a way as not to look too suspicious. There's an art to all that.

Illarionov cited another example. He had been down to Ulyanovsk, a conservative town in central Russia whose concentration on heavy industry left it particularly vulnerable to the reforms. Ulyanovsk's greatest claim to fame is being Lenin's birthplace. Illarionov had just finished a visit to an aviation factory when its director asked him to hand a letter over to Chernomyrdin. 'He was asking for a subsidized long-term credit of three billion roubles. I gave it to Chernomyrdin, suggesting that I should hand it over to the Finance Ministry. He grabbed it, said: "No, no, leave it to me, I'll deal with it." This is not a question of bribes but goodwill. To anyone like Chernomyrdin who had worked in Gazprom such amounts are laughable. It's called the purchase of political support.' There was nothing underhand in what happened with the Ulyanovsk factory. But this is how many of the subsidies were decided. The management of the factory, and the local government, would from then on feel indebted to Chernomyrdin, and, as he learnt from Yeltsin's experiences, support from the regions was always extremely important in helping to determine the balance of power in Moscow.

For all their apparent nonchalance, both sides were beginning to see the political damage that corruption could cause. It was not so much that each sought to cut down on its own dodgy actitivies as that it sought to capitalize on its rival's. According to Poltoranin, Rutskoy was one of the first off the mark. 'The whole business, Rutskoy and the suitcases, it was my fault,' Poltoranin confessed. It was October 1992.

> I was walking past Rutskoy in the corridor. He was pacing up and down, smoking cigarettes, as was his wont. He grabbed my jacket and said 'Misha, come in here a minute.' I went into his office. He opened the safe and said, 'Look at what the bastards are doing now. Shokhin's had his hand in the till . . . Nechayev's done this . . . Aven's done that . . .' And he started showing me files of documents. The safe was stuffed full of them. So I said to him. 'You're Vice-President, why haven't you reported all this to the President? This should be investigated officially.'

A few days later Yeltsin summoned Poltoranin to the *dacha* for a get-together. They sat by the fire. Poltoranin brought up Rutskoy. 'I told him: "He's always on my back, wanting to show me documents. But he never gives them to me so I can read them properly, he gives me a quick glance and shoves them back in the safe. He's supposed to be with us but he's beginning to work against us. We should push him into action." ' Poltoranin said Rutskoy's anger should be channelled into an official investigation into corruption. The Inter-Departmental Anti-Corruption Commission was to be headed by Rutskoy, and to include politicians as diverse as Burbulis, Skokov and Barannikov. It was a heavyweight team, with access to the resources of the Security Ministry and armed forces and with a brief to 'get to anyone who steals or takes bribes'. If these four couldn't get to the bottom of the dirty dealings, nobody could.

Instead of working together, the group fragmented. Rutskoy and Skokov accumulated material for one side, Burbulis for the other, with what he assumed was Barannikov's cooperation. He would find out only months later that Barannikov's loyalties were not what they seemed. Rutskoy's Kremlin office was frequented by businessmen friends who would barge in unannounced, calling him 'Sasha' and giving him orders. Rutskoy began summoning various officials, only his political adversaries, to his office, telling them that he was in possession of *kompromat* against them. 'He was trying to blackmail them into giving his *Vozrozhdeniye* foundation licences to trade in gas and oil,' Poltoranin said. Their methods were crude. On one occasion Rutskoy told Poltoranin he needed a particular building that was still in state hands. 'I said "you must be joking."' But out of curiosity, Poltoranin accepted an invitation to meet some of Rutskoy's friends.

> We got into a Mercedes with some guys who came along, and drove out of town. It was a strange kind of office, there was a big room with a table in it, all set with food and drink, grapes, fruit, cognac and vodka. They were all slapping him on the back, we had a couple of drinks. Then he said to me: 'For God's sake, come on. What are you digging in your heels for? You give me the building, and we'll build you an apartment, 700 square metres in Serebryanny Bor [an exclusive *dacha* area close to the city]. You'll get a Mercedes into the bargain.' I listened, took Rutskoy to one side and told him: 'I'm leaving now, and if you take my advice you'll go to the President yourself tomorrow and tell him about all this. I'm giving you two days. If you don't go and tell him yourself, I'll go and tell him.' So three days passed, no phone call, nothing. I met the President on some other pretext and asked him if Rutskoy had spoken to him. I told him what had gone on. A few days later when I passed Rutskoy he hissed at me 'Traitor!' And ever since then he's viewed me as his enemy.

Poltoranin was in no doubt that certain unsavoury business structures were 'running' Rutskoy. 'There was no one there I knew. They were all businessmen, traders. No one from the government. They were just a load of sleazy types, clustering round him, setting him on a pedestal in the hope of using him as a battering ram when the time came.'

Poltoranin's interpretation of dirty dealings would naturally have been highly selective. He was hardly whiter than white himself. The trouble with his Rutskoy stories is not that they might be untrue, but that he failed to mention what his own side was up to.

In public, Yeltsin stuck with his commission. He and Rutskoy chaired a special Kremlin conference in February 1993. Yeltsin's speech writers had done their work. It was the most frank admission yet of the extent to which organized crime had penetrated all areas of society. The mafia, he said, had bought off politicians and bureaucrats at all levels, infiltrated the armed forces, the banks and other state institutions to the extent that they no longer bothered to act discreetly. The people were scared to walk the streets at night. At the workplace, white-collar fraud was out of control. He cited an array of figures. Some 40 per cent of businessmen and two-thirds of private companies were involved in corruption, Yeltsin said. A record 2.76 million crimes had been registered in 1992, with the murder rate up by 40 per cent and robbery up by 60 per cent. Some 4,000 organized criminal gangs had been exposed, a quarter of which had international links. The same number were protected by corrupt officials. More than $1.5 billion in hard currency had disappeared from Foreign Trade Ministry accounts in the first nine months of 1992. 'All that time we were running around after pickpockets. I would like to know which Western banks are "working" that money and who, possibly in the government, is profiting from it. Organized crime poses a direct threat to Russia's strategic interests and national security. Corruption is literally eating at the body of society from top to bottom.'

It was a headline-grabbing performance, heralding what many hoped was the start of a much-awaited clampdown. One newspaper took a more sceptical tone. Alongside Yeltsin's warnings, it reprinted extracts of speeches made by Soviet leaders from Lenin to Gorbachev. They all pledged to crack down on the corruption of the elite – and they all gave up.

This was the context to which Yakubovsky returned. From his luxurious exile he kept abreast of the machinations – who had which documents about whom, who was accusing whom, and, most important of all, who was ahead in the power struggle. Yakubovsky knew that he should sit on the fence for as long as possible, playing one side off against the other.

Rutskoy fired the first shot. He didn't often attend ordinary parliamentary sessions, and when Khasbulatov gave him the floor as a matter of urgency everyone knew that something dramatic was about to happen. Even for the times it was an astonishing speech, one which finalized his break with the presidential administration. His voice breaking, his temper unrestrained, Rutskoy said that he had eleven suitcases of incriminating evidence showing that every cabinet over which Yeltsin had presided had been riddled with corruption. He began to name names. Gaidar, he said, had sold gold reserves and issued licences to foreign firms involved in the export of natural resources. (His aides would later admit that he had simply misunderstood the workings of the gold industry). He had proof, he said, that Burbulis had authorized $3 billion worth of illegal metals exports from the Sverdlovsk region. Shokhin had overseen the loss of $12 million worth of Western aid. Chubais had sold state property at knock-down prices to Western firms and the mafia, while

Poltoranin had sold off the former Soviet House of Culture in East Berlin for a pittance, and a presumed back-hander.

Yeltsin realized that Rutskoy was using the commission for his own political purposes. The solution was simple – relieve Rutskoy of the job of chairman and put himself in overall charge. Yeltsin then proceeded to do exactly the same, using the investigations purely to undermine his opponents. The invective sharpened. Rutskoy called a press conference to reveal more details of corruption. But as the invited correspondents gathered at the Spassky Gates at the appointed time, a Kremlin guard said that Rutskoy was not in his office. Then he admitted he had received orders not to let anyone in. Andrei Fyodorov, Rutskoy's chief aide, came rushing out, saying the Vice-President was waiting inside. 'Unfortunately we are obliged to state that the head of the President's administration and the Commandant of the Kremlin have forbidden the press access for a meeting with the Vice-President,' Fyodorov said. 'Human rights have been violated, the law on the press has been broken.'

The farcical scenes played into the opposition's hands. Yeltsin was looking churlish, petty and vindictive. Such, however, were the tactics of the presidential team. A few days later Yeltsin ordered a drastic reduction in Rutskoy's staff and withdrew his personal doctor, most of his bodyguard and his official limousine. Rutskoy could not be sacked under the constitution, so Yeltsin did what he thought was the next best thing. Rutskoy shot back, accusing Yeltsin of presiding over a 'state mafia machine'. 'I am a stubborn man. I will remain in office and prove to society who has been robbing it,' Rutskoy said. Filatov responded by saying the Vice-President would soon be 'provided with' new offices outside the Kremlin.

The corruption quarrel had left the public cold. Even journalists were losing interest. They understood that the accusations were less a matter of rooting out ill-doers than a settling of scores. After displaying so much enthusiasm, Shekochikhin said he would no longer accept any tapes or incriminating documents from accusers on either side. He compared them to squabbling families in a communal apartment. 'Enough is enough. Spare the long-suffering people your private affairs and your personal sympathies and antipathies.'

Sergei Glazyev was a victim of the vicious campaign that both parliament and the presidential team were waging. An original member of the Gaidar team, he had set his views apart from the others. He was suspicious of the philosophy of *laissez-faire* and, like the centrists, was an advocate of considerable state involvement in industry. He had kept his job as Foreign Trade Minister because he was seen as effective and, by the barometer of the times, relatively honest. By the end of 1992 he had openly gone over to the Rutskoy camp and, unlike Barannikov, had made no secret of it. Glazyev believed the radicals were doing considerable harm and asked Chernomyrdin to close Illarionov's Centre for Economic Reforms. It would not have been difficult or dishonourable to ask him to move on, because his views were at variance with those of the rest of the team. Instead, they chose more underhand means.

Glazyev had just left for a tour of several African states. He would be the highest-ranking Russian official to visit South Africa. This was August 1993, at the height of the power struggle. Before departing he had received indications that a campaign had begun to undermine him. His plane had just entered Moroccan air space, three hours into the flight, when a call came through to the pilot to change course immediately and return to Moscow. Glazyev tried to find out what it was all about, but they had little time before landing, so he agreed that the plane should go back. On arrival in Moscow, he found out that the order had been given by a medium-ranking official in the government department that looked after arms sales. The official had been working on behalf of Shumeiko, who was at loggerheads with Rutskoy. Glazyev quit in fury but made no public statement. Chernomyrdin refused to accept his resignation, saying he had played no part in the scam, and so, despite the humiliation, Glazyev stayed on. When he did finally go it was in protest at Yeltsin's dissolution of parliament two months later. That time not only was his resignation accepted but his office was immediately sealed and searched. He was not allowed back to collect his personal possessions, including even his photographs. From then on Glazyev went on the warpath. There was no better example of a moderate being turned into an out-and-out enemy.

Yuri Boldyrev was a democrat, another with a reputation for honesty. An electrical engineer with an economics degree, at the age of twenty-eight he ran in the elections for the Soviet parliament in 1989. He was elected in Leningrad, alongside Sobchak, and was a colleague of Chubais. He had been a strong member of Yeltsin's Presidential Council and was considered a natural choice for the post of Chief Inspector of the Control Administration of the President's office – a job created just after the 1991 coup to keep a tab on the behaviour and financial dealings of top state officials. Boldyrev was appointed in March 1992 but lasted only a year. He had been warned that his 'resignation' would not be voluntary.

Boldyrev antagonized the presidential team by refusing to work exclusively for them. He tried hard to prevent his administration from becoming a tool in the political fight. He was answerable personally to the President, and nobody else, but was consistently handed down orders by people like Filatov. He was being asked to pick and choose, to direct all his efforts against the Rutskoy camp, to conduct an *à la carte* investigation. Lists were compiled. Probes were ordered against the heads of the local administrations in Novosibirsk and Irkutsk. The reason was that, according to a league table of voting patterns at Congress drawn up by presidential experts, the two governors in question came out as the most strongly anti-Yeltsin. 'There was another situation when I was told by the President that a certain person must be got rid of, and I didn't do it. They got rid of him anyway, but not as a result of anything I did.' Boldyrev said Rutskoy had several times approached Yeltsin, in his capacity as head of the inter-departmental commission on crime, and asked for certain documents. On each occasion Yeltsin refused.

Boldyrev discovered 'corruption on an unprecedented scale' in the elite. He confirmed the reports of financial scandals in the military, especially among commanders of the Western Group of Forces withdrawing from East Germany – those same officers with whom Yakubovsky had been dealing at the very start. But Yeltsin needed the military and had no interest in antagonizing its top brass. The investigation was stopped. Boldyrev pressed on. 'I repeatedly tried to persuade the President to promulgate a decree disallowing organs of state power to accord special privileges to any individual firm or enterprise, and to institute a system of sanctions against those who violated it.' His first full-scale row with Yeltsin came in the summer of 1992 when he tried to check up on the privatization programme in Moscow, arguing that the mayor had sold off several buildings well below market levels. He claimed Yeltsin told him to stop the investigation, saying: 'We support Luzhkov.' The relationship deteriorated fast, and Boldyrev was told his post was being abolished. As soon as he left it transpired that the post had been retained and given to Alexei Ilyushenko, a far more pliant figure. Immediately on taking office, Ilyushenko signed a statement saying no evidence had been found of abuses by the military. Little sympathy was shown for Boldyrev on either side. Many politicians wondered how he could have been so naïve.

A few months after Boldyrev's resignation, the campaign against Rutskoy reached its peak – with the help of the Yakubovsky evidence. In retaliation, the opposition turned its attention to two of Yeltsin's allies, Poltoranin and Shumeiko. Shumeiko was accused of transferring $14.5 million to a Swiss-based company to buy baby food for Russia. The contract, it was said, was never honoured and the company used the money for its own purposes. Shumeiko said the contract was not actually to import large quantities of baby food, but to launch factory production of it in Moscow. This, he said, was already up and running. 'They want to show that I can't work in the President's entourage, that I'm a thief. Their chosen tactic is to 'take out' certain figures close to the President.' Shumeiko's immunity from prosecution was lifted by parliament and criminal proceedings were initiated. Poltoranin's offices were investigated over the question of the East Berlin building.

Yeltsin used the accusations to act against Rutskoy. He suspended him from his post as Vice-President, and Shumeiko from the job of Deputy Prime Minister, pending the investigations. The linking of the two was intended to show the President as being an impartial arbiter, but as a ruse it fooled nobody. Prosecutors quickly admitted they had found nothing to back up charges against Shumeiko and Poltoranin and followed that up with a similar judgement on Rutskoy. Rutskoy never did deliver his eleven suitcases of incriminating evidence. His aides said he still had the *kompromat*, but was waiting for the right moment, the one that would produce maximum effect, before releasing it. They were hinting at the next presidential elections.

13

Beyond the Ring Road

The Kremlin's writ, it was often said, did not extend beyond Moscow's outer ring road. The more obsessed the various branches of power in Moscow became with fighting each other, the more Russia's eighty-nine regions and republics drew themselves away. Open defiance of President, parliament and government in Moscow came only from Chechnya and Tatarstan, the most powerful of the autonomous areas; elsewhere the local leaders had settled on an unwritten code with Yeltsin's administration. In return for expressions of support in the power struggle, the regions would be left alone to run themselves. In a country spanning eleven time zones the *quid pro quo* had always been logical. In Communist times, leaders of the outlying Soviet republics were allowed virtual autonomy to run their fiefdoms as long as the parades were held and loyalty was expressed. The pace of change under the new system was much slower in the regions than at the centre. The local Party building would become the governor's headquarters; the old political enlightenment centre was turned into a commodities exchange. The local hotel acquired a casino, and the high street a couple of private restaurants. The criminals who operated underground during the Party days came out into the open. Otherwise it was generally business as usual.

The main point of contention was money. The richer regions saw no reason why they should be net contributors to the state exchequer while less productive areas were receiving handouts. The conflict led a swathe of regions in Siberia and the three regions in the Urals to threaten to go it alone. Yeltsin knew that most of these warnings could not be carried out, but it was seldom wise to push the local leaders too far.

Of all the government edicts handed down from the centre, none caused more of a furore than a decision to phase in a ban on all right-hand-drive cars. The news caused near panic in Vladivostok. Throughout the Russian Far East there was hardly a traditional Russian car in sight. Millions of old and new right-hand-drive Nissans and Toyotas had been brought over from Nagato in Japan, and if it had have been possible to change the road regulations to allow people to drive on the left, as they do in Japan, the local authorities would have done it. Five thousand miles from Moscow, Vladivostok has always been frontier territory, the Wild East as it liked to call itself. The locals have their own explanation: when the Tsar despatched his pioneers to open up his vast territories, the weak ones ended up in Siberia, the tough ones reached the sea. Moderation was a word lost on locals. Thousands travelled to Japan, South Korea and China to import cars or leather jackets. As an old port, there was always money in abundance, and crime. It was the merchant traders, the men in tracksuits with fistfuls of notes, pocket phrasebooks and a knowledge of the market that would put any Western street trader to shame who were behind the region's revival of the past few years, not the politicians. They just tried to copy the businessmen's lead. In most areas of Russia local power struggles were more sedate than in Mosow. Not so in Vladivostok.

The protagonists were the Mayor, Viktor Cherepkov, and the Governor, Yevgeny Nazdratenko. The town wasn't big enough for both of them. The trouble with Cherepkov, a former submarine captain, was that he ruffled too many local feathers. Nazdratenko was an official from the gold mining industry, a friend of the factory directors. He had got the job only because the previous incumbent had let it be known in Moscow that he wanted to become a big shot in the Foreign Ministry: he was made consul-general in San Francisco, hardly the fast track but a cushy little number nonetheless. Nazdratenko and Cherepkov had never liked each other. Cherepkov rose to fame when he helped uncover a scandal involving the commanders of the Pacific Fleet on Russia Island, a few miles out to sea, which they had turned into a slave camp. Several conscripts died of malnutrition. The officers were reprimanded, and Cherepkov used the affair to propel himself into big politics. Rather than look after the roads and the rubbish collection, he preferred to run his newspaper *Big Vladivostok*, which devoted its entire space every day to attacking the Governor, whose own daily returned the compliment.

Now Nazdratenko had had enough. It was time to apply the Moscow tactics, although in a cruder way. Cherepkov was accused of corruption. Police found 1.5 million roubles in cash stashed in a corner behind the safe in his office. The accusation might have carried more weight if the sum had been more realistic. Had Cherepkov wanted to steal a bit on the side, he would have taken more than the $1,000 in which he was implicated, a ludicrously low sum by modern Russian standards. The Governor's authorities then accused the Mayor's son of stealing a computer from his school. Father and son camped inside City Hall, 'the Grey House' as it was known for several weeks. Downstairs they were defended by sympathetic pensioners, some Cossacks and a couple of Afghan war veterans. Cherepkov's wife joined him in the vigil, ferrying in food and medicines. The Mayor refused to leave the building despite a heart condition, fearing that if he went to hospital his enemies might finish him off.

Enter the main state investigator. Going into work one Sunday to look over some urgent papers in the case, she left her four-year-old daughter with her boyfriend. The child disappeared. The word was put out immediately that it was the work of thugs hired by the Mayor to intimidate her. The truth was much more mundane. The boyfriend had got drunk with a friend. The two phoned up a local escort agency, but realized after they had used their services that they had no money to pay the girls. The firm sent round its heavy mob and kidnapped the daughter overnight until the mother should produce the money. Eventually Cherepkov was persuaded to leave the building and the investigation continued. Score settled, the matter was unlikely to go any further.

Such were the levels at which political battles were often fought. The absurdity of it all was that ideologically Nazdratenko and Cherepkov had little to fight over. Their dispute revolved around business contracts. The Governor had helped set up the Maritime Association of Businessmen and Managers in which the bosses of 213 major enterprises had clubbed together to privatize their corporations. It was an instant money spinner and others naturally wanted to join. Both sides tried to enlist the support of the Moscow big guns. It was Nazdratenko who was successful. He had meticulously preserved his good contacts with Ilyushin and Yeltsin himself, boasting how, as a member of parliament's voting commission in 1990, he had helped to ensure Yeltsin's victory in the close contest. Not even Yeltsin's enemies have ever mentioned any wrongdoings in that election. As any sensible Governor would, Nazdratenko also made sure his contacts with the other side were just as friendly.

The wooing of the regions was not discreet. As the campaign in Moscow intensified, Rutskoy embarked on a series of long trips across Russia to spread his message and drum up support. He was disappointed to find that major centres of the Urals and Siberia were safe Yeltsin territory. Instead of trying to win them over, he would lose his temper. Asked to explain why the people of Novosibirsk had voted for Yeltsin in the referendum, he replied: 'It's not surprising. They're all faggots and pederasts.'

Fresh from the ignominy of his latest indiscretion, Rutskoy flew into Vladivostok. Nazdratenko was there to meet his old chum and got a little carried away, kissing and hugging him heartily as good comrades did in the old days. He did not realize that local television was there. Misha Voznesensky, a burly no-nonsense hack of the Fleet Street mould, was head of Russian Television for the Far East and had a habit of annoying his local patricians. He took the film back to his studios and began cutting it. It wasn't a particularly sensational piece, but he hoped it might sneak in on one of the less prominent news bulletins. As Voznesensky was preparing to send it, the Deputy Governor and Deputy Head of the local KGB marched in, demanding the tape of the arrival ceremony. 'If they see this in Moscow, they'll cut off the credits to our region. You're a patriot, aren't you?' they asked of him. Being seen to be too close to Rutskoy was potentially damaging for a local leader. When Voznesensky refused, they offered money, 'as much as you need'. He still refused.

Shunned in Moscow and many of the industrial cities, Rutskoy could usually rely on a warmer welcome in the provincial heartlands where the old-time bosses held sway. There was no area more hostile to Yeltsin than the 'red belt', the agriculture-dominated regions that surround Moscow. To follow Rutskoy to Kursk and Belgorod in August 1993 was to take a journey back in time. Shorn of the trappings of office, he joined us on a regular Aeroflot flight, departing from a corrugated iron shed that is otherwise known as Moscow's Bykovo airport. The passengers aboard the Antonov-24 jet sat tight, fidgeting in embarrassed silence as they awaited their unusual companion. Rutskoy's place was at the back of the turbo-prop, near the toilets, with only the statutory plastic cup of lemonade to distract him from his musing. He was preparing his latest speech, a variation on the angry theme of an empire lost and a people betrayed.

Little over an hour's flight south of the capital, Kursk has preserved itself in a time capsule. The girls still wore their white ribbons, the boys their blue tracksuits. The streets were still relatively safe, bread was relatively cheap and meals could be acquired only with *taloni*, coupons provided by the hotel administration. This was the land of the *sovok*, Soviet Man, alien territory for the reformers in Moscow. Kursk is the site of history's largest tank battle, when the Red Army stopped the Nazis in their tracks. To celebrate it hundreds of veterans were invited. Rutskoy was guest of honour. The entire leadership had come out, flowers in hand, to meet the local boy off the plane. The traffic police had cleared the streets. Yeltsin's sensibilities were far from their thoughts. Rutskoy was leading in the opinion polls. He thrived on the attention. Welcome ceremony over, the General got down to business. 'What are you afraid of?' he demanded of the cluster of locals who had assembled on the street. 'Let's talk. Ask me questions.' A matron in a yellow dress obliged. 'Alexander Vladimirovich, when are you going to take over?' she wanted to know. 'No one's going for the President's job,' he replied, 'but he must know what the people think of his performance.' 'Bravo, bravo!' a few voices shouted. 'Keep it up!'

Rutskoy was playing on his animosity with Yeltsin. His tour was well prepared, playing to his most loyal constituencies – the military, the elderly and women of all ages. Like any politician at the hustings, his every movement was designed for maximum effect. As he stepped out of his battle bus at the start of commemorations of the tank battle, he fastidiously combed his moustache, his exuberant trademark. At the Memorial to the Fallen, a war monument of Soviet giganticism, he plunged into the crowd. A woman in her forties grabbed him by the neck and tried to kiss him. 'Help us!' screamed a man at the back, baring his gold teeth and wrestling his way to his idol. Rutskoy's lone bodyguard looked on nervously as his boss spoke. 'Dear Comrades, veterans, you saved us from the Nazi plague. Shoulder to shoulder you stood in one line in the trenches, in the tanks and planes, Uzbeks, Ukrainians, Kazakhs, Tajiks, Georgians and Russians. This we called the Great Soviet People. Now they try to divide us.' The gravelly voice resounded across the sun-drenched square. There was no need for notes, he had said it all before. He laid a wreath at the tomb of the unknown soldier and hugged a group of retired servicemen. As the national anthem of the new Russian state was played, many of the officers at Rutskoy's side failed to raise the salute. Yeltsin's Russia, a land of fast bucks, unbridled freedom and never-ending crises, was not for them.

In Kursk, unlike most cities, Rutskoy had no problems putting his views across on local television. After one more interview, he took time off to have lunch with his ailing mother, Zinaida Iosifovna. She was known around town for her years selling beer from a stand. The origins were humble indeed. Rutskoy and his three burly aides squeezed onto the sofa-bed in her one-roomed apartment, situated appropriately enough on the corner of Red Flag Street, carrying with them boxes of goodies from Moscow's cornucopia of capitalism. Outside the Rutskoy home washing hung on the line. The swings and slides on the dusty patch of grass were rusting away.

Like Yeltsin, Rutskoy sought to cultivate the image of the man next door, pet spaniel and all, working assiduously at the family vegetable patch, 'just like everyone else'. The truth was quite different. His Moscow apartment was anything but modest. The Rutskoys and their two sons were no strangers to Western tastes. His wife Lyudmila worked for Valentin Yudashkin, a leading fashion designer, and was responsible for her husband's dapper, double-breasted suits, Italian shoes and ties. Russian women love a real *muzhik*, a bloke who tells it to 'em straight and charms them with his smile, and the Rutskoy look was impeccable. Nor was he bothered about using family connections. Misha, the youngest brother, used the formal means of address, Alexander Vladimirovich, in gratitude. Plucked from nowhere to become head of personnel in the Kursk branch of the Interior Ministry, Misha made himself so unpopular by throwing his weight about that his brother had to find him a new job in Moscow.

The final stop on this leg of the Rutskoy roadshow took his cavalcade sweeping past fields of sunflower and maize to the Shepkina collective farm. Having briefly looked after agriculture (a traditional poisoned chalice at the Kremlin) until Yeltsin removed him from that job, Rutskoy took it upon himself to deliver a lecture on cereal crops to the assembled workers, who earned £10 a month, often for seven-day weeks. The sceptical ones among them raised their eyebrows. He paused for a cigarette.

The very logic of life tells us that all our problems can be solved. But these people in charge have a completely different agenda. Some talk about mistakes. But mistakes like these are not made. These are bright people. They're doing everything deliberately. They did it, they dismembered the Soviet Union. The work came from outside. The CIA, agents of other countries, along with traitors from within. They destroyed a great power. Now they're going for Russia.

His advisers tapped him on the shoulder awkwardly. Once again he had shot from the hip. Here was a man who on seeing for the first time the queue outside the brand new McDonalds in central Moscow, had yelled about young Russians' 'anticipation of Holy Communion' with the West. He once boasted how he had shouted at a delegation of US Congressmen during talks in his office, telling them if they wanted to leave they knew where the door was. 'Alexander Vladimirovich, it's time to go,' the aides implored him. But Rutskoy had not finished. 'What have they done with the workers' money? They grabbed it all, they've robbed everyone. They're getting fat on someone else's account.'

Yeltsin also visited his mother, but he had less to be proud of in Yekaterinburg – the pre-revolutionary name that had been restored to his home town of Sverdlovsk. Not far from where Klavdia lived in the centre of the city with her other son, Mikhail, stood a plaque, newly erected. It marked the spot where Oleg Vagin, aged thirty-two, and his three younger bodyguards had been shot dead. Vagin was head of a 'business centre', a favoured haunt of criminal groups. His assailants, believed to be hired assassins from the Baltic states, calmly drove away. They had not bothered to put false number plates on their car or cover their faces. The attack took place a few hundred yards from the city council and the local Security Ministry; yet it took detectives more than two hours to get to the scene of the crime. As with most murders in the city, no witnesses came forward. Nothing was done. Long ago, Yekaterinburg had already witnessed one act of violence: the murder of Tsar Nicholas II and his family. The merchant house where they were killed was razed to the ground on the orders of Brezhnev's Politburo. Yeltsin, the local Party chief, was happy to oblige, and the bulldozers were dispatched.

Modern Yekaterinburg rivalled Moscow and St Petersburg for the dubious accolade of Russia's crime capital. The pickings were great. Tens of millions of pounds were made through the export of chemicals and precious metals from the Urals. They would be taken through the Baltic states and out to the West, a lucrative business monopolized by five major syndicates, an alliance of old *nomenklatura* and thugs. Everyone, it seemed, was in their pay. Investigators were afraid of meeting in public. 'These people feed everyone in the region now,' said Vasily, a crime squad investigator who agreed to meet at a cooperative café as long as his identity was not revealed. A female colleague in the nearby town of Pervouralsk was doused with petrol and set alight as she waited for a contact. The 32-year-old captain suffered severe burns but she soon went back to work, earning £15 a month. It was hard to understand their motivation. Even on the rare occasions when they caught somebody red-handed and survived to tell the tale, they would have an extremely tough job persuading the prosecutor's office to proceed and the courts to convict. And even after that, the criminals were often released very early on parole.

Konstantin Tsyganov was one of the best-known mobsters. He was in charge of the city's Uralmash region, a small outpost that during the Communist days had been run first by Ryzhkov, then by Ilyushin. Tsyganov's arrest in the summer of 1993 led to protests from sports groups, pensioners and other lobbies who depended on his philanthropy. He was also popular among local businesses, who saw him as a vital link with an otherwise obdurate bureaucracy, opening doors, providing signed documents and affording protection – for a fee. He was held in a jail in the neighbouring town of Perm, because local prison guards were deemed unreliable. He was eventually released on bail of 150 million roubles, little more than £50,000, a ridiculously small figure for a man as rich as he. Tsyganov's company was helping to collect money for a memorial to the Tsar.

One night I happened to bump into Tsyganov in Yekaterinburg's main casino. He was playing poker, surrounded by his henchmen who carried their guns openly. There was only one other gambler, who kept himself and his bodyguards to an adjacent table. He was the head of the central district, in whose patch the casino was situated. Neither man acknowledged the other. Something had obviously happened earlier on in the evening. On the ground outside the entrance there was a pool of blood.

Yeltsin did not stay long when he visited his old fiefdom. He would go to his mother's two-roomed flat and bring her medicines. For him it was humiliating to acknowledge that basic antibiotics were not available in his home town. If she was well enough she would make him his favourite dish, *pelmeni*, piping hot dumplings filled with meat. There were no airs and graces about Yeltsin's family. His matronly wife Naina was the polar opposite of Raisa Gorbachev, with her credit cards and taste for French designer clothes.

The village where he was born was like any other in Russia, an idyll ruined by human hand. Beyond Yekaterinburg, down a long and rutted road, past the chemical works and nuclear power plants that blight the landscape and turn the snow black, stood Butko. It took five hours to cover the 150 miles. Yeltsin's only remaining relatives there were Stanislav

Glebov, a second cousin, his wife Lena and mother Anna. Their two-storey wooden house, on the corner of Krupskaya Street (named after Lenin's wife), was a cut above the rest. It was not, Stanislav insisted, the result of privilege but of hard endeavour. Four years after retiring as an electrical engineer, Stanislav started out as a private farmer, with nine cows and a horse. The directors of the collective farm, which continued to control life for the 5,000 villagers, denied him land and machinery. While the state sector received large subsidies, Stanislav was left to fend for himself and his family by selling milk and eggs to his neighbours. His battle seemed a microcosm of his cousin's. Both shared a pugnacity that, it seemed, would see them through.

For Stanislav the fate of the nation came down to the work ethic. 'Yeltsin can't feed the nation on his own. People should learn to live for themselves. We should throw out all the members of parliament. All they do is get drunk in their posh flats and hotels,' he posited as we tucked into meat and potato soup, followed by meat and potatoes, and a glass of milk. From her armchair, Anna took up the gauntlet, grinning a toothless grin and hitting her walking stick against the table leg for dramatic effect. 'What we need is hunger therapy. People have got sloppy. If they know there's no guaranteed food around the corner, they'd work. If Peter the Great had held negotiations with the *boyars*, his reforms would have failed.' Yeltsin's mistake, she said, was not his decision to undertake radical reform but his failure to push ahead once begun.

Stanislav joined us on the journey back to the city. He had packed his best grey suit. He was off to appeal to the regional court for his land. He had never told his cousin about his problem, because he knew he had more important matters to deal with. Three days after my visit to Butko a telegram appeared at my door in Moscow: 'Refused again give land/tell world impossible receive land in Butko/Stanislav.'

14

Worms and Cockroaches

'Evil always originated in the Kremlin. We should withdraw presidential and government structures from here and turn the Kremlin into a national museum.' Khasbulatov was in top form. Whatever their shortcomings as politicians, Russia's leaders had acquired a talent for the colourful put-down. Yeltsin had brought it to the forefront, albeit with more bluster than wit; Rutskoy had taken it on with his 'boys in pink trousers'. The undisputed masters were Khasbulatov and Kostikov, Yeltsin's spokesman, who regarded circumspection as a dereliction of duty. Khasbulatov struck the first blow in April 1992 when asked in Congress for his views on Gaidar and the government: 'I have the same open contempt for such people as I do for worms.'

Kostikov likened Khasbulatov to Stalin. 'The results [of his policies] are known,' he said: 'Mass terror, deportations, gulags,' to which Khasbulatov replied: 'If the press secretary dares to say just one more word against me, he'll be thrown out and done away with.' Kostikov was then asked why Yeltsin had left it to him to round on the opposition, and in a *tour de force* replied: 'Profoundly aware of his status as leader of the nation, he simply cannot take part in cockroach races with the Khasbulatovs and Rutskoys of this world.' The timing was perfect. The gambling business had found a new lease of life with parasites.

Invective against one's own was acceptable. When it came to foreign dignitaries, and one in particular, there was a limit. Margaret Thatcher was an absolute taboo. The Iron Lady was adored by the people of the old ideological enemy. During her prime ministerial visits to the USSR local journalists would gush at her. When she was thrown out in the Conservative Party's Politburo-style palace coup, Russians simply could not understand it. How ungrateful we Britons were; we did not know what was right for our country, we were admonished, by Communists and anti-Communists alike. Ironically, her fate was similar to that of the man she 'discovered', Gorbachev, who was feted in the West as a world statesman well after his political demise in Russia. Thatcher came to Moscow soon after she was forced to leave Number Ten, safe in the knowledge that there was one place where she was guaranteed adoration. Politicians queued up to be included on her agenda. Her most striking appearance was at MGIMO, the college where children of the Soviet *nomenklatura* were trained to become diplomats. Crush barriers were overturned as Russia's bright young things, who had waited in vain for tickets, tried to charge past the doormen. In subsequent years, only Michael Jackson received such a mobbing.

Thatcher returned again, with less fanfare, to Moscow and St Petersburg in July 1993. During the trip she gave a series of television interviews, and naturally was given an easy ride. Asked her views on Russia's power struggle, she made clear her support for Yeltsin and said he would be justified in taking tough action against parliament. The remarks would have gone largely unnoticed – they broke little new ground and fell into the mainstream of Western opinion – had it not been for Khasbulatov's reaction. Thatcher, he told a television reporter the day she left, had no right to lecture Russians about democracy, especially as Britain did not have a written constitution of its own. (It was becoming fashionable to cite this historical 'omission' as an example of the fallacy of Western democratic traditions.) Why had Thatcher's interviewers not challenged her on this point, Khasbulatov asked? 'You can humiliate yourselves if you want to. But don't humiliate your own people, your own politicians, who are not in the slightest bit inferior to the various old bags who pay us visits.' The word, *babyonka*, would have been used by a peasant about his nagging wife, mother or mother-in-law.

The presenter of the programme was shocked at the outburst. Khasbulatov was unrepentant: 'I said that deliberately because I knew what your reaction would be! Why should I think she is cleverer than I am? I see no grounds for it at all.' An opinion poll the next day showed that Russians trusted Thatcher more than any other foreign politician to put their sorry affairs in order. Next up was Boris Fyodorov, Finance Minister and avowed Westernizer, who said with all the sanctimoniousness he could muster: 'I would like to apologize on behalf of all Russians to Mrs Thatcher, who was insulted by our Speaker. I hope Britain and the rest of the world do not think that all of us in Russia are such boors.' Thatcher was advised that such language was a normal part of the political process and kept clear of the fracas.

The year had started with an attempt at reconciliation by Yeltsin: 'Let us proclaim 1993 the year of a moratorium on all political punch-ups. If we don't deal with the economy, then it will destroy us all.' Yeltsin had been chastened by his defeat at Congress, by having to drop Gaidar. But, as part of the compromise package, the referendum on Russia's political future was going ahead in April, as agreed by all sides. Therein lay his hopes that the constitutional mess might be finally resolved. Russia had been operating under a basic law drawn up in 1977, when Brezhnev was in charge. It was not a particularly bad document for its time; it was just that the Communists never saw fit to abide by it. After Russia declared sovereignty in 1990 it was amended so many times that it had become completely unworkable. Once Russia became a fully fledged state and the Soviet Union was no more, all sides recognized that an entirely new constitution was needed. Yeltsin had had the chance in the autumn of 1991, when his powers were unchallenged, to dissolve the Supreme Soviet and Congress of People's Deputies and force through a constituent assembly which would have worked out the framework for a new political arrangement. There would have been considerable discussion over many of the basic aspects, most notably the relationship between President and parliament, but he would have got his way if he had acted quickly.

In 1992, as he dithered, the opportunity slipped away from him. By the start of 1993 it seemed all but lost. Parliament's own draft constitution sought to maximize the powers of the legislative branch, and minimize those of the executive. Yeltsin did not want to return to a Soviet-style rubber-stamping parliament, but he believed that corners should be cut to push through radical change. Speed was of the essence. He needed no reminding of the chances for economic reform that had been wasted by Gorbachev. In any case, with its strong representation from the provinces, any legislature would by definition tend towards conservatism. There should have been a mature, healthy debate with compromises on both sides. But parliament had the upper hand. Guaranteed a majority in Congress, Yeltsin's opponents could pass laws restricting the President's powers, or take swipes at his government with impunity. They could make up the rules as they went along, and as long as Zorkin was behind them, hiding behind the legalistic niceties, Yeltsin became their prisoner. Whenever the occasion required it, deputies thought up amendments and passed them at the press of the electronic button. Once the situation had deteriorated into personal vendettas, Yeltsin had two choices – to give in to Congress, or to fight. And he could no longer fight while abiding by the constitution.

Zorkin had been widely praised for the truce he had negotiated between Yeltsin and Khasbulatov. One television station called him the man of the year. It all seemed to go to his head. Within weeks of the deal at the December Congress, parliament, with Zorkin's blessing, double-crossed Yeltsin and demanded that the referendum be postponed indefinitely. The reason it gave – that a vote would exacerbate social tensions – was spurious. Most voters were sick of the games and wanted politicians to concentrate on what mattered, the standard of living. Opinion polls gave Yeltsin low ratings, and parliament even lower. Yeltsin's forces were paralysed. Chernomyrdin's new government, like Gaidar's before him, had little freedom to operate.

As the next Congress, the eighth, began in March, many commentators were talking for the first time about the 'post-Yeltsin era'. With the referendum plans scuppered, the path would be open for parliament to pick off the remaining reformist ministers, push through an entirely different economic and foreign policy, and enshrine their dominance by passing their own draft constitution at a special conference that autumn. Yeltsin cut a forlorn figure. Prompted by Burbulis, he decided he had no choice but to declare war on parliament. Addressing his supporters at a political rally, Yeltsin said he was preparing for a 'final option'. The following day, in a meeting with the army General Staff, Yeltsin was urged to take 'decisive measures' to end the constitutional crisis. The warning was deliberately leaked to make the President look tough, but a crackdown still seemed implausible. Kozyrev and other ministers were ordered to cancel trips abroad and to turn up at the Grand Kremlin Palace for Congress. Parliament responded by demanding that the 5,000 strong guard annexed by Yeltsin be put back under its control. Grachev, the Defence Minister, said military units had been put on a low state of alert.

Khasbulatov needed no prompting. In his keynote speech, which suggested he would stop at nothing, he described the December truce as 'the work of the devil', demanded the sacking of Kozyrev and Chubais and threatened to freeze the salaries of government ministers. Yeltsin stormed out. The talk was of cataclysms ahead. 'The smooth reformist period has ended,' said Shakhrai. 'The Congress has led the country to the threshold beyond which lies the path to revolution, street rule and chaos.' Congress closed after four days, having scrapped the referendum and issued a declaration accusing Yeltsin of 'political adventurism'. It was not expected to meet again until June. It did not need to. It could sit and wait.

Yeltsin mulled over the options with his aides. They decided to fall back on a trusted Communist tactic: to lay the ground in advance of a crackdown, just as Gorbachev did in the Baltics. Kostikov issued a statement. 'The President of Russia, B.N. Yeltsin, is deeply worried by the threat to democracy and reform. He has received numerous appeals from the regions, from factories, social organizations and individual citizens, asking him to defend democracy and stop the restoration of Communism,' it said.

On the evening of Saturday, 20 March, on prime-time television, Yeltsin addressed the nation to announce the imposition of 'special rule'. He ordered government forces to protect strategic buildings and said any decision by parliament that challenged his powers was invalid. The measures, he said, were vital to safeguard the referendum, which would go ahead whether parliament liked it or not. Opposition leaders rushed to the White House. Rutskoy, Zorkin, Stepankov and Khasbulatov's number two Yuri Voronin rushed in their black limousines to Ostankino, television headquarters. Brushing past bemused guards, they demanded to see the duty editor of Russian Television. The future of the country was at stake, they insisted. Twenty minutes later they were on television, sitting awkwardly together on a sofa to read out statements. Zorkin, the supposedly neutral arbiter, said: 'The announcement which the President made today presents us with an attempt at a coup.' The gang of four appealed to the people and security forces not to carry out the President's orders. To the Yeltsin camp, that move smacked of treason.

A special session of parliament was called the next day. The aim was the impeachment of Yeltsin, nothing less. For that, though, they needed the support of the security forces. The three ministers concerned were summoned, but each refused to commit himself. Barannikov, the Security Minister, was playing his usual double game, but it was the army Khasbulatov needed and Grachev, the Defence Minister, was studiously staying neutral. Thousands of protesters gathered, the pro-reformers at the Mayor's office, the anti-Yeltsin mob outside the White House, separated by a thin line of police. Guards loyal to parliament were joined by vigilantes in leather jackets. Many of the deputies had bedded down for the night, convinced that Yeltsin would strike again.

But Yeltsin had disappeared from view. Within hours of delivering his speech, he heard that his mother had died of heart failure. The news left him distraught. According to Alya Tanicheva, a family friend from Yekaterinburg, Klavdia had been reasonably well that day. 'When we talked on Saturday she was completely normal and fairly talkative. After his television appearance she became nervous and stressed. She was a bundle of nerves – she always worried about him.'

Much depended on the Constitutional Court, although with Zorkin in charge a decision against Yeltsin was virtually a foregone conclusion. Zorkin, who had broken off a trip to the USA on being told that the President was up to something, said that after the television appearance Yeltsin's office had refused to hand over the text of the actual decree. After sitting through the night, the judges decided on their ruling, finding by a majority of nine to three that Yeltsin's decree had violated the constitution. It would be for a Congress to decide his fate, they said. Zorkin had once again allowed himself to get carried away. A judgment of such import was passed without the court seeing one piece of paper. It had relied entirely on a tape of Yeltsin's broadcast. Yet under its charter, the court was forbidden from delivering verdicts without seeing the signed documents. As one Moscow newspaper put it: 'Court declares television sets unconstitutional.' With a nod from the court, the hardliners prepared to finish off Yeltsin's career as he went to bury his mother. As he paid his last respects at an Orthodox rite at Kuntsevo cemetery, Yeltsin wept and clung on to Naina for support. Attending the funeral were the entire political elite, including Rutskoy and Zorkin. Both men shook Yeltsin's hand; Rutskoy looked away as he did so. The main evening news said Zorkin presented Yeltsin with a copy of the verdict at the end of the funeral. This Zorkin would later deny.

Yeltsin loathed the judge, perhaps more than his other adversaries. Neither sought to conceal the one telephone conversation they had had immediately after Yeltsin's declaration. According to Zorkin, Yeltsin needed to find *kompromat* against him. He asked his security forces to investigate. They reported that they had spotted the judge bringing arms illegally into Russia. Zorkin said he and his wife had been asked by the Russian Ambassador to Washington, Vladimir Lukin, if they would take a parcel containing two hunting rifles back to his son in Moscow. In their conversation, Yeltsin allegedly told him: 'You've been in America. I understand your wife brought back things she shouldn't have done. I know about it.' 'Political and constitutional language was being reduced to the level of kitchen conversation,' Zorkin said. 'Can you imagine a situation where the President of the USA would start phoning the Chairman of parliament or the Supreme Court and blackmail them on the basis of conversations he'd had with one of his chief bodyguards?'

The impeachment process was put in train. Khasbulatov spoke openly of Rutskoy assuming office. But everything depended on a decree that no one outside Yeltsin's office had set eyes on. Yeltsin's team did some sharp footwork. By the time the decree was published, the wording had been entirely changed. Gone was any reference to special rule, and the whole tone was milder. It was not an act of great political inspiration, but a result of in-fighting in which the moderates outwitted the radicals. Yeltsin himself had gone into virtual hiding, to mourn for his mother.

Two weeks after Yeltsin's declaration, an emergency ninth Congress convened. All sides warned of open confrontation. Yeltsin appealed to deputies on television: 'Remember, if the Congress takes historically incorrect decisions, it will plunge the people into an abyss of confrontation.' The Patriarch, stepping reluctantly into the fray, appealed for calm. The Defence Ministry issued a statement calling on servicemen to observe military discipline and the law 'which forbids any political agitation or activity in the armed forces'. Khasbulatov urged Yeltsin 'to apologize for his mistakes'. Such were the fears of violence, with the army perhaps being split in two, that it looked for one moment as if Congress would step back from the brink and allow Yeltsin his referendum. If the deputies managed to doctor the questions, Yeltsin stood a good chance of losing it anyway. Then he would have to go. The hardliners had done their arithmetic. It was touch and go whether they had two-thirds of the 1,033 deputies on their side to impeach Yeltsin. They suspected they would only have one chance, and maybe they needed to wait.

Just as it seemed the Congress was running out of steam, Yeltsin made the most extraordinary appearance. It was in the last hour of the Saturday session. He had been out of the hall for most of the day. Suddenly he returned and asked for the floor. He was looking haggard. His mat of thick grey hair had been swept forward, instead of back as usual. He mumbled incoherently about his opponents paying a price, about consequences and about reform. Was he drunk or was he ill? Whatever the case, he enraged the deputies, who started jeering him off the rostrum.

Yeltsin stormed out. He told reporters he had not slept for three days and was suffering from grief. Minutes later, however, he appeared to have regained his composure. He went on a walkabout along Tverskaya Street, flanked by Viktor Yerin, his Interior Minister, and Barannikov. Nobody has ever found out exactly what happened that evening. Yushenkov was convinced that drink had not played a part.

> He'd just had a shower after playing tennis. He'd been listening to the Congress proceedings on the relay system and he hadn't combed his hair yet. So he came into Congress like that, looking rather unkempt. Then suddenly everyone's saying he's drunk. We advised him to go and talk to the journalists, to prove he wasn't. Everyone was pressing around, trying to get as close as possible, to smell him. One of the Communists burst through past his bodyguards and grabbed hold of his suit. When he came away I asked whether Yeltsin had smelled of booze, and he said, churlishly, 'He's probably eaten something to get rid of the smell.'

The next morning Khasbulatov told deputies he and Yeltsin had met and had agreed on a compromise. The referendum would be cancelled and joint elections for President and parliament would take place in November. His announcement caused consternation. Many in the chamber felt that, following the débâcle the previous evening, they now had Yeltsin within their grasp. Their Chairman was trying to let him off the hook. So furious were the hardline factions that they forced on to the day's agenda not only the impeachment of Yeltsin but a vote of no confidence in Khasbulatov too.

After the coup, Yeltsin's close shaves with the hardliners had aroused little passion on the streets. Muscovites had learnt to take the power struggle in their stride. This time the stakes were higher. A demonstration in defence of the President was called for the same morning. The turnout would be a key test. The march began outside city hall early in the morning. By the time it had wound its way past the Lubyanka, the home of the KGB, down Ilyinka Street where several ministries were housed and on to St Basil's Cathedral, the numbers had swelled. As they made their way through the centre they gave vent to the ritual chant of 'down with Communism', which had not been heard since the golden year of 1991. They came in their droves, up to 100,000 people of all ages. Most of them stayed all day, eating ice cream in the sunshine as the Congress proceedings boomed from a giant loudspeaker. They kept their spirits up. There was none of the venom or viciousness of the rival hardline rally that was taking place simultaneously on the other side of the Kremlin. The warm-up acts for the radical protest were the old stalwarts, Popov, the former mayor, and Bonner, Sakharov's widow. 'There is no constitutional crisis because we have no constitution,' Bonner said, holding up a little booklet of the constitution. 'What I have in my hand is a piece of toilet paper for people's big and little needs.'

It was late in the evening by the time the result was announced. The pro-Yeltsin rally had dwindled but several thousand had stuck it out. Many sat on the cobbles in trepidation. They couldn't bear to think of the fate that awaited Russia without Yeltsin. For all his faults, he was the only guarantor of continued change. The hardliners fell short by only seventy-two out of more than 1,000 votes. Khasbulatov escaped impeachment by a more comfortable margin. The demonstrators cheered when Yeltsin clambered on to the bus parked below the cathedral to address them. 'The Communist *coup d'état* did not succeed. Democracy won. Young Russia won,' he told them. Chernomyrdin stood by his side, as he had done throughout the crisis. His role was pivotal. He had convinced many waverers that to support Yeltsin did not necessitate being part of the radical camp. Parliament didn't know how to deal with him. They would have loved to denounce him as a traitor to the cause, but knew that was impossible. Almost uniquely among the main figures, he had remained loyal but independent.

Congress was despondent when it convened the following day for its final session. One obscure deputy appeared with a large bloodstained bandage covering his head. He said he had been hit on the head with a metal object by an elderly man as he walked from his hotel past the pro-Yeltsin demonstrators. The crowd, he said, had been made up of 'drug abusers and people with mental diseases'. It was an unconvincing attempt to wrest back the moral high ground. With great reluctance, deputies gave the final go-ahead to the referendum. But they were determined to stack the questions and rules in their favour.

For the first time in a long time, Yeltsin's position did not seem so bleak. Yet his camp realized the going would be tough. Of the four questions in the referendum, the only one in which victory seemed likely was the first, the question of confidence in the President. It was the most important, but on its own it would not have amounted to a victory. The second question asked voters whether they approved of the government's economic record. This had been inserted by parliament, and with so much hardship in the country there was little hope of success there for the President. The final two questions asked whether parliament and the President should submit themselves for early election. Originally a valid vote on each of the four questions required a majority of all eligible voters. Yeltsin's lawyers challenged this in the courts and Zorkin, possibly realizing that the tide was turning away towards the President, ruled that the first two questions required a majority only of votes cast.

Yeltsin based his campaign on the use of media that were slanted heavily in his favour. He made only three forays into the provinces, one of them *en route* to his Vancouver summit with President Clinton. Burbulis supervised all the President's appearances on television. There was no shortage of volunteers among the radicals. Poltoranin was prominent as ever, as was Gaidar, the deposed Prime Minister, and Mstislav Rostropovich, the world's leading cellist, who had earlier demonstrated his democratic credentials by returning from exile at the start of the coup and going straight to the White House to support Yeltsin.

The Yeltsin team enlisted the services of Western advertising agencies and fund raisers. The results were mixed. A dinner organized by two young Americans backfired when there were too few takers for the $1,000 tickets. The reluctance to fork out money at this level was hardly surprising, even for Russia's spendthrift rich. The tactics adopted to woo the poor were equally brazen. A series of decrees were signed increasing social security benefits for students, war veterans and children, and promising greater support for workers whose firms were threatened by bankruptcy. Later, ministers were to say that implementation of the decrees would be delayed due to insufficient resources. State television broadcast news that was heavily biased towards the President. One special programme showed the Yeltsins 'at home', with the lord of the manor scolding his wife about the tea being cold in a carefully designed package to make him look like a typical *muzhik*.

The opposition resorted to the tactics of desperation. Parliament issued an unsigned statement claiming Yeltsin was planning to introduce presidential rule on the night of the referendum after falsifying the results. He had been told by the Security Ministry that he was unlikely to gain above 40 per cent in his favour. Khasbulatov accused the presidential team, *inter alia*, of buying votes and 'working on' election officials. The parliamentary press office then distributed a report claiming that falsified voting slips had already been prepared. No attempt was ever made to provide evidence for these claims.

The highlight of the Yeltsin campaign was a pop concert staged in his honour under the domes of St Basil's. Anybody who was anybody in the showbiz world was invited. Yeltsin made a brief appearance to acknowledge the support and deliver a short speech. He looked frail, leaning on the shoulder of his Interior Minister for support. He promised that if he lost he would resign. If he won he would interpret the vote as a mandate to force through a new constitution. Banners appeared in Moscow and other cities advising the electorate how to answer the four questions. Yes, yes, no, yes. It was a matter of memorizing the order.

The gods were on Yeltsin's side. Not only was the weather unseasonally hot for April, but the electorate found time to vote on the way to or from their *dachas*. The results exceeded the most optimistic forecasts in the presidential camp: 59 per cent on question one (vote of confidence in the President), 53 per cent on question two (approval of economic reform),

32 per cent on holding early presidential elections (which corresponded to 49 per cent of those who voted), and 43 per cent on early parliamentary elections (or 67.2 of voters). The outcome was comparable to Yeltsin's election victory in June 1991, before times became hard.

Even before the results had been collated a 'war of interpretations' had started. The opposition said the referendum had solved nothing. Yeltsin had acquired no new legal or constitutional rights, it said. Yet, no matter how they tried to massage the figures, to the broader public the results *were* seen as settling the issue of 'who rules Russia'. Yeltsin, after all, had now received two popular mandates in less than two years. As Poltoranin put it: 'The President has received from the hands of the people a *carte blanche* for decisive action.' Yeltsin's more radical aides urged him to move quickly. They reminded Yeltsin of the mistakes made after the coup when he failed to neutralize his opponents.

A new constitution, drawn up by an expert group under the leadership of Shakhrai, was presented. It was an amalgam of the French, American and German variants, adapted to Yeltsin's requirements of a strong executive. The President would be elected for a maximum of two five-year terms. There would be no Congress and no Vice-President. A new parliament, the Federal Assembly, would be formed, consisting of two chambers, the State Duma and the Federation Council. Parliament would have limited rights to impeach the President or reject his nominations for the government. The document contained weaknesses but was a good basis on which to build. The presidential camp knew that however good it might be, it would not be passed by the obdurate parliament. Other means would have to be found.

Yeltsin responded characteristically to his referendum victory. He did nothing for several days. The only aspects of policy carried out with zeal were the personal vendettas. Anybody who had anything to do with Rutskoy was either to be won over with incentives or punished. Zorkin found that the gas, electricity and water were suddenly turned off at his *dacha*. 'A special group was set up with the task of going through all my records, including my medical record and bank accounts,' Zorkin recalled. 'One of the chief bodyguards came up to me and said: "We're going to privatize all these dachas." The implication was: join the team, get your dacha, but after that you must do as you're told. From this I understood that the old Bolshevik methods of dictatorship were still in operation.'

Yeltsin carried out a limited purge in the government, sacking his old friend Skokov, who had gone over entirely into the Rutskoy camp. Chernomyrdin, for all his support for Yeltsin, was taken aback by the high approval rating for economic reform. He had been on the point of closing down the radical Centre for Economic Reforms, but quickly changed his mind.

Yeltsin was being advised to bypass parliament and simply sign a new constitution into being, ignoring what parliament and Zorkin's court had to say about it. This plan was considered too confrontational, so Yeltsin opted for a more gradual method of bypassing the hardliners. The Constitutional Assembly opened in the Kremlin on 5 June. It was handpicked, with representatives from all the regions, as well as from business, political parties, the legal profession, the Church and the trade unions. There were around 700 delegates in all. Opening the conference, Yeltsin warned that he wanted results, not 'the political chattering we have seen at Congress'. The first day ended in farce. Khasbulatov staged a walk-out after being refused the floor. Then a Communist delegate tried to approach the platform. He was lifted off his feet by security guards, bundled out of the room and deposited at the door of the hall. The diminutive protester waved one of his shoes defiantly at Yeltsin as he was being carried out. Yeltsin described the antics as 'a planned provocation' and ordered that the proceedings be continued in secrecy. For the purists, the gathering left much to be desired. Its very location was unfortunate. The Marble Hall was where the Party's Central Committee had held its plenums.

At this time Yeltsin's attention was focused on 'General Dima' and the battle to discredit the opposition. Economic reform was grinding along, but with little sense of direction. Monetary control was lax, while no strategy had been devised to help industry. The optimism produced by the unexpected referendum results dissipated. Khasbulatov was back to his old tricks. In a series of resolutions passed just before the summer recess, parliament voted to double the planned budget deficit, in an attempt to undermine attempts at keeping a grip on financial policy. Undeterred by the referendum, they were planning the next Congress for the autumn. This time they would change the procedure, making it easier to remove the President.

Vigorous in crisis, so listless in normal political life, Yeltsin had once again allowed the momentum to slip away. Poltoranin took up the theme. 'I told him: "You have everything at your disposal and you're doing nothing. You're not working, you're simply lording it about." He didn't like it when I spoke to him like this. He'd already grown accustomed to everyone telling him what a great and wonderful President he was.'

One incident best demonstrated the trough into which the administration had fallen that summer. This was the great rouble fiasco. The announcement early one Saturday in July of the withdrawal of all banknotes printed before 1993 did more to damage confidence in the government than any other of its decisions. The motives for it were understandable. There were simply too many roubles in circulation, most of the old ones in the hands of the outlying republics. The Central Bank had warned it would enact currency reform, but had made it clear that the process would be gradual. Suddenly Russians were told that all notes printed before the start of the year were invalid. They had two weeks to change up to 35,000 roubles (about £15) into new money. The rest would have to be deposited in savings banks for six months. With inflation running at 750 per cent a year and interest rates at a sixth of that, the measure amounted to confiscation. Millions would suffer losses, not as high as might have been imagined, because inflation had ensured that people kept as few roubles in cash as possible, but still losses. And, as with Pavlov's confiscation of cash in 1991, it was the poorest who suffered most.

Many people on trips to Moscow found they no longer had the money to get home. As police struggled to control crowds outside savings banks, some sleeping there overnight to secure their place in the queue, Yeltsin announced a softening of the conditions that would leave fewer people out of pocket. Then the recriminations began in earnest. The reformers homed in on Gerashchenko, the Central Bank Chairman. Among Western financiers and diplomats, Gerashchenko was known as 'the dreaded G-word'. 'We did not have any vicious plot in mind,' he pleaded. He said his main objective had been to force other republics to decide whether to stay within the rouble zone. Fyodorov, the Finance Minister, was apopleptic. The currency was, after all, largely his responsibility, and he had been on holiday in the USA when the decision was taken. He had learnt about it from American newspapers.

More staggering than the government's disregard for its citizens' well-being was the ludicrousness of the decision-making process. Nobody denied that a cabinet meeting had taken place on the eve of the announcement. The reformers claimed Gerashchenko had outlined the idea only in theory and set no date for it. Yeltsin was given only an outline briefing. On his return, Fyodorov suggested that corruption and money laundering might have been part of the equation. Both he and Gerashchenko survived. No apology was made. Addressing Western bankers at a convention a few days later, Gerashchenko used one word to describe his country: *bardak*. Its literal translation is 'brothel', its figurative one 'a complete mess'. Everyone started using it. It summed up the situation perfectly.

15

The October Revolution

<hr style="width:20%;border:2px solid black" />

Konstantin Zlobin handed me a book from his shelves in his sitting room. 'It's all in there, read it.' He had passed me a copy of Freud's *Beyond the Pleasure Principle*. In it, he maintained, lay the answers to why the second October Revolution had taken place. In the heat of the moment the mentality of the mob takes over; irrational actions become infectious.

I had last seen Khasbulatov's spokesman on Sunday night, 3 October 1993. Yeltsin's siege of the White House had been broken. Moscow was on the verge of civil war as the hardliners marched towards the television centre. This was the denouement of the two-year struggle between President and parliament. This was Yeltsin's moment of truth. Zlobin was running down the sixth-floor corridor. 'We've done it. Yeltsin's on the run. Hundreds of police are coming over to our side,' he shouted, gasping for breath. 'The army is never going to obey him.'

Less than twenty-four hours later, Zlobin walked out of the building and into the afternoon sun, hands on head. The opposition had been routed. More than 150 people were dead. As the President himself admitted later, the army chiefs almost disobeyed him. Had they done so, he would have been out of power. At the last moment they fought his battle, surrounding the White House with tanks and pounding the rebels into submission with artillery fire. Rutskoy, Khasbulatov and the other ringleaders surrendered. They were put into an armoured bus and taken to an unknown destination. Zlobin was frogmarched in the bright sunshine towards the river. He believed he was about to be shot. Nothing happened. The cordon opened a chink and he was free. Zlobin hailed a cab home, hugged his wife and daughter and slumped into the bath.

There was nothing extraordinary about Zlobin. He had worked his way up through the ranks of official Soviet journalism, watching his step all the way. When offered the post of press secretary to the Supreme Soviet, he grabbed it, as anybody else would have done. In the weeks following the uprising, 'coup two' as it became known, he would sit on a bench in the playground outside his very ordinary block of flats and ponder those moments of madness. In between reflections he was haunted by another unpalatable truth. He was out of a job, and had never had to look for work before. If he and his friends had been paying attention, they would have started scanning the jobs columns a couple of months earlier. They had, after all, been warned.

'Ladies and Gentlemen. The President of the Russian Federation. Boris Nikolayevich Yeltsin. Let the press conference commence.' Kostikov, the spokesman, took his seat deferentially alongside Yeltsin. Presidential press conferences were a rare occurrence and Kostikov liked to squeeze all the pomp he could out of them. It was 19 August, the second anniversary of 'coup one'.

Yakubovsky had been and gone, leaving behind his *kompromat* against Rutskoy and company. For once, Yeltsin was inclined to believe the conspiracy theorists. Congress was preparing another, perhaps final, onslaught. The courts were against him. The army was an unknown quantity. The KGB was back to its nefarious ways.

Yeltsin acknowledged that he had wasted the referendum victory. He now had to make up for lost time. In the coming months, he told the assembled journalists, he would prepare his 'artillery fire' – metaphorically speaking, we presumed. 'I will use different means to bring about early parliamentary elections. An action plan is being drafted. It spans two and a half months – the rest of August for the opening volleys, September as the crucial month, October and possibly part of November. Parliament has become hostile to the people and is threatening Russia's security. It must be stopped.'

Yeltsin knew his limitations. He spent weeks looking around for a successor to Barannikov as Security Minister. He was toying with the idea of scrapping the ministry altogether and replacing it with a smaller, more manageable security service; but now was not the time for that. He eventually settled on Barannikov's deputy, Nikolai Golushko, an old-timer, a man of little vision but, Yeltsin hoped, a steady hand.

The President had tried brinkmanship twice already. His declarations of 'special rule' in December 1992 and March 1993 had failed. The first time he confined himself to threats, the second he made the mistake of informing waverers and enemies in advance. This time he was determined to plan well in advance but give away as few details of his intentions as possible. He played to the army, visiting several regiments traditionally deployed in crises. With his army coat slung over his shoulders, and in the presence of a few chosen photographers, Yeltsin was making a deliberate point. He sounded out his more reliable ministers. They knew, and he knew, that if nothing was done, their powers would be steadily eroded. There was no turning back.

Khasbulatov and Rutskoy had prepared themselves for confrontation. They didn't know exactly when it would come. For Yeltsin, there was no right time to strike. On 21 September Yeltsin appeared on television, sipped from his cup of tea, and announced he was dissolving parliament and calling elections to an entirely new legislature, within an entirely new constitution, on 12 December. The state networks had been given two hours' warning of the speech. Deputies were already inside the White House when it began.

An emergency Congress was immediately convened, even though it fell well short of a quorum. Deputies stripped Yeltsin of power for violating the constitution and appointed Rutskoy as Acting President for three months. Shortly after midnight, four hours after Yeltsin's statement, Rutskoy was 'sworn in' by a solemn but jubilant chamber. The Constitutional Court, true to form, voted by nine to four to endorse parliament's decision. Rutskoy's first act was to annul Yeltsin's decree. Not for him the niceties of debate: his own first decree provided for execution by firing squad for 'illegal actions' taken by top officials.

Outside parliament, several hundred diehards waved red flags and cheered as the new 'President' promised to reverse most of the previous two years' economic and political changes. They erected barricades of iron rods and concrete. Khasbulatov called on soldiers to mutiny and come to the defence of parliament. The defenders of the White House this time bore little resemblance to those in the coup of August 1991. The talk now was of lynching, of taking no prisoners. There was hardly a sympathetic character among them. Arms stashed away by Khasbulatov's private army inside the building were being handed out to all-comers. 'Dangerous weapons are getting into the hands of extremists, tramps, people with unstable psyches, criminals and mafia elements.' For once, a remark by Yeltsin's spokesman, Kostikov, had a ring of accuracy.

Both sides slid inexorably towards conflict. The city authorities disconnected gas, electricity and phone communications to parliament. Aeroflot was told not to sell tickets to deputies trying to come to Moscow from the provinces, but to find seats on the first available plane for any who wanted to leave the capital. Police closed off streets surrounding the White House, but didn't prevent people from coming and going. Chernomyrdin rallied the government behind the President. Pressure was applied wherever possible. The Prime Minister sent telegrams to regional leaders warning them of the 'personal consequences' of failing to obey Yeltsin's orders. 'The only way to remove the malignant tumour of double leadership is by surgery. Conservative medicine has done no good,' said Chernomyrdin. Grachev accompanied Yeltsin on a walkabout, assuring him that commanders of all ranks had 'declared full support' for him. Yeltsin told the crowd that parliament no longer existed. 'Therefore there is, cannot and must not be any dialogue. But there will be no blood. I tell you. I think we have had enough of parliament making fools of us and the people. Enough.'

Tucked away on the third floor of the White House was room 3-110. It hardly befitted the chambers of head of state of a world power. Even though not one country had recognized his accession to office, Rutskoy was keeping up appearances. He was hard at work, issuing decrees and stern warnings to those who ignored them. Khasbulatov had given him the best office at his disposal, bar his own. In the corridor, several bodyguards in well-pressed suits checked all-comers. Inside they tried to make it as grand as possible. A large Russian tricolor stood behind the desk. A new name plate had been fixed – Rutskoy, Alexander Vladimirovich, Acting President of the Russian Federation.

Rutskoy stood hunched, signing papers, as his half dozen most faithful aides stood over him. Despite sleeping for two nights on a bed in an ante-room, without lighting, heating or telephone, he appeared in good shape, impeccable as usual in a grey double-breasted suit. 'My role, as acting leader, is to ensure that elections take place, democratically,' he said, with feigned disinterest as to their outcome. Yeltsin and his entourage had broken the law and deserved to be punished. 'These games at compromise have brought the country to this. Another tragedy. Shame before the world. The people believed in Yeltsin, they believed the country would follow the path of law, the path of democratic transformation, but in the end the very idea has been discredited. It's time to begin living normally, like human beings. Laws, laws and laws again. Then society will be stable.'

One floor immediately below Rutskoy's office were those of his 'power ministers'. Barannikov had been 'given back' the Security Ministry. Andrei Dunayev, who had been sacked by Yeltsin at the same time as Barannikov, was 'promoted' to the post of Interior Minister, while Vladislav Achalov, who had worked closely with the coup leaders in 1991, was put in charge of the army. This *troika* tried to convince their erstwhile allies in the ministries and general staff to come to their defence. The guerrilla-style operations from the White House were organized by the extremist Makashov, a far more dangerous figure. Up and down the stairs between the two 'command posts' shuffled deputies and sympathetic regional bosses. Some were accompanied by Cossacks in studded shoes and a succession of men in dark glasses carrying mobile telephones, the only means of communication with the outside world.

Yeltsin tried the odd carrot, announcing that deputies' salaries would be paid all the way through until the expiry of their original term in 1995. Such an incentive was enough to win over some of the more respectable members of parliament, but not the diehards. He also pledged to submit himself for re-election in June 1994, six months after parliament but two years before he needed to. Next he tried the stick, deploying lorry-loads of troops in bullet-proof jackets and armed with sub-machine guns on the streets. The pretext had been an attack one night by a group of thugs on the headquarters of the CIS joint command. Two people died. The victims were a policeman and an elderly woman, who had peered out of her window to see what was going on and been hit by a single bullet.

On the first weekend of the uprising, as the few hundred bedraggled diehards, with their bloodshot eyes and angry faces, huddled around bonfires and sang tired old ballads, Yeltsin and the rest of Moscow were witnessing a music spectacular without rival in recent years. On Red Square, the bells pealed and cannons boomed in a free, open-air performance of Tchaikovsky's *1812 Overture*, evoking a glorious imperial past. Thousands of people turned out to watch Rostropovich conduct the National Symphony Orchestra from Washington. The symbolism said it all. The previous evening Rostroprovich had begun his tour at the Conservatoire. The soloist was none other than Ignat Solzhenitsyn, son of Alexander. Ignat was coming home for the first time. At the end of their performance of Shostakovich's Piano Concerto No. 1, the elderly conductor and young pianist hugged each other in an embrace that said volumes about their allegiances. The audience rose in rapture. The support lent by Rostropovich, a moral beacon in this wasteland of sleaze, was invaluable for Yeltsin. Rostropovich supported him not only in his times of trouble, but also of relative calm.

Inside the White House, the rebels were whipping themselves up into a frenzy. Barely an hour passed without a rumour of an ultimatum, a potential storming. Luzhkov, the Mayor, warned them to hand over their arms. But the threats were not taken seriously, because they were accompanied by public promises from Yeltsin to Western leaders to refrain from using force. The number of deputies was gradually whittled down to 150. With access to the building blocked, those inside took turns to rally the dwindling forces. The talk became ever more desperate. 'We have information that the American Congress is taking Clinton to court for supporting Yeltsin,' declared one speaker, to cheers from the motley crowd of supporters outside. Another said a plan had been hatched to starve out Russian farmers by importing rice from Taiwan.

The longer the siege went on, the less likely it seemed that a way could be found to end it peacefully with neither side emerging humiliated. Yeltsin seemed at a loss. The so-called ring of steel around the building was constantly being broken. The supply of weapons was never cut. Rutskoy and his allies went on walkabouts in the grounds, trying to talk the troops on the outside perimeter into changing sides. From a megaphone perched on a bright yellow armoured personnel carrier, the government forces played the popular rap tune Happy Nation by Ace of Base over and over again. Was this Yeltsin's idea of intimidation?

One of the aims of the rebels was to disrupt Moscow life. They were galled at the lack of public engagement in their struggle. Just beyond the police cordon people went about their daily business contemptuous of the scenes around them. Parliament's few hundred sympathizers did what they could. They took to the streets not far from the White House night after night, between the appropriately named 'Barricades' Metro station and Uprising Square, from where the workers had tried to march from the slums on to the centre of Moscow in 1905 but were beaten back by the Tsar's forces.

The mob of 1993 should have been a pushover. They played cat and mouse with the police. These young officers tried to appear hard by thumping their truncheons on their riot shields, but they didn't look up to the job. The flak jackets tucked inside their cumbersome greatcoats made them look even more absurd. A few heads were cracked, the odd person was led away, but night after night the police allowed the crowds to build barricades and disrupt city life. The demonstrators erected barricades by unloading rubbish skips and commandeering trolley buses, blocking the Garden Ring Road around the American Embassy. Women wailed 'fascists – fascists' each time the police charged. Each mini-insurrection gave the besieged deputies heart. One policeman was crushed to death. The determination of the one side was in stark contrast to the confusion and listlessness of the other.

As the crisis dragged on towards a third week, all sides seemed to resigned to sit it out for as long as it took. With the Constitutional Court compromised, the only plausible mediator was the Orthodox Church. The Patriarch had not wanted to get involved. That the Church had to be brought in demonstrated how feeble the political structures were. Representatives of both sides were invited to the Danilovsky Monastery, the headquarters of the Church in the south of Moscow. For two days they talked, but it was clear they were getting nowhere.

It was during those negotiations that the violence took on new proportions. A major rally was called in support of the rebels. Beneath the walls of the Foreign Ministry in Smolensk Square up to 1,000 protesters erected barricades. Police tried to intervene but soon withdrew. The mob, chanting 'Victory is ours' and 'Yeltsin – fascist', armed themselves with molotov cocktails. Some were boys of under ten years old, looking for a good time. Some were elderly women in pink lipstick and matching woolly hats. Some were labourers, their bloodshot eyes, puffy faces and recognizable breath betraying their liking of the bottle. They tore sheets of corrugated iron off roofs of derelict houses, raided building sites and removed tyres from parked cars. With petrol dragged along in canisters, they set fire to their booty, sending plumes of smoke into the crisp afternoon sky. And all the while the flimsy lines of badly armed officers stood by. It was a moral victory for the rebels. It was clear that these people would stop at nothing. But still no extra measures were taken. More violence was expected the following day.

The demonstration, between 5,000 and 10,000 strong, began quietly enough outside the October Metro station. The turnout was not particularly impressive for a Sunday morning. The crowd gave vent to its spleen as usual, while police with loudhailers asked them to disperse.

Luzhkov had signed a temporary order banning marches. It was all fairly innocuous to begin with. Grandmothers approached nervous militiamen, spotty young boys with their helmets and shields, telling them they were being led astray by Yeltsin's government. The crowd then started to move. The route was simple: along the Garden Ring Road, towards the White House. At every step, the police retreated, firing tear gas, their truncheons flailing. They had no stomach for the fight. Reinforcements arrived at Smolensk Square, but by then it was too late. The crowd was charging, bricks, stones, metal staves in hand. The police answered back, firing automatic weapons into the air. They had been told not to fire into the crowd. Undeterred, the mob ran on. Men were at the front – ordinary workers and teenagers in balaclavas and jackboots, spoiling for a fight. It all happened within minutes. As the police vans sought to retreat, they reversed into each other. Policemen jumped out in a desperate attempt to flee. Some succeeded but were disarmed by the mob. Others were pummelled to the floor. Only the intervention of a few demonstrators prevented dozens of officers from being beaten to death. *Babushkas* were among those taking swipes. 'Please, in God's name stop,' shouted one man, lying on a policeman.

Those lorries whose tyres had not been punctured were requisitioned. Teenagers at the wheel and red flags waving from open windows, they zigzagged along the main road and headed down the hill for the White House. The foot soldiers followed behind them. The police retreated over the bridge, occasionally thumping their riot shields, more to keep their own spirits up than to instil fear into the fearless. Shots rang out from the Mayor's office next door, sniper fire from the upper floors. I asked one unit commander why they weren't taking on the mob. 'Our boys don't want to be here,' he replied, as he radioed in vain for orders from his equally hapless superiors. 'We never expected this.' They must have been the only ones who hadn't. His men seemed most concerned about repairing the punctured tyres of their vehicles to help them get the hell out of the mess.

Within minutes, the mob had trampled over the barbed wire and on to the grass. The doors of the White House sprung open amid a deafening roar. After a week's siege, it was finally theirs. The throng flocked to the back of the building for communion with Rutskoy and Khasbulatov. Bystanders posed for photographers, apparently unaware of the dangers. Some women stood frozen and sobbed. Then came the moment they were waiting for. Their two leaders appeared. Rutskoy, loudhailer in hand, was in his element. 'Dear comrades, you have shown courage. Now you must take by storm the Mayor's office and Ostankino.' 'Rutskoy – President!', the crowd replied.

There was no time to lose. 'Comrade men, form lines to the left in readiness for taking the Mayor's office,' one uniformed man shouted.

'Why can't I have a gun?' cried an elderly woman. Freud was right. By this stage in the siege, the extremists had taken over. Barkashov was putting his mini 'battalions' of neo-Nazis through their paces. With a *Sieg heil* arm upraised, they shouted 'down with fascism' before taking their place in the front. Their role in the events was acutely embarrassing for the opposition, rendering absurd its claim to represent the real democratic forces.

Oleg Rumyantsev, one of the few rebels who could not be termed an extremist, offered a conspiracy theory to explain the fascist phenomenon. The Barkashovtsi, he said, had been deliberately placed in the White House by the Yeltsin team and orchestrated by 'special agents'. 'The government did not feel it could simply take on the Communist forces in parliament. It needed a "brown" element as well as the reds to justify their actions. That was why they were prepared to wink an eye at the activities of Barkashov's men and others like him. I'd even go as far as to say they were being discreetly financed,' Rumyantsev said. It was a good try, but hardly convincing.

As the battalions were forming, I came across Zlobin. He was running down the corridor with papers in his hand, perhaps the text of an announcement they were planning to read out once the television station was in their hands. The mood inside the White House was euphoric. I also spotted Baburin moving briskly towards the balcony. There was a new spring in his step. Would Yeltsin survive, I asked him? 'No chance, he's got no guts.' He smiled, and flicked a 'V for victory' sign. It took the rebels, Kalashnikovs in hand, minutes to march the hundred yards to the Mayor's building opposite and up the stairs. The first line of police surrendered, cowering in doorways. They were allowed to go after handing over their weapons. A lorry reversed into the barricaded front entrance, sending plate glass flying. The volunteers marched in. They found several of Luzhkov's aides and dragged them out. Some had their faces butted by rifles. A huge pool of freshly spilt blood lay on the ground. Others were taken across to the White House as hostages.

Yeltsin had been that morning in the Kremlin with Gaidar, whom he had just reappointed to the government. The President then went off to the *dacha* at Barvikha for Sunday lunch. The casualness of the leadership was extraordinary. The Kremlin was all but deserted as the White House was taken back by the demonstrators. By mid-afternoon the President had been brought back to his office by helicopter, as the roads were not deemed safe enough for him. The aides hurriedly assembled but nobody knew what to do.

Sergei Parkhomenko was one of the top political commentators in the country. He had arrived at the Kremlin, at the office of a friendly presidential aide, and was astonished by what he saw. His original newspaper article was censored for two days in the Russian press, so he merely handed it on to Westerners. Parkhomenko described in trenchant detail the paralysis that had beset the Kremlin that evening. Advisers sat around, sometimes arguing among themselves, sometimes each alone with his thoughts. Nobody knew what to do. He claimed that it was only the arrival of Poltoranin and Burbulis, the two old stalwarts who had fallen distinctly out of favour, which galvanized the bureaucrats. His was the first revelation of its kind, and brought furious denials and warnings from the presidential press service. A few days later Yeltsin would all but admit Parkhomenko's version. 'There is a lot of talk that the authorities dragged their feet, were hesitant, did not know what to do. I must tell you straight – not everyone had enough self-control, not everyone had enough strength and nerve to cope with the gigantic pressure at the most critical moment.' Parkhomenko found out afterwards that it was not his criticism of the aides that had most annoyed them but his praise for Poltoranin.

After the event, much was said by Rutskoy sympathizers about Yeltsin's 'grand conspiracy'. From the August press conference to the September announcement of the dissolution of parliament – Decree Number 1400 as it was known – to the humiliating retreat of the police in the face of the mob to the deployment of troops, every move, they conjectured, was choreographed to allow Yeltsin to crack down on the opposition. Yet the facts never bore out the theory, and as time passed it was gently dropped. Yeltsin was at the mercy of a hostile Security Ministry. The army was deeply divided and disillusioned, while Interior Ministry forces had little experience of crowd control, and little desire to become involved. Most of all, however, any conspiracy presupposes a level of organization and efficiency that time and time again had shown itself to be beyond both Yeltsin and his opponents.

If Rutskoy had taken stock of the situation once his mob had broken the siege of the White House, he would have concluded that the best option was to stay put. Such was the prevailing apathy that Yeltsin would have had little chance of reimposing any blockade and would have been forced into a humiliating political withdrawal from which he would have had great difficulty recovering. With the White House up and running again, the hardliners would have been able to dictate terms. But by calling for an attack on the television station Rutskoy delivered Yeltsin a lifeline, because hitherto parliament's actions could have been construed as purely defensive.

Yeltsin's first act was to decree that in the event of his death his powers would be assumed by Chernomyrdin. The Prime Minister played a crucial backroom role that evening. He was one of the most adamant advocates of the use of force and it was he who ensured that enough troops were sent to Ostankino to fend off the attack. There was much that day that was surreal. A chaotic convoy of armoured personnel carriers dodged the traffic along the Garden Ring Road as it made its way to the next field of battle. Some displayed the hammer and sickle, others the nationalist flag of black, yellow and white. Some kept their affiliations to themselves: these were government forces, part of the same cavalcade. When the Rutskoy mob arrived at the television tower just off Peace Prospekt, it was strafed by automatic gunfire. Tracer bullets lit up the night sky. Much of the shooting was coming from inside the building and was aimed indiscriminately. Several passers-by who were injured alleged they had been deliberately picked off by government snipers, even though they were quite clearly civilians and hiding where they could, such as behind plastic bus shelters.

As the battles raged, the leading reformers gathered in Gaidar's office on Old Square. They knew that whichever side controlled television would eventually win out. The First Channel had been taken off the air by the fighting. Russian Television, the second channel, also broadcast from there, but it had made provision for such a crisis and managed to operate from a secret location. The radicals wanted Yeltsin to communicate directly with the people, but he had no time. Gaidar was chosen, and rushed off to the makeshift studio to address the people. He was followed by a phalanx of politicians, businessmen and artists who declared their support for Yeltsin. Gaidar appealed to Muscovites to gather at city hall, the next presumed target of the hardliners, to defend democracy with whatever they could. Hundreds turned up that night, building their own barricades and preparing molotov cocktails. As he returned to his office Gaidar was met by Vladimir Gusinsky, a prominent banker. He was trying to gather a snatch squad to send to the White House to rescue one of Luzhkov's assistants who had been taken hostage. 'We have to fight. With guns. Otherwise we're doomed,' Gusinky shouted.

Yeltsin declared a state of emergency. He spoke to Grachev, the Defence Minister, who promised him troops were on their way. They didn't come. Eventually, a column of at least forty armoured vehicles moved in to defend the Kremlin and Defence Ministry, and went no further. Over at Ostankino, the rebels, armed with grenade launchers and armoured personnel carriers, had burst through on to the ground floor. The fighting there was the most intense, with corridor to corridor gun battles that lasted for many hours. This was the nearest Russia came to civil war. Dozens died in the pandemonium on the streets, but by the middle of the night the rebels' advance had been repelled. Many of them made their way back dejectedly to the White House, across the city. Police cars had been taken over by hoodlums. There was not a policeman in sight that night. For a few hours there was a complete absence of power: anarchy, in other words. Yeltsin's loss of grip was there for all to see. The man who had once promised a new era of reform and democracy had no option left but to turn to the army for his political salvation.

It took Yeltsin all night to persuade Grachev and the military high command to obey him. He had to go to them in the ministry in the early hours to implore them to move the forces already in the city to the White House, and to bring in more. According to Yeltsin's memoirs, the interventions of Chernomyrdin, his Prime Minister, and Korzhakov, his bodyguard, were crucial in swaying the doubting generals. But Grachev held out. He wanted a written order from the President. He got it. Again according to Yeltsin's memoirs, even his loyal Alpha Group had told him they wouldn't take part in any assault, and it took a bizarre shooting for them to change their minds. Barsukov, the Kremlin Commandant, persuaded a few of the men to drive up to the building to take a look. As they approached, by chance they came across a man lying wounded on the road. As a lieutenant climbed out of his vehicle to tend to him, a shot rang out from a sniper. The soldier died instantly. On hearing the news, the remaining men needed no further persuasion. Such was Yeltsin's account.

Even before then, the mood inside the White House had soured. The defeat at Ostankino was a bitter blow. The rebels dug themselves in for another war of attrition. Even when they saw tanks surround the building they still didn't believe the troops would fire on them.

The assault began at 7 a.m. and ended ten hours later. Troops from the Dzerzhinsky division, the Kantimirovsky motorized infantry division, and paratroops from Tula and Ryazan gathered outside the White House. From the river, from positions close to the American Embassy and less important approaches, the tanks began their shelling. For hour after hour the dull thud of tank fire was interrupted only by sniper fire – and by the noise of hundreds of sightseers. They climbed scaffolding, sat on roofs, gazed out of windows – all for a grandstand view of the drama unfolding before them. Elegantly dressed old ladies mixed with teenagers in leather jackets and mini skirts, academic-looking men wheeling their bicycles, even couples walking their dogs. Nobody had gone to work. Most people watched the live coverage on CNN; the more intrepid or foolhardy wanted to get close to the line of fire. Few people showed emotion, except when police tried to clear them out of the way. When pressed on their allegiances, almost everyone came out for Yeltsin.

In the early afternoon, the pounding stopped. Attempts were made to negotiate a surrender. I found myself among a few dozen youngsters who decided for a dare to 'storm' into the building, through an entrance that had been pounded by shells. Into the darkness they ran, lighted matches in hand, their feet crunching shards of glass. They had no way of knowing whether a solitary rebel might be hiding. There was no one left, so, frolicking and giggling, the kids started to remove whatever they could find. They hauled ugly brown chairs over their heads. Raincoats were snatched from the cloakroom, leather jackets, policemen's hats – everything was taken, down to the fuseboxes. When the mob sauntered out, they saw two young secretaries being frogmarched out by soldiers. 'Tarts,' the boys and girls shouted, 'Red sluts.' It all seemed such a laugh at the time.

While the Barkashovtsi and the other motley extremists crouched by windows or in corridors in defence of the building, the remaining deputies, their secretaries and assistants, cleaners and cooks and their children were rushed downstairs to a debating chamber, a room as far away from the outer windows as possible. Zlobin was one of them.

We sat there with only two candles in the room. We debated a few things. We sang old Soviet songs. Rutskoy came in once shouting slogans. Khasbulatov came in three times to jolly us along. 'No surrender. The ultimate victory is ours,' all that stuff. They then went back to the gunmen. But with pounding and shooting below us, we knew it was only a matter of time. Then Yeltsin's Alpha troops came in, men from outer space with all their wires on their backs and high-tech. They said they could guarantee our lives, nothing else.

16
The Poisoned Pen

The dilemma was acute. I was sitting in the offices of a friend, a senior journalist at *Izvestia*, chewing over the issues of the moment, as we did from time to time. It was the summer of 1992. I had just returned from one of those summits of CIS leaders. This time the venue had been Tashkent, capital of Uzbekistan, an instantly forgettable meeting had it not been for Yeltsin and the saga of the airport steps.

Yeltsin certainly looked the worse for wear, bawling and stumbling as he stepped off the plane. The scene was captured by state television on the peak-time evening news. Next morning in parliament, Isakov told deputies the pictures showed Yeltsin 'falling over the camera'. 'Deputies must discuss the important issue of the President's drunkenness,' Isakov said. He demanded that the President undergo tests to ascertain his 'sanity and health'. Khasbulatov switched off the microphone, demanded an inquiry into Isakov's behaviour and instructed the television network to omit the exchange in its reports on the day's proceedings. Obediently they did. It would be one of the last occasions in which the speaker displayed deference to the President.

Everybody had his own Yeltsin and drink story, or claimed to. At a later summit in Minsk I was sitting with a group of Russian journalists who told a tale of Yeltsin slurring his words and having to lean on Korzhakov during a speech to open a Russian University in Bishkek, capital of Kyrgyzstan. In London, in November 1992, something had clearly happened to the President between a friendly but very correct lunch at Buckingham Palace and the concluding press conference in the Hyde Park Hotel, where he was staying. 'The mini bar,' chuckled one Russian reporter as Yeltsin waxed lyrically, and somewhat incoherently, about the marvels of the British royal family.

Presidential aides argued privately that the sedatives he habitually popped turned the effect of one glass of wine or shot of brandy into something much worse, that he did not drink to excess, that claims to the contrary were part of the opposition conspiracy. It was seldom possible to separate fact from rumour, and it was not difficult to spread a story disparaging the other side. Rutskoy's aides would brief Western journalists with 'exclusive' information. Yeltsin, they said, woke up in the middle of night and needed a glass of cognac to get him back to sleep. There were several others. No evidence would ever be offered.

My colleague at *Izvestia* had checked several of the stories. To his dismay they were true, at least in part. 'Everything depends on Yeltsin,' he said. 'In any normal society I would publish and be damned. But I believe we've a higher task than sensationalism. I'm probably displaying my Communist upbringing so I'll say no more.' I told him that I agreed. At least I did then. Self-censorship did not come easily at the time. After decades of disinformation, servility and planted questions many of Russia's journalists, especially the younger generation, took to the new freedoms and powers of the Fourth Estate with relish. Of all the areas of Russian life there were few as heartening as the endeavours of local reporters trying to prise the truth from recalcitrant officials.

Under *glasnost*, it was all about stretching the bounds of the possible, challenging official Soviet history, breaking taboos. It was a period when the *shestidesyatniki* – the men of the 1960s – came to the fore, men such as Vitaly Korotich and Yegor Yakovlev, whose dream of humane socialism was all but extinguished by the crushing of the Prague Spring in 1968. Gorbachev would often fight their battles for them inside the Politburo, clearing the way for new revelations about Stalin's atrocities in Korotich's *Ogonyok* or Yakovlev's *Moscow News*. Like most in the intelligentsia, the editors never took the risk of full-blown dissidence. They had little time for what they saw as the destructive anti-Communism of Yeltsin and the radicals in the late 1980s, and were keen to avoid embarrassing Gorbachev or the liberals around him.

It took one of Yakovlev's deputies to break the mould. Vitaly Tretyakov amassed a small team of bright young writers, some of whom had had no experience of the Soviet journalistic system, with the idea of creating a new newspaper. *Nezavisimaya Gazeta*, the Independent Newspaper, began its life at the end of 1990 with a small office on the street behind the KGB headquarters and with a start-up grant of 300,000 roubles, given by Popov and Stankevich in city hall. During the coup, when all but the most servile newspapers were closed down, the journalists put out a flysheet and distributed it on the street, evoking memories of the *samizdat* publications of the pre-*glasnost* days. *Nezavisimaya* would round on Gorbachev for the Baltic massacres, for his equivocations. It would praise Yeltsin, never unquestioningly, for his vigour in challenging the establishment.

Tretyakov broke with Yeltsin over the Belovezhskaya agreement. In a front-page editorial, he accused him of mounting a palace coup against Gorbachev. With each month that passed the animosity intensified. Tretyakov would write open letters to Yeltsin, entreating him to change course. The other journalists had never intended the paper to become a one-man soap box. At the end of 1992, Dmitry Ostalsky, one of the deputy editors, led a mass exodus. He took with him almost all the paper's best writers, among them Parkhomenko. Together they founded the newspaper *Sevodnya*, Today.

The demise of *Nezavisimaya* marked the end of the age of innocence. Ostalsky knew that total independence did not exist. The future lay in corporate financing in the Western mould. The best hope was to find a proprietor who would produce the money but not insist on interfering. He thought he had found him in Gusinsky and his multi-million business. Gusinsky's was a remarkable success story. He started out, as so many of his contemporaries did, by exploiting the opportunities presented by the small-scale liberalization introduced by Gorbachev. A former student at Moscow's most prestigious theatre school, he began by selling bracelets, ashtrays and other knick-knacks in street markets. Some of the stalls were frequented by Western tourists and brought in considerable profits. Until then the only souvenirs to be found were mass-produced and sold in unattractive large state shops. He went on into the import–export business and then on to property and construction. By the start of the 1990s Gusinsky had befriended Popov, the sitting Mayor, and Luzhkov, his eventual succcessor. With those links it was a short hop to huge wealth. His Most Group, a finance conglomerate, became one of Russia's most powerful corporations. His bank was the first to issue internationally recognized credit cards.

Gusinsky travelled the world. Money was no object for him or his third wife, Lena, a law graduate whom he met while she was working in his company's legal department. She spent much of her time at their Chelsea flat, with a swimming pool in the basement, and in the summer the two would pop over to their house in the Algarve. When she was about to give birth to their second child, at one of Harley Street's most expensive clinics, he block-booked first-class airline seats every day to make sure he would make it. He was late.

Gusinsky was a workaholic, driven by the desire to expand his empire and his influence. What Silvio Berlusconi could do in Italy, he could do in Russia. *Sevodnya* was a start. With Most money behind it, it came out early in 1993, a sober, well-presented broadsheet with an emphasis on business and leisure, aimed as much at the new upwardly mobile Russian as at the traditional intelligentsia. Its political line was pro-reform but not necessarily pro-Gaidar. Gusinsky was a strong supporter of Yavlinsky and other reformers who were outside the government.

Deprived of his top guns and forces of moderation, Tretyakov allowed his anti-Yeltsin ardour to get the better of him. He would show no compunction about joining *Pravda* and *Sovietskaya Rossiya*, the two traditional Communist stalwarts, in supporting parliament. I went back to see Tretyakov in the summer of 1993. Yeltsin, he complained with no attempt at humility, had not consulted him. 'I am disappointed in him as a person and as a leader. He has shown no ideas, no vision. It is not my ideas that have changed, but his.' Yeltsin had not defended Russia's vital interests and had allowed the Harvard-educated 'boys' to destroy the country. I put to Tretyakov the remark Rutskoy made to me at his collective farm in Belgorod about the CIA and its 'role' in the destruction of the USSR. I assumed that he would laugh, would explain that his friend 'Sasha' was prone to such indiscretions but didn't really mean them, or perhaps that it was a useful piece of electioneering. Instead, Tretyakov stared me in the eye, and said, in all seriousness: 'He's absolutely right.' It was a desperately sad revelation to me, that even the most intelligent, well-travelled and sophisticated Russians had still failed to accept that they, and they alone, were responsible for the mess they were in. It spoke volumes for the state of the political process.

Inconsistency was not an accusation that could be levelled at Yuri Nikolayev. My first meeting with the deputy editor of *Sovietskaya Rossiya* took place during Yeltsin's 1991 presidential election campaign. After an all too brief period in the mid-1980s as a radical newspaper, *Sovietskaya Rossiya* switched sides and became a maverick anti-establishment organ from the other side, the national-patriotic standpoint. It rarely minced its words. Nikolayev, a burly, greying man, had just published another 'scoop' and was in exuberant form. 'Got him this time,' he said, as he inhaled from another of his *papirosi*, the cardboard unfiltered cigarettes that became a style statement in the face of the Marlboro invasion. While everybody else was saving up to buy Italian moccasins, Nikolayev wore his grey plastic Soviet shoes with pride. To decline 100 grammes of vodka in his company at lunchtime was more than a touch wet.

I would try to see Nikolayev every couple of months, usually at one of Moscow's dwindling number of Soviet-style restaurants such as the Prague or the Tsentralnaya. His mood would change depending on the state of play in the power struggle. Only on one occasion was his appetite spoilt, by the conversation at an adjoining table where a sleazy Frenchman was discussing with his Russian partner how to get precious art works past the customs. The West, he reminded me, was buying up Russia, bleeding it dry. At the end of that meal his driver and black Volga failed to turn up at the appointed time. I took Nikolayev back to his office. As we drove up the hill up Tverskaya Street, past the shops that had aspirations to Bond Street or Fifth Avenue, past the advertising hoardings showing handsome women and men, their teeth whiter than white, Nikolayev scowled, muttering darkly 'speculators, robbers'. The problem for Nikolayev was that his newspaper was losing its niche. It was too old-fashioned. The more rabid nationalist newspapers such as Prokhanov's *Dyen* were simply more racy.

The odds in the media battle between Yeltsin and parliament were stacked heavily in Yeltsin's favour. The only newspaper that would be regularly seen in the provinces on the same day as publication in Moscow, or just a day late, was *Izvestia*, which had its own printing presses in dozens of towns. Other titles would arrive only after considerable delay. *Izvestia* also happened to be staunchly pro-Yeltsin. Citing as an excuse *Izvestia*'s original mandate in Communist times as an official newspaper, parliament voted to take over its premises and remove its editorial board. Khasbulatov sent in his guards, but after threats from the government they were removed. The opposition's real problem was its lack of clout where it really mattered – on television. Newspapers played a role, but as soon as subsidies were drastically cut circulation across the board plummeted and cover prices soared. Television was the prime opinion-former, and Yeltsin's team were determined not to let go of it.

Channel One, or Ostankino as it was called on its relaunch, was the only station which could be received throughout the CIS. The second station, Russian Television, was created as a pro-Yeltsin bastion in early 1991 and was the most loyal propagator of the presidential line. Nevertheless for sixty minutes every evening, Channel Two handed over its airwaves to the opposition. *Parliamentary Hour* was devised by Khasbulatov and hosted by Nina Berdnikova. Nina was many Russians' idea of the perfect woman, with carefully styled long blonde hair, copious amounts of make-up, long legs, a gushing voice, fluttering eyelids and a penchant for flowers. Her drooling interviews with Khasbulatov made her the darling of the deputies, so much so that the speaker of parliament, who fancied himself as a Russian version of Don Juan, began one programme by presenting Nina with a bunch of red roses for her birthday.

Parliamentary Hour was scheduled too early in the evening to enjoy a mass audience, despite Nina's best efforts. The one anti-Yeltsin programme that carried weight was *600 Seconds*, presented by Alexander Nevzorov, a former movie stuntman and son of a KGB officer. His programme, broadcast on Leningrad Television immediately after the main nine o'clock evening news, broke new ground in reporting. With the seconds flashing behind him on the screen, Nevzorov would uncover true crime stories. No detail was too gruesome. Within weeks of its first broadcasts, Nevzorov had picked up an audience of 80 million across European Russia. In a land of grey suits, his leather jacket became a cult object. Nevzorov would expose the corruption and vice of small-scale *apparatchiks*. Although we did not know it then, his revelations were careful not to antagonize the real crime bosses. Still, it was compulsive viewing for all, irrespective of political affiliation. Nevzorov's political development was symptomatic of the difficulties the democratic movement faced.

By the start of 1991, Nevzorov had broken ranks with the democrats, startling them with his version of the events in Vilnius and Riga. Not one single person, he claimed, had died at the hands of the heroic Soviet forces. His film, *Nashi*, Our Boys, depicted the soldiers as loyal defenders of the faith and the Latvians and Lithuanians as un-reconstructed fascists. Nevzorov had provided a compelling tabloid touch to the new nationalism, far more popular than anything the old-style Communists could do. During the parliamentary uprising he filmed from inside the White House, and to the strains of Rakhmaninov urged his fans to come to the building to resist 'the dictatorship of former President Yeltsin'.

Yeltsin had assigned to Poltoranin the job of guarding the faith, especially on the two main state channels. He did this assiduously, haranguing media chiefs for deviating from the line. Yegor Yakovlev was his most prominent victim. The old man of the Gorbachev era had been seen as an enlightened choice to replace Leonid Kravchenko (the toady who had ordered the screening of *Swan Lake* on the first day of the coup) as chairman of Ostankino. Yakovlev tried to ensure reasonably objective reporting, especially on the sensitive issue of inter-ethnic conflict. Ostankino, after all, was supposed to be serving all the former Soviet republics and not just Russia. Poltoranin would often call Yakovlev on his direct line with orders. Yakovlev did his best to ignore the most dictatorial edicts. Poltoranin didn't appreciate being countermanded and sought any pretext for getting rid of him. He found it in a news report on the small local war between the Ingushi and the Ossetians in southern Russia.

Yakovlev was called in to Poltoranin's office, given a dressing-down on the subject and informed that Yeltsin had signed a decree dismissing him. Yakovlev would find out later that it was not the plight of the Ingushi, and the alleged bias shown by his reporters, that had sealed his fate. 'I was told by a friend in the presidential administration that I had been seen going to Gorbachev's *dacha* one evening for dinner. I asked him how they knew; he smiled as if to say "don't be so naïve". I didn't realize that seeing former Soviet Presidents had become a sackable offence.' Once again, Yeltsin misread the signs. The media reaction to the dismissal was so furious that Yeltsin forced Poltoranin to issue an apology and offer Yakovlev a job as an adviser. Yakovlev politely refused.

As long as television remained in state hands, Poltoranin felt safe. When Gusinsky applied to start up Russia's first major private network, he panicked. NTV, Independent Television, started broadcasting a week after the assault on the White House, with several top presenters and reporters that Gusinsky had brought across from the other networks, at fees that were extremely high by Russian standards. It started off with a few hours a night on the Leningrad channel, ensuring that its reach was minimal. Poltoranin sought to keep it that way, and the two fought it out for Yeltsin's ear. The power of money talked loudest, and Gusinsky was allowed to take over a little-used national frequency. From there his information empire grew. NTV became easily the most popular station, its news programmes interspersed with top-quality films.

Poltoranin's abrasiveness was becoming a liability for the President. Just before the December 1992 Congress, Yeltsin shunted him aside. As a consolation, he allowed his old friend to establish a new quango, the Federal Information Centre. He was hoping that Poltoranin would stay more in the backroom. But within weeks Poltoranin had turned the agency into a more powerful institution than the ministry itself, into a watchdog whose remit was to defend the 'democrats' in the media from the hardline onslaught. For journalists and editors the pressure from Poltoranin was relentless. According to Alexander Nekhoroshev, head of news and current affairs at Russian Television, it came not just from the combatants themselves. One top businessman called offering him millions of roubles, cash in hand, to grant airtime to a top politician whom he was 'promoting'. 'It was the first time that had happened to me. Until then it was the politician who rang up on the hotline himself to ask if we could "possibly help".'

Svetlana Sorokina was the queen of Russian broadcasting, a single-minded yet reassuring face for tens of millions of viewers. Only a few years earlier she had been a close colleague of Nevzorov in Leningrad. After the coup, the two barely spoke to each on their rare encounters. Most nights Sorokina would read the main evening news on Russian Television, adding her own thoughts for the day as she went along. Whenever she was momentarily off-camera the phone would ring. It would be her boss, the manager of the network, ordering her to insert this or omit that, in obeisance to the latest edict from the Kremlin. Most of the time she ignored the commands because she was one of those figures that nobody dared sack. On the fateful night of 3 October when the rebels were storming Ostankino, Sorokina was one of the first to appear at the secret hide-out, immaculately turned out in a sailor suit. With Sorokina back on the box there was no need to worry. So feared was she by the hardliners in parliament that one promised to hang her by the ankles. Despite the fan mail, the fame and the dangers, Sorokina and her cameraman husband Volodya were forced to spend their first three years in Moscow in a very ordinary hotel. Her employers couldn't find her a flat. The couple would travel on the overnight train most weekends to see his mother in St Petersburg. Only in the spring of 1994 did they move into an apartment, a pleasant three-roomed flat close to the office. She was one of a few who could have made it rich very quickly, but had other priorities.

Alexander Lyubimov was equally famous, equally glamorous, but brought up in an entirely different school. The son of a former KGB operative in London, Lyubimov was one of the first young, brash television voices of *glasnost*. He had all the confidence that came from having protectors in the top echelons of power. He used it for a different purpose than the narrow propaganda of the nationalists. Unlike Nevzorov, he did not jump across to the hardliners, but maintained a deep scepticism about all the political combatants. Lyubimov incurred the wrath of the authorities by telling viewers on the night of 3 October, a couple of hours after Sorokina's appearance, not to bother heeding Gaidar's call to defend Yeltsin, and to stay at home.

'I didn't think it was right to risk people's lives to defend our politicians,' Lyubimov said. 'It's all about lining pockets, and one group is no better than the other. A lot of these people were quite decent before they entered the Kremlin. Something seems to happen once you start working there. You have to abide by the rules.' Lyubimov said that in recent months, whenever his programmes said something the authorities did not appreciate, he would not, as had been the rule, receive a formal warning from an appropriate official. 'Their methods are more obvious now. We get threatening calls from criminal gangs whom they've obviously hired.' Corruption, he said, was no longer an exciting theme for viewers. 'Everyone's at it, so what's the point of accusing one person or another? That just looks as if you have an axe to grind. There's much I could reveal, but it will only destabilize things further, and for the moment keeping Yeltsin in power is in most people's interests.'

The criminal world was achieving what the Communist Party bureaucrats had failed to do in their final years: to instil fear among journalists. I remembered meeting Troitsky, my old rock promoter friend, one day in 1986. He had just been to the Central Committee to apply for permission to stage a rock concert. The Party's grip on information and entertainment was beginning to slip. For the best part of a decade afterwards, journalists enjoyed virtually untrammelled freedoms. That was before the new mafia had taken hold. 'No one dares to tease, let alone investigate, the real masters of the new Russian reality, the barons of organized crime,' he wrote.

All kinds of irrelevant small fish get caught, and often let out shortly afterwards. But there is a conspiracy of silence when it comes to the big shots, although it is pretty well known that famous entertainer X or sports promoter Y or businessman Z are, in fact, the godfathers of the Moscow mafia. They are often on television and in the papers, perfectly admired by presenters and interviewers [who know]. I am afraid I am no exception in this conspiracy. So far there is no underground dissident anti-mafia movement in Russia. Which means that, in a way, we now have less freedom of speech than in 1984.

17

The Plan Backfires

It was 11 December 1993, the eve of election day. I had been invited to dinner at the home of the Gusinskys. I had been warned that security would be tight; I didn't realize just how tight. No sooner had we parked in the courtyard of the building, one of those brick structures that are home to many in the elite, than the tracking began. The two men at the ground-floor entrance asked for our identity cards – they already knew who we were and whom we were visiting. A third man took us in the lift. When we arrived at the Gusinskys' floor he told us to wait while he rang the bell. All safe; we were allowed in. Lena had once described it to us a 'gilded cage'. The Most Group employed 680 security officers, more than 10 per cent of the staff on its payroll. Vladimir and Lena had eighteen bodyguards between them, who would accompany them and monitor their phone calls round the clock. If they went out to a friend's house, the guards would loiter around the entrance. When Lena drove herself in Moscow, as she preferred to do, the guards would follow behind her bumper, trailing her. The concern was understandable. Bankers were being seen off by criminal groups with alarming regularity, so much so that Gusinsky and four colleagues appealed to Yeltsin to help them. The mafia, they said in their open letter, had gobbled up the small firms; now they had their sights on the big corporations. The police, they added, regarded financiers as no better than gangsters. 'Society and its new financial and entrepreneurial institutions find themselves looking down the barrel of the gun of well-organized bandits armed with state-of-the-art weaponry.'

Gusinsky was polite and hospitable that night, but something was troubling him. I presumed it had something to do with the election.

The first fully democratic vote should have been a cause for celebration. After the assault on the White House, the reformers had gained the upper hand. In conjunction with the election, a referendum was to be held in which voters would be asked to approve a constitution for Yeltsin that would considerably strengthen his position. Although the leaders of the uprising had been banned from taking part, the thirteen groups involved in the election covered the entire political spectrum, from neo-fascists to Communists to state interventionists to radical monetarists. The joker in the pack was Vladimir Zhirinovsky, the man who had surprised everyone

168

by coming in third in the presidential elections of 1991 that brought Yeltsin to power. Zhirinovsky was expected to improve on his strong 8 per cent of last time, but not by much. In any case, his voice would be drowned out by Russia's Choice, the main pro-government party led by Gaidar, and by rival groups of reformists led by Yavlinsky, the maverick economist, and Shakhrai, the increasingly ambitious Deputy Prime Minister.

Opinion polls had been banned by the Electoral Commission for the ten days prior to polling. The last surveys released to the public had put Russia's Choice well ahead; but the vast majority of voters remained undecided, many of them declaring they couldn't be bothered to cast their ballots. Apathy was the main problem for the reformers. The machinations of the summer and the siege of the White House had soured the mood markedly since Yeltsin's referendum victory that April.

Gusinsky explained that he had just received information that not only was Zhirinovsky going to do well, he was going to beat Russia's Choice. 'I have many friends in the Security Ministry,' Gusinsky said. 'For some time they've been investigating the links between their colleagues and Zhirinovsky. It's not easy. It seems to go high up. As for other bankers, God knows why they're supporting him.' Something had gone very badly wrong. After weeks of calm resolve, some would say smug over-confidence, the radicals began to panic in the final days of the campaign. Russia's Choice issued a statement warning that the man 'who seemed to all of us to be a political clown' was now 'threatening the existence of the nation'. With hours to go before polling stations opened in eastern parts of the country, Russian Television suddenly changed its scheduling. It was Saturday afternoon in midwinter. Millions had been settling down to a feature film, only to discover they were watching a heavy-handed documentary about Zhirinovsky. Using original footage, it showed Zhirinovsky celebrating his birthday with a host of unsavoury friends such as Iraqi diplomats and German neo-Nazis. It allowed him to opine about Great Russia and racial purity. The documentary was produced by Shura Skodo, the man I had met at the *Zadvorki*, the millionaires' ball back in 1991. It was an attempt to portray Zhirinovsky in the worst possible light, but as a piece of propaganda it was dreadful. It smacked of desperation. He actually looked quite convincing, more charismatic than the others who had graced the television screen night after night during the campaign. The tactic was to backfire terribly.

Yeltsin had said it himself. Nobody had emerged with credit from the battle of the White House. For many, the reality sank in the following morning, once the adrenalin had ebbed. They had just watched the President destroy his own parliament. Many felt ashamed that it had come to this. The building itself was a charred ruin. Around the perimeter, a wall of soldiers stood guard. Crowds converged, day after day: some were looking for a souvenir, perhaps a spent cartridge, perhaps a piece of twisted metal; others were looking for their loved ones. I asked Georgy, a soldier from a division that had come up from Tula, whether he was proud of what he had done. 'We carried out our duty, and we did it well,' he said, 'but it shouldn't have had to be like this.' As we talked, a young man approached him. He was polite but in a daze. 'Excuse me, comrade,' he said to Georgy, 'I think my two brothers were in there. Could you tell me please who's in charge of sorting out the dead?' 'Go to Petrovka 38 [the city police headquarters a couple of miles away],' Georgy replied. 'I've been there,' said the boy, 'they said to come here. My mum's sick with fear. I've come all the way from Oryol.' He was almost the same age as Georgy – nearby towns, opposing allegiances. Georgy took a puff of his cigarette and swore, not from anger. An hour later, when it was time for him and his colleagues to leave, for the tanks to roll back out of town, he was the first to jump down the hatch. On the far side of the building, where the Russian flag was blowing incongruously into the autumn sunshine, two corpses lay side by side on a stretch of grass by the embankment of the Moscow river. One was covered by a stretcher, the other by a white blanket. People gawped, but even the voyeurism of the past few days had its limits. Nobody dared to lift the veils.

A state of emergency and night-time curfew had not been the best way to usher in the 'new era'. Even though the uprising had been put down, Yeltsin was taking no chances. Riot police and vigilante groups patrolled the streets. Anyone caught without a permit was liable to a beating and arrest. The main victims were 'non-Russians' – anyone with a dark skin. To most Muscovites that rough justice was all the Azeris, Chechens, Armenians and Georgians deserved. They were all tarred with the same brush as their countrymen who controlled the street markets and the other small rackets across the capital. Many in the authorities allowed their 'victory' over the White House rebels go to their heads. Whatever else it had done, parliament had provided checks and balances of sorts. Now, free from the legislators' obduracy, the presidential administration went into overdrive to make up for lost time. In the four weeks following Decree 1400, his fateful dissolution of parliament, Yeltsin signed another 233 acts of law.

With most of the ringleaders safely in prison, the government stepped up its campaign against the opposition. Several of the ringleaders were on the run. Police and Security Ministry agents scoured the country for them. Anpilov was picked up in a village in the Tula region, south of Moscow. Several of the Barkashovtsi had managed to escape through a network of tunnels and sewers under the White House. Most were eventually picked up. The rebel leaders could have been charged with treason, which allowed for the death penalty. But the prosecutors settled for the crime of mass disturbances, with a maximum prison term of fifteen years.

A special job centre was established for displaced and contrite deputies. Their demands were high. One member of the dissolved parliament, a former lorry driver, suggested a senior job in the Transport Ministry, while five vied for the post of Deputy Foreign Trade Minister, a job that carried considerable foreign travel and many a lucrative perk. About 150 of them were found sinecures in the government. The presidential administration grew so fast that it expanded from the Kremlin into other buildings in the city. Next, Yeltsin rounded on the compromised judiciary. Zorkin was sacked as Chairman of the Constitutional Court, and the court itself was effectively closed down. Stepankov was replaced as Prosecutor General by Alexei Kazannik, a retiring lawyer from Omsk who became a hero of the radical cause by giving up his seat in the Soviet parliament to Yeltsin in 1989.

Most radicals believed the clampdown could not be tough enough. They reminded Yeltsin of his failure to act decisively after the 1991 coup. The President took the warning to heart, but was also under pressure from the West to go easy. He started by banning all political parties and groups that had taken part in the uprising. *Pravda*, *Sovietskaya Rossiya* and other newspapers that had sympathized with the rebels were taken off the streets. They were told they could re-register under different titles and with new editors. Shumeiko, who had taken charge of the Information Ministry, advised journalists to behave more responsibly in future and exercise self-censorship. One of the main tasks of the media, he said, was to help form a 'new ideology'. 'The ideology of the democratic rebirth of Russia must be built on the ideas of patriotism, on the huge potential of the country, on its spirituality and culture,' he told bemused ministry employees.

Several liberal newspapers, fearing the long-term consequences of the radicals' zeal, came out in support of their adversaries in the 'red-brown' press. *Izvestia* went one step further when it published a sensational document: a draft decree giving the security forces the right to turn back any citizen who entered any Russian city without permission to do so; to stop anyone, or search any property, without a concrete reason; and to make 'preventative arrests' for up to thirty days. According to *Izvestia*, Yeltsin refused to sign the paper and had warned his aides about going too far; but the fact that it had reached his desk was alarming enough.

It was in this context that the registration of political parties began. The supporters of the old parliament were initially split. Some advocated an election boycott; others, like Baburin, said they should at least try to work in the new legislature. The punitive measures taken against them were often petty, and invariably counter-productive. Baburin had been invited to the International Press Club, an American-run press centre located in an American-run hotel. When Baburin arrived he was was told by the club's president Harry Bohdan that the meeting had been cancelled.

Bohdan apologized profusely but said he had been 'advised' by the Kremlin that it would 'not help working relations' with the club if Baburin were allowed to speak. The order was handed down anonymously. Baburin shrugged his shoulders, smiled and walked about ten yards along the hotel lobby where, flanked by designer clothes shops, bewildered guests and hordes of journalists, he put his views across to much greater effect than if he had been allowed in.

The first group to apply for registration was Zhirinovsky's Liberal Democratic Party. The groups were given three weeks to gather 100,000 signatures and submit them to the Central Election Commission for checks. Altogether thirty-five groups applied, but most people saw the election as a foregone conclusion. Russia's Choice was the presidential party, and the President was back in full control, for the first time in more than eighteen months. The party's coming to power was to be sealed at a lavish inaugural conference at the House of Cinema, the very building where the democratic movement had come into being with the Inter-Regional Group. The night before the conference I happened to be eating with some colleagues in the film industry in the House of Cinema's restaurant when I bumped into several of the great and the good staggering into their waiting limousines. Their spirits had never been higher. There they all were: Burbulis, Kozyrev, Poltoranin, Gaidar. 'It's going to be great tomorrow,' said Burbulis. 'We've finally got the upper hand.'

It was not my idea of entertainment. The meeting was as depressing as the one in 1989 had been uplifting. Perhaps it was naïve romanticism on my part. The shaggy pullovers and the emotional rambling talk of human rights had been replaced by pinstriped suits and calls for discipline. The raw energy of old had been replaced by Western-style marketing and stage managing. As they arrived, delegates were each given a fake leather attaché case replete with paper, diary and credit-card wallet. The poachers had become gamekeepers. The motto for the meeting was attractively vague – Freedom, Property, Legality. The conference was opened by church bells and a children's choir standing next to a giant screen of sixteen Japanese televisions. The organizing committee had made a clever choice as first speaker: Sergei Kovalev, a member of the outgoing parliament, a dissident, and one of a minority to complain about the crackdown. He reminded the assembled throng not to become smug and lose sight of the original goals of the human rights activists. 'Russia has paid for the lack of morality of its politicians over the past two years,' Kovalev said. He studiously averted his gaze from the front row, which contained several top Yeltsin aides.

Kovalev's was the only speech worth noting. Indeed, what mattered most at that conference was not what was said but what wasn't said. Yeltsin had not turned up. In failing to appear, he was dissociating himself from Russia's Choice.

Riots in Moscow, May Day 1993. (*Yuri Kozyrev*)

Rutskoy addresses a loyal crowd in Kursk, August 1993. (*Jeremy Nicholl*)

Dzhokhar Dudayev (with moustache, second from left), self-styled leader of the breakaway region of Chechnya, praying with local mullahs in Grozny, the capital. (*Jeremy Nicholl*)

Rich and poor. *Above*, The first Rolls Royce purchased at the Moscow showroom parked alongside the city's largest monument to Lenin, designed by the sculptor Lev Kerbel. (*Yuri Kozyrev*); *below*, Scavenging for food on a rubbish dump near Moscow, March 1993. (*Peter Andrews*)

Moscow's Tumba golf club, the first to be opened in Russia. (*Jeremy Nicholl*)

Lotto Million, one of the most popular game shows on Russian television.
(*Jeremy Nicholl*)

Yeltsin addresses a crowd outside St Basil's Cathedral on the eve of the referendum in March 1993. With him on the podium are Popov, Yelena Bonner (widow of Andrei Sakharov), Sergei Filatov, his chief of staff, and Father Gleb Yakunin. (*Jeremy Nicholl*)

October 1993: the White House – the parliament building – pounded with tank fire by the Russian army. (*Jeremy Nicholl*)

The siege of the White House, October 1993. (*Jeremy Nicholl*)

A woman holding a poster of Khasbulatov celebrates as she waits outside Lefortovo prison for the release of the leaders of the October 1993 uprising. (*Yuri Kozyrev*)

Soldiers resting during a pause in the fighting around the White House, October 1993.
(*Robert Wallis*)

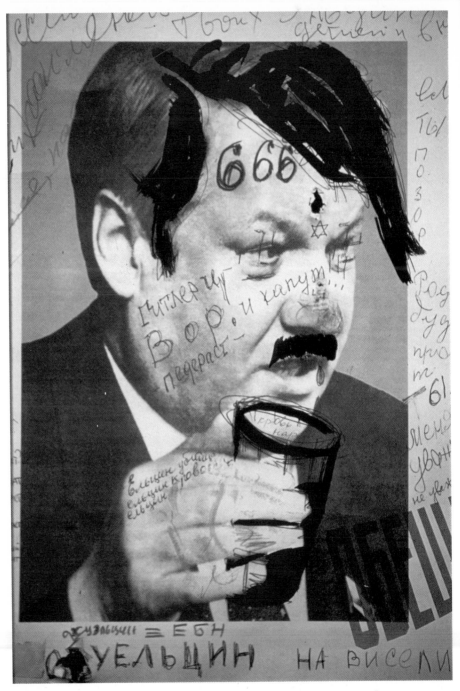

Defaced poster of Yeltsin in Moscow, October 1993. (*Jeremy Nicholl*)

That day I wrote about the disappointing start for Russia's Choice, how it had failed to present itself in a morally cleaner light than the other groups. Later that week I received a phone call from a Russian journalist friend. He had just read my article. 'Now you're deserting us as well,' he said. 'You don't understand anything. All your talk about playing it by the rules – we did that before, and look what happened. They came back at us. They're fascists. If they come to power our lives will be over. And you're a traitor.' Once again the old dilemma had reappeared. Could a strong democracy be built in Russia by entirely democratic means? Many radicals said it couldn't. They cited Lenin's old maxim about two steps forward, one step back.

Yeltsin was under pressure from the West to relax his grip, to allow all sides to have their say. Of the groups that had applied for registration, only thirteen met the requirements of the Electoral Commission. Among those that failed was the Party of Economic Freedom run by Konstantin Borovoy, one of the first entrepreneurs. He was said to have obtained signatures illegally. Baburin was another. He claimed that on the eve of the deadline armed uniformed men burst into the offices of his Russian All-Peoples Union and stole 20,000 petitions. His party rushed to make up the numbers but was disqualified for forging names. With so many accusations and counter-accusations flying back and forth, and with the organization of 95,000 polling stations in such a short time a logistical nightmare, all sides were relieved to see the hundreds of foreign monitors who descended on Moscow's five-star hotels.

Yeltsin's top priority was the referendum. The Yeltsin camp had sneaked in several changes at the last moment. These made it clear that the President should serve out his full term, until June 1996, finally dispelling any idea that Yeltsin would submit himself for re-election in June 1994. It was also stipulated that for its first term only, the Federal Assembly would sit for two years, not four.

The campaign ended where it began – on television. State broadcasting provided two one-hour prime-time slots each night, to be divided strictly among the contending groups. With little else to do in the evening, almost everyone watched television at some point, providing a captive audience of tens of millions. The order was drawn by lot. First off was Civic Union – or, to give it its new catchy title, Civic Union for the Sake of Stability, Justice and Progress. Volsky, the man for all seasons, was still there in charge. Rumyantsev, still smarting from parliament's defeat, believed Civic Union shared many of his social democratic ideals. He would regret his choice. The party gained 2 per cent of the vote, one of the lowest shares, a result explained more by its shortcomings in public relations than by its policy. Volsky and his chums droned on in a monotone about how the monetarists would bring social collapse. A man called Igor Yorgens said everything Russians had been told about the success of Poland's economic reform was wrong. There were some Polish cities, he said, that had no workers other than postmen and policemen. Realizing that the presentation was not going too well, a third Civic Union spokesman urged viewers not to switch channels. The Mexican soap opera had not begun yet, she told them. She forgot to say they could tune in to a football match on another station.

The unfortunate viewers were then subjected to another half hour with former Komsomol members who clubbed together under the curious title The Future of Russia – New Names. They had youth on their side but just about nothing else. These were followed by a film of the well-meaning ecologists, sitting in a circle around a log fire in a cosy sitting room, and another of the Communists, whose star attraction was not their leader, Gennady Zyuganov, but the stunning Nina who was fronting the programme. Nina's associations with Khasbulatov failed to damage her career. A few months after the elections, she would be back on Moscow's local third channel.

Early indications suggested that very few people had made up their minds. Millions were planning to stay away from the polling stations. The fact that the new parliament had not been assigned a headquarters did not add to its or the election's credibility. Yeltsin wanted the two chambers to sit separately in buildings consonant with their more humble status. He was determined that the deputies would not move back into the charred and derelict White House. Once it had been repaired, it would be given over to Chernomyrdin's government. Up to a dozen buildings were earmarked for the new legislature, but in each case the existing occupants fought staunchly against eviction. An outbuilding of the Academy of Sciences was among those mooted, as was Gorbachev's Foundation. Eventually Yeltsin settled on two sites: the Mayor's office, a 1960s eyesore which in Communist times housed the headquarters of Comecon, the East European trading bloc, for the State Duma, and the House of Press for the Federation Council. Journalists were up in arms about losing their home, but their appeals were ignored.

It took a film-maker, Stanislav Govorukhin, to inject some confrontation into the dull campaign. Govorukhin was a leader of Travkin's Democratic Party and director of some of the most telling films of recent years. *We Can't Live Like That* was a devastating exposé of the sleaze and hopelessness of modern life, a slap in the face to Gorbachev and his promises of a better future. That was followed in 1992 by *The Russia We Have Lost*, which set a new trend of anti-Communist nationalism, giving a rose-tinted view of the era of the Tsars and further demolishing the Lenin myth. The film was laced with much that was threatening about the new Russia, with its heavy doses of anti-semitism and embittered sense of a fallen empire. Nicholas II was depicted as a man of brilliance and compassion, Lenin as a slit-eyed fanatic who had to be Jewish.

Govorukhin was always angry. A Victorian-style dandy who believed that happiness for Russia ended in 1917, he snarled at the sight of shoppers jostling outside a Western store that was opening for the first time. He snarled at the rich; he snarled at the poor. Govorukhin had a pithy little line to remind audiences that the most ardent reformers had in their day been ardent Communists. 'I hate all Communists – Yeltsin, Gaidar, Poltoranin . . .' he said. 'Werewolves they are, all of them.' Extracts of his new film were used as propaganda for Travkin's campaign. He travelled to towns on the border with China and described how everything was being sold off – raw materials, skilled labourers, women. Then, in a reference to the assault on the White House, Govorukhin described Yeltsin as a traitor. This was breaking new ground in the campaign. Having minded their words at the start, the Communists now joined in the attack. Nevzorov, who was standing as an independent but allied to the Communists, called Yeltsin a mass murderer and claimed several hundred had died in the storming of the White House. (The authorities put the death toll at around 150.) Yeltsin's spokesman demanded that the government intervene to stop 'the lies, distortions, demagogy and insults' on television.

There was a steely determination about the Communists. Nevzorov apart, there was precious little charisma among their candidates. Zyuganov was a dour mathematics teacher, whose dogged determination was not to be underestimated. He and his comrades were camped out in the shabby offices of *Sovietskaya Rossiya*, making do with a couple of rooms, three telephones and dozens of helpers. They were reliving 1917 all over again, quoting their mentor for inspiration. 'As Lenin said: these elections are fraudulent. If we cannot stop them we must take part in them,' said Dmitry Volkov, the Communist candidate for Moscow Central, at a rally which consisted mainly of pensioners. He chose to omit the fact that the elections held immediately after the October Revolution had been comparatively free and fair, but the Bolsheviks had not done too well, so they closed down the Constituent Assembly after its first morning. I asked Zyuganov whether such direct criticism of the President might not backfire. He said he had received hundreds of telegrams of support since Nevzorov's broadcast, especially from small provincial towns. Yeltsin had destroyed his aura of invincibility by sending in the tanks, he said. Now he would pay. 'We're going to be particularly strong in the heartlands – in those regions which they haven't yet quite ruined, whose people they haven't managed to turn into idiots, those regions which have saved Russia from past invasions and troubles.'

With television news weighted heavily in favour of Russia's Choice, and with only a couple of formal slots in which to put over their message, the parties knew there was no way out of paying for commercial advertising space. The rates were extremely low by Western standards, but still they had to find sponsors to help their cause. One firm specializing in collecting and analysing commercial information said publicly that it was looking to adopt a 'promising and compliant' party.

Russia's Choice had the most money. Its campaign headquarters in Herzen Street were housed in the Liberal-Conservative Centre, a Russian umbrella organization allied to libertarian and right-wing groups in the West. One of its main sponsors was an American think tank called the Kriebel Foundation. The head of the centre, Murashev, the former police chief and radical ally of Yeltsin's, coordinated the election campaign. He sat at his computer for eighteen hours a day, working out who should be speaking where, where the big guns should be focused. Behind him, providing inspiration, was a large framed photograph of Thatcher. Russia's Choice called upon Western advertising companies. The product they came up with was slick – perhaps too slick. One image featured young people dancing happily in a discotheque when a band of sinister-looking men in black suits and dark glasses stormed in and ordered the place shut down. The message was clear: this is what will happen if the Communists or the other hardliners take over.

Many of the hardline groups proved adept at coordinating their campaigns. The Communists and their allies in the rural areas, the Agrarian Party, made sure they didn't put up candidates against each other or criticize each other. The reformers, meanwhile, allowed personal rivalries and ego conflicts to get the better of them. There were policy differences, but not enough to merit splitting the vote, even among members of the government. Russia's Choice contained the largest number of ministers, but the ambitious Shakhrai had persuaded several top names to join his newly established Party of Unity and Accord.

One of Shakhrai's electoral stunts was to portray himself as one of the few incorruptibles. He wrote in a newspaper that he had earned an average of 138,000 roubles (£70) per month over the year. All his earnings had come from his government salary; he had no foreign bank accounts, no property holdings or additional sources of income. He, his wife and their two sons owned a three-room cooperative apartment and were hoping to trade it in for a five-room apartment in a different part of town. The family also occupied a government *dacha* with four rooms but no sauna, cooks or maids. He and his wife shared a Volga car with the in-laws, but they had no computer. 'In addition, every member of the family has a bicycle.' He announced that he was taking a self-imposed unpaid holiday in order to devote his efforts to his campaign, so as not to conduct it at state expense.

A small, dapper man with a prominent moustache, Shakhrai had put himself in the running as a future presidential candidate after the April referendum. Yeltsin was annoyed and let it be known he did not think Shakhrai would get the post. He resigned in May 1992, warning that government policies were on the wrong track; six months later he returned as the President's personal troubleshooter on ethnic conflicts, with the thankless job of sorting out the Caucasus. He swapped his pinstripe suit for combat fatigues and received numerous death threats. During the campaign he made clear he wanted to be speaker of the new Duma, and seemed to be prepared to do anything to get the job. He even praised the old Communist Party for its success in maintaining order over the decades, keeping the trains running on time. 'Conservatism is a very good word,' he said. 'We see it as a way of preserving Russia, the family, the conscience.'

The leader of the other main reformist group would not have said anything of the kind. Yavlinsky liked to portray himself as a radical, in the true meaning of the word. According to him, Gaidar had not enacted real reform, he had merely allowed the *nomenklatura* to take advantage of economic *laissez-faire*. Yavlinsky had allied himself with Lukin, whom Yeltsin had tried but failed to remove as Ambassador to Washington, and Boldyrev, the disgruntled corruption investigator; but his was more or less a one-man show. He wanted everything he did to be different, to be the outsider looking in. I met up with him in a dingy hotel in Yekaterinburg. It was not yet dawn, the water in the bathroom was more sulphurous than usual and he had had less than four hours' sleep. There had been one consolation: no cockroaches had been spotted. He was breakfasting on sausages of a greyish hue. Yavlinsky was deliberately doing it the hard way, playing on his past as a former champion boxer. 'I don't tell the local administrations that I am coming because I don't want to stay at some posh Party hotel and be driven around in limousines.'

Logically, he and Gaidar should not have been attacking each other. But it irked Yavlinsky to know that, whatever happened next, Gaidar would always be remembered as the real reformer of the new Russia. Nobody mobbed Yavlinsky, whose squashed nose and wiry hair hardly made him a pin-up. But he knew what he wanted. He had made no secret of his aim to succeed Yeltsin, and unlike Shakhrai, he did not depend on the current master for anything. In his early forties, with a wealth of experience already behind him, he knew he had time on his side. He was sitting pretty. The latest poll had named him the most popular politician in the country. Each speech on his campaign trail was tailored to its audience: for military specialists in Tomsk he praised the army; at an industrial plant in Novosibirsk he stressed the need for a different form of privatization; in Krasnoyarsk he called for changes in the tax system. Faced with the unfortunate workers at the factory in Yekaterinburg, who produced televisions that were twenty years out of date and more expensive than Japanese models, he gave them the lot. He wanted a less painful version of reform, an idea that was popular but hard to realize. 'Ministers cannot say the ends justify the means. It would be nice to ask

150 million people to go to the moon for a couple of years while we get on with our reforms. But we can't.'

Yavlinsky had support from prominent businessmen – in Moscow, Gusinsky was firmly behind him – but all the organization was carried out by his economic think tank, Epicentre. It allowed him to keep a tight rein on the campaign, but made it harder for the message to be spread far and wide. Inside his battle bus, a souped-up American landcruiser lent by a local bank, as we listened to a particular cassette from Queen played over and over again (especially the track 'We are the Champions'), Yavlinsky would tug at my arm to ask what I thought of each speech. The private doubt was surprising for a man who exuded so much confidence in public. Speeches over, and generally well received, we boarded a Yak-40 plane. It had been sent by an entrepreneur to take the team to Voronezh, where we were putting up at a training camp of the local football team. On board the heating was not working properly and we kept our coats on. We cracked open cans of beer and tucked into buns. Yavlinsky opted for tea from a battered vacuum flask, and we discussed politics. We began with Westerners. Yavlinsky was fluent in English and very much at home in the West, but like many Russians was appalled at the ignorance of foreigners who prescribed advice from their five-star hotels. He opened his latest book, *The Lessons of Economic Reform*, and pointed to a line: 'Russia is not a virgin you can spend some time with and then move on to the next.'

Another maverick was Lukyanov. The last time I had seen the former Soviet parliamentary speaker had been in court with Pavlov. Unlike Khasbulatov, Rutskoy and their fellow conspirators in 'coup two', the leaders of 'coup one' were free to campaign. Lukyanov had to notify the judge each time he wanted to leave Moscow, and then could do so only at weekends. Each Friday night, he would make the 200-mile journey by car along the Minsk Highway to Smolensk, his home town, part of the 'red belt'. He was standing for the Communist Party. I joined him one morning at the House of Culture of the Smolensk Aviation Factory. There was barely an empty seat in the house. Of the seven candidates for the city constituency, Lukyanov was the only one who really tried to win people over. He was rewarded for his labours, cheered wherever he went. He played on his status as a victim of the new establishment. 'Don't worry, comrades, I'll speak the truth in court. I'll tell them who ruined the Soviet Union. The only person who betrayed anyone was Gorbachev, who betrayed his party. My conscience is clear.'

Smolensk had been razed by the Nazis as they advanced on Moscow. Lukyanov was a young boy then. 'I met the war here,' he declared. 'At the end of it there was virtually nothing standing. We rebuilt this town over forty years; now they want to return it to rubble.' 'Shame!' the audience cried.

Perestroika should have been about the perfecting of the Soviet socialist structures. It was not about destroying what we had. The government tells the IMF it is planning for an army of ten million unemployed. Prices are rising twenty per cent a month, seven hundred factories close a month. Half a million have died from ethnic conflicts, people are too frightened to leave their homes. These, comrades, are the boys' achievements over the past two years.

It was not difficult to be a speech writer in Smolensk for any of the anti-government parties. The factory proudly built the small Yak-42 aircraft. By the end of 1993 a quarter of the 8,000 workers had been put on compulsory 'holiday' until the New Year, receiving the equivalent of £25 a month as compensation. More would lose their jobs.

Lukyanov was to win comfortably. So would Vasily Starodubtsev, a fellow conspirator in 1991 and head of the state agricultural lobby. Starodubtsev stood in the Tula region, close to the collective farm where he remained adored by the locals throughout his imprisonment. The pair were only two of a range of colourful characters in the election, many of whom were brave enough to fight for the 50 per cent of places that were assigned constituency by constituency and not by the safer system of party lists. In Tver there was Eduard Limonov, an exiled writer who saw himself as a punk rebel hardliner; in Yaroslavl there was Anatoly Kashpirovsky, whose televised 'treatment' of the ill by hypnosis made him a cult figure in the late 1980s. Many of the most charismatic were standing in Moscow. Yuri Vlasov, a double Olympic heavyweight weightlifting champion, was pitted against eight other candidates in north-west Moscow. The centre of the city saw the toughest race, with sixteen would-be politicians fighting it out for one place. The most famous of these was Tarasov, the millionaire hounded into exile in London on suspicion of fraud, and Gazmanov, the slushy pop singer. Nobody doubted that some of these figures would be elected. That would be no bad thing: they would inject some colour into political life, something that had been sorely missing.

Yeltsin had a one-track mind. What mattered for him was that the constitution question, the third on the referendum, was passed. He assumed, as most others did, that the pro-reform groups would divide up the lion's share of the vote between them, and somehow come to a pact. The Communists would not do badly, and Zhirinovsky would probably improve slightly on his 8 per cent in the presidential elections. The broad red–brown front would amass a quarter to a third of the vote, a sizeable contingent, but would be well outnumbered by the likes of Gaidar, Yavlinsky and Shakhrai. That was that, and there was no need to worry.

What particularly rankled with Yeltsin was criticism of his draft constitution. He put it to the popular vote but had no intention of allowing a full discussion on it. As the attacks intensified, he summoned the leaders of the thirteen contending parties to his Kremlin office for a dressing-down. He ordered them to stick to their election programmes. 'I warn you that your free television time will be taken away if you deviate from the theme. Your theme is your manifesto. We will fight for the constitution and I ask you not to trample on it.' Sitting on either side of Yeltsin were Gaidar, naturally enough, and Zhirinovsky. Zhirinovsky was the first to stand up when the President walked in, and nodded his head, while others scowled, as Yeltsin held forth. Apart from Russia's Choice, his was the only party to speak out unequivocally in favour of the new basic law. As a result he was treated with kid gloves by the President.

Zhirinovsky's campaign was streets ahead of the rest. He kept it simple and kept it interesting. It was not much more sophisticated than his cheap vodka pledges of 1991. Every Saturday morning he stood outside the entrance to his local metro station, Sokolniki, loudhailer in hand. He invited questions and had an answer for them all. His was a genuinely fresh face, one of the few never to have been a member of the Communist Party or tainted by *nomenklatura* privilege. He lived in a two-roomed flat in a Moscow block like any other. The windows on the ground floor were boarded up, having been smashed by vandals. The corridors reeked of urine. The LDP's offices, on the fourth floor of a pot-holed lane in the centre of the city, were nothing if not accessible to the ordinary man. They were cramped and dingy. Just inside the entrance was a kiosk selling accoutrements such as black leather jackets and heavy metal T-shirts. Down the hall early every morning the queue began of aspiring members who were asked to pay only 100 roubles for the privilege of joining his party. Inside, Zhirinovsky held forth to any journalist who wanted to hear. Always he would bring out *the map*, showing all the lands over which that Russia would once again reign.

But his real forte was television. He told Russians that under his leadership they would live well, no longer in fear of their lives on the streets, and be citizens of a proud and mighty nation. He was careful not to insult Yeltsin personally, but he made clear that everything he stood for was rotten. He provided a perfect package of humorous and convincing promises.

On the eve of polling, Yeltsin appeared on television, urging the 107 million voters to opt for 'worthy, competent, responsible and intelligent' candidates. 'It is your decision – is Russia to be, or not to be, the country we voted for in the presidential election and the April referendum? It is your decision; is there to be, or not to be, peace and calm in Russia? Vote for those who put action first, not words or sweet promises.' They didn't listen.

18
Great Russia

S ergei Krasavchenko was staggering punch-drunk up and down the
hall. The election results service had stopped. The President's deputy
chief of staff was asked what was going on. 'Nothing special,' he replied.
He became more and more incoherent. 'Russia is a Titanic only if you
want it to be a Titanic,' he said. 'Yeltsin is no Hindenburg.'

Polling stations in western Russia had just closed. The first exit polls
were making depressing reading. Russia's Choice was level-pegging with
Zhirinovsky's LDP, with the Communists featuring strongly in third
place.

Still, it was not over yet. The all-night gala in the Palace of Congresses,
decked out especially for the occasion, went ahead. The motto for the
night was The New Political Year. Politicians of all sides were to come
together in a symbolic act of reconciliation and responsibility in front of a
live television audience of tens of millions. As the show opened, the two
young comperes, teeth whiter than white, smiles pure Hollywood, did
their best. But they kept on fluffing their lines. Nothing was going
according to plan. The interviewees had not shown up and the right
people were not looking jolly. The first figures came in from Vladivostok
and other points in the Far East showing Zhirinovsky well in the lead,
with Russia's Choice and the Communists vying for second place. 'Our
computer seems to have been infected with a virus,' Tamara Maximova,
the gala host, giggled into the microphone. It was not what was supposed
to happen, so the results suddenly dried up. In their place came cabaret
turns and viewers' telegrams, 'wishing democracy well'.

The Yeltsin camp fell back on the other issue at stake, the constitution.
But even there there was precious room for comfort. Turnout was
hovering just above the 50 per cent required. Kostikov was quick to
display public bonhomie. 'Dear Russians, the constitution has been
passed. We live in a new state. Democracy has triumphed.' The assembled
looked on, bemused. What made him so sure? The *real* victors had already
begun celebrating. Zhirinovsky went over to Zyuganov and began
slapping him on the shoulder. The Communist leader was not sure how
to respond, whether he should be seen cosying up to the neo-fascists. The
man of the moment then went over to the table assigned for Women of
Russia, the rank outsiders who had surprised everyone by surmounting

the 5 per cent hurdle needed to gain seats. This selection of middle-aged former Communists with *bouffants* and purple rinses were an interesting variation on the feminist theme. Not that they espoused feminism particularly: more a nostalgic homeliness that many obviously found reassuring. The Women were delighted to join in the eating, drinking and toasting with Zhirinovsky's henchmen. 'Here we have some good-quality grape juice, called champagne. I suggest we drink to Russian culture,' proffered Zhirinovsky. The Communists and the Women sipped their sparkling wine. Zhirinovsky drained his.

Telman Gdlyan had taken on bigger fish in his time. A radical anti-Communist lawyer who believed the ends justified the means, he took on the entire establishment in the late 1980s in an attempt to have Ligachev investigated for corruption. Now he went over to Zhirinovsky and called him a scoundrel. As he walked away, Zhirinovsky, who was by this time considerably the worse for wear, lunged at him with a punch that missed by yards. So much for reconciliation. Just below the podium was the table reserved for Russia's Choice – the longest, naturally. It was all but empty. Chubais and his wife had made a brief appearance, scowled at the sight of the revellers and headed for the door. Zhirinovsky marched up to the remaining few and screamed, 'This is not a party – this is your wake.' They pretended not to hear him. He then began introducing his 'shadow cabinet', mostly shady young men in brightly coloured sports jackets.

The election party was taken off the air, much to Zhirinovsky's chagrin. The Election Commission said it had never intended to issue results so quickly. Any figures that might have been given out on television were unauthorized and potentially inaccurate, it added. In desperation, the loyal Ryabov and his Commission were making up the rules as they went along.

Next day, a chastened Gaidar called for a popular front against Zhirinovsky. 'The presence of fascists in parliament is in itself a defeat for Russian democracy.' But within Russia's Choice the recriminations had begun to fly well before polling day. The main target was Shumeiko, for his attempts to censor the press. The problem went far deeper, however. The new establishment had lost touch with the bulk of the voters who had yet to see the benefits of the reforms. It had hardly tried to talk to them, in stark contrast to Zhirinovsky. The radicals in the government realized after the election that it might not have been particularly wise to apply the financial squeeze during the campaign. It was hardly surprising that an army that hadn't been paid for several months had voted for the 'sweet promises', as Yeltsin had put it. Around 130,000 officers withdrawn from Eastern Europe and the Baltics were having to endure lives in squalid and cramped train carriages and huts because no money could be found to build them houses quickly enough. The Germans had paid a few million to get the process going. Rostropovich had chipped in with funds for 100 homes just outside Moscow. But it was small beer. Within that context, the protest vote was entirely understandable.

Activists for Russia's Choice had been saying just that in the weeks up to polling day. Nikolai Matveyev stood, and lost, as a candidate for the Duma in Tula, a proud old city 120 miles to the south of Moscow that came of age when chosen by Peter the Great as the site for his first arms factory. Tula was virtually a one-industry town, like hundreds of others in Russia. At least there it made samovars as well as guns. With the military–industrial complex in decline, the mood was always going to be hostile. 'I knew people were angry,' said Matveyev. 'What I didn't realize was the extent.' As polling day approached, as Zhirinovsky's persuasive television appearances were the talk of the town, Matveyev bombarded Russia's Choice headquarters with alarmist faxes. They told him not to worry, everything would be all right. In the event, the result there was even more alarming than in the country as a whole. Nearly one in three of Tula's 1.4 million strong electorate voted for Zhirinovsky, more than double the proportion that backed Russia's Choice. 'Those people in the capital are completely out of touch. They simple don't talk the same language as people we know here,' he said.

A visit to the town's bazaar bore that out. It was a Dickensian picture of degradation. Old women hawked pullovers they had knitted or socks they had darned, knowing that, ultimately, they were unlikely to emerge with more than a bob or two. Several said they had stood on the perilous ice and in the pelting snow all morning and had earned only 3,000 roubles (£2 at the time). Inside the main market hall, hundreds of young men and middle-aged women were doing the same. They paid a proportion of their earnings to the local thugs, who watched them from the balcony, for the privilege of having a roof over their heads. To ask any of them for whom they voted was to invite a torrent of invective. With the odd exception only two answers were given – either Zhirinovsky or 'I didn't bother to turn up.' 'This is why I went for him,' said one young man, punching his fist into the air. 'We Russians can't live without the fist.' One woman travelled once a fortnight to Poland to buy a bit here, sell a bit there. She was trying to offload a box full of polyester shell suits and tinny Taiwanese radios. She was an alto at the local conservatoire, but couldn't make ends meet. Despite it all, she had voted for Russia's Choice. Her companion on these *shopturi* abroad had opted for Zhirinovsky. They teased each other about their loyalties, but the difference didn't seem to matter too much. I had found the same in Moscow on polling day, with several families content to split the vote. In many constituencies, voters had gone for a reformer as their local candidate, and the LDP as their chosen party. If there was a lesson to be learnt it was that where the reformers kept their feet on the ground they did not fare too badly.

The man who had most betrayed them was Yeltsin himself. He had never resolved his perennial dilemma. Was he the non-partisan President of all Russians? Or was he the leader of the reformist wing, the representative of those who had brought him to power in 1990 and 1991? In his darkest hours he would veer towards the latter, as in December 1992 when, on Burbulis' advice, he charged towards the car factory at the start of his referendum campaign. Yet the storming of the White House pushed him back towards the conciliators. He had gone to the brink and stared political oblivion in the face. He needed to win back the consensus. Having skipped Russia's Choice's election meetings, Yeltsin spent most of the final week out of Moscow, looking at ethnic conflicts in the northern Caucasus and visiting NATO headquarters in Brussels. Had he known the consequences of his failure to support Russia's Choice, he might have thought again.

Gaidar said Yeltsin had once again been badly advised.

I think the President had a misplaced confidence that the main battles had already been won, that Communism as a realistic option was a closed book after the October events, that the nationalists were weak. The only questions remaining in his mind were tactical ones, the finer points in the various reform programmes. He could see no point allying himself to one particular party. He'd wait to see who the people voted for. This feeling was very widespread among the people who had Yeltsin's ear at the time.

Burbulis, the perennial advocate of confrontation, went public against Yeltsin for the first time. The President, he said, had put his own ego and historical reputation above the needs of reform.

It took Yeltsin several days to respond to the results. When he did, he spoke of the need to guard against fascism, but avoided mentioning Zhirinovsky by name. Sacrifices had to be made. First to go was Stankevich, a fairly pointless dismissal from a fairly pointless post. Stankevich was formally Yeltsin's adviser on political affairs, but for more than a year he had hardly ever got to see him. The other sackings had more consequence. First he abolished Poltoranin's Federal Information Centre, which had managed to annoy just about everyone. Then he went for the head of television. Vyacheslav Bragin had been made Chairman of Ostankino following the unseemly hounding out of Yegor Yakovlev. The appointment of a former district Party chief ('not even a regional boss', his staff would scoff) had been greeted with universal disdain. Bragin's main contribution to Russian broadcasting was to give more air time to the Mexican soap operas that had had the country transfixed for months. When it came to politics, and the storming of the television centre in October, Bragin was found wanting on every count. He all too readily decided to shut down broadcasting as the fighting began (even though the rival station continued), and forbade his journalists to cover the fighting. He said afterwards that he had been concerned only for their safety. To compound his cowardice, he allowed the various political groups to buy space for their election broadcasts on credit. Zhirinovsky, it transpired, had been the main beneficiary of Bragin's generosity.

Rather than apologizing for ditching Russia's Choice, Yeltsin saw the election outcome as vindication of his timely move to the centre. Ironically, the biggest victor – bigger, perhaps, even than Zhirinovsky – was Chernomyrdin. His master stroke had been to ignore the elections altogether. His own rating soared. Now he was free to attack Gaidar and his radical therapy:

> I said it a year and a half ago, and I am ready to repeat it now. It was wrong to jump into the river without testing the water first, as was done in January 1992. We should face the truth and admit that many people voted against the hardships and mistakes of the current reforms, rather than for any specific platform. The election defeat is a personal evaulation of Gaidar as the person responsible for the economy. The same goes for Chubais. They should think it over hard. They have a lot to think about now.

Their thoughts, for the moment, were on Hitler. Krasavchenko's comparison of Yeltsin with Hindenburg was less than flattering, but it merited reflection. Within just over two years of invoking emergency powers, as the Nazis notched up their first election successes at the height of the recession, the ailing 82-year-old German President had ceded power to Hitler. He had tried hard to avoid him, but had been pushed into it by the inexorable appeal of the easy solution. Was the ageing Yeltsin about to do the same?

Zhirinovsky and Hitler had much in common, not least their ideological tracts. *The Last Leap South*, Zhirinovsky's latest offering, had become required reading. He described how as a boy in Kazakhstan he had had to live in a communal flat, how his mother could not afford to feed him properly, how he was discriminated against at school, how he had barely kissed a girl by the time he made it to Moscow aged eighteen. He was painfully shy and convinced of his personal inadequacy. Sex and politics, in the Zhirinovsky mind, were inextricably linked. The advent of Lenin was likened to rape. Stalin's time was the 'epoch of homosexuality'. The Khrushchev years were dominated by 'uniform masturbation', the Brezhnev era was marked by 'orgies and mass fornication', while the Gorbachev and Yeltsin reigns suffered from 'political and economic impotence'. Like Hitler, Zhirinovsky was obsessed most of all with ethnic purity. He had trouble convincing others of his 100 per cent Slav pedigree. His father Wolf provided awkward ancestry. Zhirinovsky had a trite little line to disavow his Jewishness. 'My mother is Russian, my father is a lawyer,' he would say.

Roman Spektor, President of the Jewish Cultural Association in Moscow, remembered a somewhat different Zhirinovsky from the rabid nationalist of 1994. In February 1988, the Anti-Zionist League, one of the KGB's many front organizations, decided to set up a more 'pro-Jewish' organization called Shalom. Spektor and his friends took part in the founding congress to try to ensure the KGB did not hijack the meeting completely. Of the 100 participants, 'all of whom I assumed were at least partly Jewish', it was Zhirinovsky who stood out. 'His was the most sensible speech. He went over the group's charter item by item, making a lot of constructive and democratic suggestions. I was amazed. Afterwards we exchanged phone numbers.' Zhirinovsky was elected to the committee, but not to one of the top positions. Immediately afterwards he apparently lost interest. Spektor called him a few times, but he said he was busy. Obviously, Judaism was not for him.

A few months after the election, an enterprising journalist in Alma Ata said he had uncovered Zhirinovsky's family records which showed his full name to be Vladimir Wolfovich Eidelstein, not the most convincing of Aryan credentials. He received permission to change his name in 1964, at the age of eighteen. Zhirinovsky denounced the findings as lies. Paradoxically, Spektor pointed out, the reformists' best line of attack on him was to concentrate on his alleged Jewish origins. However reprehensible, the tactic was bound to pay off among the Russia public. 'On the trolleybuses they're already saying "a Jew has come to power."'

Those who claimed to know Zhirinovsky well said he abandoned moderate policies in the late 1980s because he saw they would not get him noticed. Andrei Zavidya was a former comrade. The two had fought the 1991 presidential race on a joint ticket. They soon fell out. Zavidya's own background is murky. He financed *Sovietskaya Rossiya* for a while, while never quite coming clean on its activities. There were many such characters around Zhirinovsky, including a sizeable contingent from the KGB. Zavidya said that in the early days he had provided much of the LDP's funding. As for the finances behind the election campaign, he would refer obliquely to 'commercial structures'. There was considerable speculation, but little hard evidence, that the KGB had systematically promoted the LDP. 'He was useful and he was bright,' Zavidya said. 'Anyone who speaks five languages well is no fool. All this nationalism, all this screaming and shouting was just to give him a platform. All the other positions on the political spectrum were occupied. I made Zhirinovsky and when the time is right, I'll destroy him and become President myself.' Zhirinovsky's links with the KGB were the worst-kept secret in Moscow. There were enough indications to suggest that the KGB and the Party had helped create the LDP and encouraged its progress. Oleg Kalugin, a former officer who became one of the security apparatus's most outspoken critics, explained: 'Zhirinovsky's appearance in Russia as a political figure is entirely artificial. If you look at his record, his education, his army service, everything, a man with his origins, half Jewish, would never have stood a chance of getting anywhere.'

Zhirinovsky's first press conference after his election success was a sight to behold. His party had just secured 23 per cent of the vote for the Duma, 9 per cent ahead of Russia's Choice. The Communists were in third place, with Yavlinsky, Shakhrai and Co. trailing even the Agrarians. The great rabble-rouser suddenly became the great statesman, the man who would work for peace and harmony around the world. In full evening dress, matching bow tie and cummerbund, he patiently sought to explain that he was no anti-semite, he did not want to extend Russia's borders, he would not dream of intimidating its neighbours. 'We will never tell people of any race that they cannot live in Russia. Everyone who was born here and works here is, in my view, a full-blooded Russian citizen. No one will throw them out.' He soon gave up with the pretence and reverted to type. 'Many of our voters come up to me and tell me they are tired of seeing so many presenters on television who are representatives of non-Russian peoples. What they really want to see are kind Russian faces speaking good Russian.'

Everything boiled down to *the map*. Russia would regain most of the territory of the former USSR, but not by force. The prodigals would simply see the light. 'In the coming years many of these republics will, with tears in their eyes, beg the new President of Russia to incorporate them into the Russian state.' Zhirinovsky dreamed of the two great European powers dividing up central and eastern Europe as they had done in the past. A revived Russian empire would reincorporate Belarus and most of Ukraine. *Grossdeutschland* would include Austria, the Czech lands, western Poland, Slovakia and the Baltics. Tallinn would become a city state, subservient Poland would receive western Ukraine, while Germany would be given Königsberg, its former eastern seaboard town that became Kaliningrad under Soviet occupation. But Russia was, after all, a Eurasian state that could not be denied its *Lebensraum* to the south. 'The Last Leap South', wrote Zhirinovsky,

is not only a solution to Russia's internal problems and the pacification of peoples in regions from Kabul to Istanbul. It is also the solution of a world task. How I dream of our Russian soldiers washing their boots in the warm waters of the Indian Ocean. The pealing of bells from a Russian Orthodox Church on the shores of the Indian Ocean or Mediterranean would proclaim to the peoples of this region peace, prosperity and calm.

The state media were in a quandary. The man represented one of the largest factions in parliament. Was it advisable, was it feasible to ignore him? Or, as Adam Michnik, one of the intellectuals prominent in Poland's break from Communism, wrote: 'Russia stands before a dramatic dilemma, to which no one has yet given a reasonable answer. What is better: to disrupt the rules of democracy and chase out the totalitarian parties while they are still sufficiently weak? Or respect the democratic order and open to these parties the road to power?' The media barons started by giving Zhirinovsky as little air time as possible. But the policy became ever harder to sustain as each antic became more outrageous than the next.

He towered over the early sessions of the Duma. As he entered the unprepossessing Comecon building on the first day, hundreds of photographers, cameramen and reporters dived towards him. Nobody had seen a scrum like it since the days of Gorbachev. Chairs and tables went flying. Zhirinovsky relished every moment of it, sitting at a lounge chair in the lobby with journalists kneeling on the floor below him. Chernomyrdin, who had arrived to make the opening address, searched in vain for anyone to interview him. With one of his LDP men, a gormless retired pilot called Georgy Lukava, sitting temporarily in the speaker's chair, Zhirinovsky shouted instructions from the floor. The first session was abandoned in chaos. The fight over the speaker's post dragged on into a third day. Zhirinovsky was getting frustrated. He had wanted the job for himself and promised his opponents in the chamber that, in return for their lack of trust in him, he would send them to psychiatric hospitals. As Chubais pointed at his watch sarcastically, Zhirinovsky thundered: 'You will be doing that in a prison cell to call for your lunch. I would have made a perfect speaker, an example not only for the country but for the whole world.'

Worse was to come the following day, at the buffet queue. Zhirinovsky and his henchmen barged in, demanding that they be served their lunch first. When Mark Goryachev, an entrepreneur from St Petersburg, protested, Zhirinovsky told him to shut up and threatened to throw him into jail once he had come to power. Goryachev then punched Zhirinovsky in the face. Police were called in to separate the pair. There would be more punch-ups. Several of Zhirinovsky's colleagues left him, the most prominent among them his former right-hand man and deputy Viktor Kobelev, who threatened to reveal *kompromat* on him. Many in the LDP had been acutely embarrassed by publication of a photograph of a naked Zhirinovsky running his hands along the chest of a male comrade in a sauna during a recent visit to Slovenia.

Western governments were in a dilemma. They were wary of bestowing on him martyr status, but they did not want to help him propagate his views abroad either. He had already had the Japanese and Germans up in arms by threatening to create 'new Hiroshimas and Nagasakis' if they interfered in Russia's internal affairs. Then he offended the Bulgarians by using a visit to Sofia to call on their President, Zhelyu Zhelev, to resign. He was given twenty-four hours to leave. As he waited at Sofia airport for a flight home, he shrieked to a Russian embassy official: 'Call Bulgaria's President and tell him he's scum. He takes good care of Russian prostitutes working in Bulgaria but offers no cooperation to Russian members of parliament.' While touring Serbia, to much acclaim from his fellow Slavs, Zhirinovsky boasted that he had given the Serbian leadership a secret weapon that could 'wipe out humanity'.

The French thought they had found a good compromise. Zhirinovsky's visa stipulated that he must not leave Strasbourg, where he was to address the European Parliament, and he must behave himself. He responded by barging in on a meeting of liberal legislators who had asked him to stay away. Then he started screaming at a crowd which had gathered outside the Russian consulate to protest against his visit. He ripped some plants from their pots and flung them at the demonstrators and journalists. Addressing the European Parliament, he said: 'Turkey bombs Kurdish villages. Britain fills the streets of Northern Ireland with blood. UN pilots bomb Serbia. Don't be surprised if other pilots come to bomb other European cities. We don't know how far Russia's borders will stretch. When we decide, you will have to accept this decision.'

For all his excesses, Zhirinovsky expressed the injured pride felt by millions of perfectly normal Russians. With more adept handling of Russia's foreign policy, the economic decline that was bound to accompany the start of reform could have been presented in a manner less humiliating. From 1982 to 1992 Russia went from one extreme to another. Mr Nyet, in Andrei Gromyko, became Mr Da in Andrei Kozyrev. The Foreign Minister who would oppose anything the Americans advocated at the United Nations would have turned in his grave. In the first year after the coup, the Russian representative seemed to need no prompting to put up his hand in support of Western initiatives in the UN Security Council and other international fora. Operation Desert Storm, which had been given the nod by Shevardnadze and Gorbachev, was followed by the no-fly zone over Iraq, American intervention in Somalia and sanctions against Serbia. It was not that they ought not to have backed a particular Western-inspired move, but that the decisions often failed to address the thoroughly reasonable concern of Russia's national interest.

At the start Yeltsin was happy to defer to his Western partners. After all the snubs and the mishaps on his trips abroad prior to becoming President, he was desperate to be accepted on the world stage. He was also eager to pay back the debt for the support the Americans gave him during the coup. His visit to Washington in June 1992 marked the high point in Russia's foreign policy 'love-in'. It was a time of extravagant promises. The centrepiece of the summit with George Bush was the START II agreement that was to slash the long-range nuclear warheads of the USA and the former USSR by two-thirds. Joint military exercises were planned, cooperation pledged between the CIA and the renamed KGB. It was a time of flamboyant gestures. No sooner had Yeltsin arrived in Washington than he rang Solzhenitsyn to urge him to come home. Later that evening at a state banquet he whirled Barbara Bush around for a brief waltz. Yeltsin became the first leader from Moscow to address the American Congress. He told them what they wanted to hear, and it came from the heart. 'The world can sigh in relief,' he said. 'The idol of Communism, which spread social strife, enmity and unparalleled brutality everywhere, which instilled fear in humanity, has collapsed. It has collapsed never to rise again. I am here to assure you: We shall not let it rise again in our land.' He was given thirteen standing ovations.

Yeltsin made no secret of his hope of westernizing Russia. The perennial debate on Russia's place in the world had been reawakened even before the collapse of the USSR. The nationalists had adopted a more virulent version of the vocabulary of the Slavophiles of the nineteenth century. In their eyes, Russia did not belong within Europe. That applied as much culturally and politically as it did economically. Foreign models simply would not work.

Soon after his trip to Washington, Yeltsin shifted tack. In October 1992, he addressed the cream of Russian diplomacy at the Foreign Ministry collegium. 'We are too shy in the world community,' he told them. 'Many in turn address Russia in an inadmissible way, even imposing humiliating conditions on us. Russia is not a country that can be kept in the ante-room.' Yeltsin wanted a fresh approach. He did not want to discard Kozyrev, partly because that would be seen to be bowing to his opponents. Instead he put policy formulation under Skokov's Security Council. After several months' deliberations, the Council delivered a confidential report to the President. Its conclusions were far-reaching. The world, in strategic terms, was to be divided into the 'near abroad' and the 'far abroad'. The former team referred to the other fourteen former Soviet republics, the latter to everything else, including Moscow's former Warsaw Pact satellites. After the Brezhnev doctrine, in which the USSR assumed full rights (including military) over the Eastern bloc, came a Kremlin equivalent of the Monroe Doctrine, allocating to Russia the same rights over its immediate 'backyard' (the former Soviet Union) as the Americans had done over theirs (Central America). The report also said Russia was to be referred to as a 'power' rather than a 'country' and that it would serve as 'a force counteracting the United States which aspires to the role of unrivalled world leader'. When Skokov was later sacked, it was not for his views, but for his loyalties. His concept had set the new agenda

– and it left many in neighbouring republics once again frightened of the bear next door.

The identity crisis arose out of the loss of empire. With the exception of the Baltics, which were implicitly acknowledged as different, most Russians had not contemplated having the other republics severed from them. The Soviet Union, to most Russians, was Russia with a few bits tacked on the end. Nor had many in the republics seriously believed that they would be cut off from Russia. Almost overnight, the most pressing issue was the fate of the 25 million Russians who found themselves living on 'foreign soil'. The 'Russian card' became an essential stick with which to beat the republics. None of the leaders had contemplated the economic consequences of the Belovezhskaya deal that dissolved the USSR. From Khabarovsk to Kaliningrad to Kazakhstan, factories were interdependent for their raw materials, energy and finished supplies. When the CIS was formed nobody imagined it would give rise to customs posts and visa requirements. The leaders' egos played a large part in making the divorce more painful than it needed to be.

At the centre stood Yeltsin and Kravchuk, the Ukrainian President. Their brinkmanship at successive CIS summits, especially over the Black Sea fleet, provided a useful diversion from their own respective domestic woes. Most Russians, even those who considered themselves relatively liberal, found it psychologically difficult to accept the notion of a completely independent Ukraine, and the idea that the Crimea should belong to it. It was Nikita Khrushchev who came up with the idea, in 1954 to mark 300 years of Russo-Ukrainian unity. Then, boundaries between republics were of interest purely to the cartographers. Soviet Ukraine and Soviet Russia were part of one 'family of peoples' and Crimea's golden beaches and lush resorts (by Soviet standards) were available to all. With both nations nominally independent, it was only a matter of time before Russian nationalists demanded the return of the peninsula. The Supreme Soviet in Moscow made its first move in May 1992, declaring Khrushchev's decision illegal. Yeltsin managed to dampen down the aspirations, and to persuade the Crimean parliament to suspend preparations for an independence referendum.

Ukrainian nationalists saw in the various developments a Russian-American conspiracy. Western governments, they said, were happy to indulge Yeltsin in his policy towards the 'near abroad'. Their paranoia was exacerbated by the reluctance of the West to grant substantial aid to Ukraine. 'It's a long time since we wanted to impress you,' said Mykola Mikhailchenko, a senior adviser to Kravchuk. 'If you couldn't deliver, you shouldn't have promised.' The trouble was, there wasn't much to support. Parliament and President were at loggerheads, just as in Moscow, but the difference was that the government in Kiev had barely scratched the surface in economic reform. The only man who came close to a

Gaidar, Yavlinsky or Fyodorov was Leonid Kuchma, the former director of a weapons factory, who quit after only seven months as Prime Minister in protest at the obduracy of officials all around him. A trip to Kiev was a depressing experience back into provincialism and the world of Soviet Man. Many from the diasporas in Canada and the USA left Ukraine after a few months, their hopes dashed.

In Soviet times Ukraine was referred to as 'the bread basket'. Its climate was more temperate, its harvests were comparatively bountiful, its workforce was more diligent; but the heavy industry in the east of the republic was no less of a behemoth than Russia's. Within a few months of 'gradual reform', the Ukrainian transitional currency, the *karbovanets* or coupon, had plummeted to a third of the rouble's value. So fast were the tiny banknotes being printed that the government's chief economics adviser was overheard to ask: 'What comes after trillion?' Whole parts of the country were having to do without heating. Visitors to government offices in Kiev were told they should keep their coats on. Whenever challenged by their critics, the radicals in Moscow would cite Ukraine as an example of how *not* to reform. 'Ukrainianization of the economy' was a term of mockery.

Ukraine and the West were caught in a vicious circle. As long as Ukraine refused to sign away its long-range nuclear weapons, Western governments saw the country as unworthy of aid. Yet Ukrainian leaders feared that once they had ratified the START treaty, they would not be taken seriously in negotiations. Among radical Ukrainian politicians, distrust of Russia was endemic. Bohdan Khoryn, deputy head of parliament's foreign affairs committee, was typical of them. Ukraine, he said in the autumn of 1993, needed its nuclear missiles as an antidote to Russia's. Khoryn believed that Yeltsin and his foes were united in one purpose – to restore Russian hegemony over the territory of the former USSR. 'If we hadn't had these weapons, Russia would have behaved differently. Look at Georgia, Moldova, look at the way Shevardnadze went on his knees asking for the help of the Russian army to fight rebels who were backed by the Russian army.' Yet Kravchuk was determined to rid Ukraine of the pariah status it had found itself bearing, mentioned in the same breath as North Korea as a nuclear outcast. In return for his signature to a deal pledging to relinquish Ukraine's 1,800 nuclear warheads, Kravchuk was given centre stage with Yeltsin and Clinton at their January 1994 summit in Moscow.

In the same month the other main focus of discord between Russia and Ukraine intensified. Presidential elections in Crimea, populated predominantly by Russians, saw victory for Yuri Meshkov, a nationalist who had promised in his manifesto to work to reunite the peninsula with Russia. In May, parliament in the capital, Simferopol, passed a declaration of sovereignty, putting itself on an equal level with Ukraine. Within hours, the Ukrainian parliament had overruled the vote. Twenty armoured personnel carriers rumbled through Simferopol in a show of strength by the Ukrainian authorities. Yeltsin warned Kravchuk against threatening Crimea. The Ukrainians knew themselves that their hand was extremely weak, that the only way of staving off the loss of the peninsula was confrontation. Only a few extremists thought that was a price worth paying for holding on to Crimea.

Ukrainians had precious little to show for their three years of independence apart from a national flag and anthem: land that was still collectivized, exhausted heavy industry, huge debts to Russia for its energy supplies, monthly inflation of more than 150 per cent and little of the entrepreneurial spirit seen in Moscow or St Petersburg. So discredited was the non-reform that in parliamentary elections early in 1994 the Communists emerged as the largest faction. At Kravchuk's behest, they appointed Vitaly Masol as Prime Minister. Masol had held the post from 1987 to 1990 but lost support after backing Gorbachev's efforts to hold the Soviet Union together. The wheel had turned full circle.

Among the smaller former republics, economic hardship was appreciably more acute in than Russia. Their problems had been exacerbated by mischief-makers in Moscow, stoking ethnic conflict or applying economic pressure, as in the rouble fiasco the previous summer. But, for better or worse, many in the poorer republics were coming round to the realization that links with Russia, economic and political, had to be restored. Nazarbayev, the Kazakh President, who had never got over Yeltsin's snub to him in December 1991, was one of the first openly to advocate a new union, a Eurasian Union he called it, with a single parliament, single currency and open borders, along the lines of the European Union.

Many of the dissidents, the uncompromising independence fighters of the late 1980s, were voted out, or pushed out, of office. Vytautas Landsbergis, who more than anyone else was responsible for bringing to an end fifty years of Soviet occupation in the Baltics, was defeated in Lithuanian elections by Algirdas Brazauskas, the former Party boss. That result was mirrored across the former USSR and Eastern Europe. In Poland and Hungary, the two most successful exponents of the move to the market, new-look Communists were making a comeback. The labels, however, were sometimes misleading. While never as fiery as Landsbergis, Brazauskas had during his first tenure of office steered the Lithuanian Communist Party determinedly away from its Soviet big brother.

The Belarussian leader, Shushkevich, one of the three original 'conspirators' who finished off the USSR, fought a losing battle against the forces of reaction. He was ejected as speaker of parliament, de facto leader of the country, in January 1994 and replaced by Vyacheslav Kebich, the Prime Minister and a more typical proponent of old-style politics.

Kebich was happy to sign away the country's modicum of independence for a modicum of financial stability, directed by Russia.

The process was even more pronounced in Azerbaijan, where an armed uprising led by a disgruntled army colonel, Surat Guseinov, brought to an end the rule of Abulfaz Elchibey, a former dissident whose one year in power had seen a dramatic chill in relations with Russia and military setbacks in Nagorno Karabakh. Guseinov's forces met no resistance on their long march from Gyandzha, the second city, eastward to Baku, the capital. But the real playmaker was Geidar Aliyev, who came back into big-time politics at the age of seventy. Aliyev's career went back to Brezhnev's time. As Party First Secretary in Azerbaijan from 1969 to 1982, he did what the smartest of republican bosses did: he ran some of the most lucrative rackets in the USSR, while ensuring his fiefdom's complete servility to the word from Moscow. He would shower Brezhnev with gems and paeans whenever the Soviet leader visited the oil-boom town of Baku. He was just the kind of henchman Gorbachev wanted to be rid of, and although it took him considerable efforts, eventually Aliyev was ousted from the Politburo amid accusations of corruption, which naturally went uninvestigated. Aliyev moved back to the small Azeri enclave of Nakhichevan, where he lived well and bided his time. When he returned, he toned down his act. To make money in the new capitalist environment required a more subtle approach to palm-greasing. The lesson for Azerbaijan was clear, as one of Aliyev's aides told me: 'Elchibey made the mistake of not telephoning Yeltsin often enough and trying to go it alone. That can't be done any more.'

Of all the brave ventures into independence, the most disheartening was Georgia's. In Communist times, Georgia was the most sought-after of all holiday destinations to which only the lucky few would be able to escape the monotony and squalor of most Soviet cities. By the time the old union collapsed, Georgia was embroiled in civil war. Zviad Gamsakhurdia, a former dissident and translator of Shakespeare who had turned himself into a despot, was forced to flee after tank battles which saw much of the centre of the capital, Tbilisi, destroyed. The victorious commanders turned to Shevardnadze, who had retired to his political institute in Moscow following Gorbachev's fall. Shevardnadze was a controversial choice. In his years as first KGB then Party chief in Georgia, he had not flinched from cracking down on his opponents. But he was seen as the only hope. Georgia's economy had been virtually destroyed by wars in the breakaway regions of South Ossetia and Abkhazia. The hand of Russian nationalists was everywhere to be seen, goading rebel leaders and supplying them with weaponry in their bid for independence from Georgia. Independence, in reality, meant links with, or rather dependence on, Russia.

When Aliyev took Azerbaijan back into the CIS, Georgia was left the only former republic – apart from the Baltics, who were seen as an entirely separate case – to remain outside the bloc. When Abkhazian rebels overran Sukhumi, the regional capital and one of the jewels of the Black Sea coast, Shevardnadze flew to the city to be with his people as it fell. His appeals to Yeltsin for help fell on deaf ears. Not only was the future of Abkhazia at stake, but also the very existence of Georgia as a single entity. For followers of Gamsakhurdia had regrouped in the west of the republic and were notching up significant gains. Shevardnadze then took the ultimate gamble, the ultimate U-turn. He announced that Georgia was entering the CIS. In other words, it was ceding considerable sovereignty to Russia in order to survive. He was denounced as a traitor by many, but he had no choice. Kozyrev responded by saying, with typical Russian condescension: 'I think we'll be able to restore order now.' Within weeks, hundreds of Russian marines had swept ashore on the Georgian coast, where they were greeted by Shevardnadze, bringing with them armoured vehicles and other heavy weaponry. As soon as they did so, the war with Gamsakhurdia's rebels went Shevardnadze's way. This was the more respectable form of Russian 'peacekeeping'.

One republic gave up the pretence earlier than the rest. Tajikistan, the poorest of the fifteen, had been torn apart by the most violent of all the mini wars in the former USSR. The rebels comprised an unlikely alliance of Islamic fundamentalists and secular anti-Communists. Tajikistan had long been a final redoubt for Russian influence in the Near East. It was across a bridge and into Tajikistan that Soviet troops completed their humiliating retreat from Afghanistan. It was in Afghanistan that the anti-government rebels were receiving succour in 1993. One event tipped the balance towards direct intervention from Moscow. The murder of twenty-five Russian border guards by insurgents from across the frontier led to the first sorties into Afghanistan since the end of the intervention.

In Tajikistan, the Russians did not bother to conceal their role as colonial protectors. Russia claimed the external borders of weak CIS states as its own. Russian officers in Tajikistan displayed none of the defensiveness that was the result of an unwanted presence. They were affable and open, as I discovered when visiting the headquarters of the 201st Motorized Rifle Division in Dushanbe, the capital. One senior officer could have been speaking about 'the white man's burden': 'If we don't stop the fundamentalists here they will reach the Russian heartlands. They never wanted independence in the first place. We threw it at them. Now we have to teach them how to deal with it.' The Americans, whose embassy was one floor directly above the Russians' in a Dushanbe hotel, seemed content to go along with Russian hegemony. It was the lesser of two evils and at least they were trying to seal the border. The Tajik government was happy to see itself as a client state. Said Rashid Alimov, the Foreign Minister: 'Russia is water and air for Tajikistan.'

Exactly two years after the collapse of the union, another of those CIS summits took place. This time twelve countries were present, and the venue was Ashkhabad, capital of Turkmenistan. The most remote of all the Central Asian republics, Turkmenistan had not embarked on the risky path towards democracy. Its President, Siparmurad Niyazov, had been a loyal Party chief. With the revenues pouring in from his country's bountiful reserves of natural gas, the Turkmenbashi, as the leader was known, had taken to being flown in a leased Boeing, with an American crew, and to renaming most of the capital's main streets after himself or members of his family. His people enjoyed a reasonable standard of living as well as complete tranquillity, a rare commodity in Russia's outer reaches. In return for giving them an easy life, Niyazov enjoyed absolute power. The Yeltsin of old would have poured scorn on such an arrangement. But when the honoured Russian guest flew into Ashkhabad that December, it was like the good old days. Both presidents exchanged the triple kiss on the cheeks, no fewer than four times.

The Russian army demanded a reward for its participation, albeit reluctant, in putting down the resistance in the White House. A relieved Yeltsin was happy to deliver. That reward was a new military doctrine, which had been discussed *ad infinitum*. It marked a radical break with the past. Among the main changes were the removal of the long-standing pledge never to be the first side to use nuclear weapons in battle, which everyone knew was cosmetic; allowing troops to help police quell internal conflicts; omission of previous references to reducing troop strengths to a target of 1.5 million personnel; formation of rapid deployment units for regional wars, now considered the main threat to Russian security; the dropping of an undertaking not to go beyond Russia's borders in repelling an attack; and granting the army the right to undertake peacekeeping missions under UN auspices or as a result of bilateral or multilateral deals.

The new Monroe doctrine was thus enshrined as policy. Russian forces were now formally seen as the mainstay of the defence of the whole territory of the former USSR. The only exceptions, as far as the West was concerned, were the Baltics. Nobody was left in any doubt after the Soviet assaults on Riga and Vilnius in January 1991 what the Russians were capable of if they felt they were losing face. Yeltsin's support of the independence aspirations of the three nations had won him many friends there as well as support from Russian radicals. Russians came to believe that the people of the Baltics should show their gratitude for the magnanimous gesture of handing them back their independence. Instead, their countrymen had their noses rubbed in the ground by new citizenship laws adopted in Estonia and Latvia. Lithuania didn't need to take such measures as its population was more or less homogenous. In the other two states, Russians made up around half of the population, most of them having moved across after the Second World War, attracted by the considerably higher standard of living and the more Western feel of the republics. Ethnic dilution by Russians was part of the Soviet policy of colonization. That the process should somehow be reversed was an understandable aim. The question was how.

Suddenly these Russians were told they were 'non-citizens'. They could apply for citizenship if they had sworn allegience to their newly adopted states, passed a stiff language exam, had lived there for a specified number of years and had not had any affiliation to the Soviet 'occupying' army. Alla Chiiz was the least nationalist kind of Russian that could be found. She was a computer analyst who worked as a volunteer for local women's groups. Her husband Zhenya trained as a mathematician but spent much of his time as a concert singer. Whenever I visited St Petersburg, they would put me up. Once a month, they drove across to Tallinn to visit Alla's father, Mikhail. He was a retired army colonel who lived well, had never learnt a word of the language and had never doubted the Russians' right to be there. In 1959, at the age of thirty-two, he was sent to guard Estonia's border with Finland. He retired at fifty-five and supplemented his pension by working as a clerk in a shipbuilding firm in Tallinn. At the time of independence and market reforms, his firm was looking to rationalize. He was one of the first to be made redundant. He was told he could never become a citizen, and never privatize his own flat, as everyone else was doing. Chiiz was not an evil man, only a man living in a generation too late. 'He was proud of living in Estonia,' Alla said, 'but he died hating the country.' One of his last acts was to vote for Zhirinovsky. For the nationalists in Moscow, these 'Russians abroad' were becoming the fifth column, accorded a kind of hero status similar to that bestowed by Hitler on the Sudeten Germans. The Yeltsin government pandered to the resentment but tried to keep it within bounds. It huffed and puffed about withdrawing its troops, but continued to move them back to Russia. Kozyrev spoke of the West's hypocrisy in championing human rights in the Soviet Union in the 1970s and 1980s while ignoring what Russians saw as the violation of their basic rights in the Baltics in the 1990s.

Western attitudes towards the Baltics were only one example of a much-heralded partnership turning sour. Disappointment among the reformers was in large part a consequence of unnaturally high expectations and a misunderstanding of both the West's ability and its commitment to help. Many Russians had lumped together state expenditure with private corporate involvement, and Western companies were not going to invest seriously just for the sake of supporting a political sea change that was to their liking. From 1990 on the debate in the West over how much aid to give to Russia, how quickly, and on what terms, often missed the point. More important than the substance was the tone, and invariably Western leaders, company directors and bankers got it wrong. Russians would not sing for their supper. Most of the time the supper was not forthcoming.

Sergei Alexashenko, Deputy Finance Minister, put it caustically but accurately: 'The real influence of Western society on Russia's economic reforms is not very great. It would be greater if there were tangible results from Western cooperation.'

The Vancouver summit of April 1993 highlighted the problems facing both donor and recipient. It was a relationship between a banker having trouble with his board of directors and the applicant for a loan. The sum in question was $1.6 billion. Most of it was money reworked through the system to make the total look more than it really was. Yeltsin got to the point: 'Too little is not very good because it is not enough to enable you to solve problems. Too much also could be bad because it can be used by Communists to target us. The opposition will say we are shackled by the West.' Clinton wanted the money to look a lot in the eyes of Yeltsin's supporters but a little in the eyes of his opponents; a lot in the eyes of America's Western allies but not too much in the eyes of American voters. This was the first summit when no attempt was made to sweep the irritants in the relationship under the table. For the sake of the hardliners back home in Moscow, they were stressed for all they were worth.

Summits were becoming increasingly pointless. They became exercises in loss minimization. Pro-American rhetoric was distinctly out of fashion; ideas such as the 'Democracy Corps', agreed in Vancouver and designed to promote 'intensive people-to-people contact', belonged to the 1970s and 1980s. When Clinton visited Moscow in January 1994 he was eager to strike the right note, to give Yeltsin a slap on the back but not to be seen to be narrowing America's options. At Spaso House, the American Ambassador's residence, Anthony Lake, Clinton's National Security Adviser, discreetly sought out many of Yeltsin's opponents, including Zyuganov, the Communist leader. In virtually every sentence Clinton referred to Russia as 'a great country'. It was all too manufactured, too transparently playing to the gallery. The most telling indicator of how the relationship had cooled, or become more workmanlike, was not in any hostility that Clinton engendered, but in the lack of interest in his presence. Russian newspapers gave the event precious little coverage, devoting their column inches instead to the discovery of a new man in the life of Alla Pugacheva, Russia's plump peroxide queen of pop.

Zhirinovsky's rise brought home to Western leaders what they should have known a long time earlier, that this was no time to antagonize Russia. Yeltsin and Kozyrev had fought an enormous battle with most of the political elite over the war in Bosnia. Pressure was mounting for Russia to break ranks, to push for an end to sanctions against Serbia and to veto further military action in defence of the mainly Muslim Bosnian government. Hardline groups with strong links to parliament were continuing to send aid and volunteers to the Bosnian Serbs. What Yeltsin needed in order to stave off some of that pressure was a signal from the

West that he was a fellow participant at the diplomatic top table, not an afterthought. He was not getting what he wanted. Even when his special envoy, Vitaly Churkin, conjured up out of nothing a promise from the Serbs to pull their heavy weaponry away from Sarajevo, on the eve of threatened Western air strikes against them, the international community did not take adequate notice. Its attitude towards Russia as an awkward intruder was laid bare for all to see when the Americans launched NATO air strikes on Serbian positions outside the besieged town of Gorazde. Yeltsin was enraged. This, he said, is obviously what you call partnership. American explanations that *technically* they didn't have to let other countries know, that there had been no time, cut little ice.

'What has happened is that Russia, Europe and America have passed the stage of romanticism in post-totalitarian diplomacy when both sides embraced each other so tightly that national security interests were left aside.' Kostikov, Yeltsin's spokesman, was responding to another of the thorny issues that had arisen in East–West relations of late. This was the question of expanding NATO, an alliance Russians believed belonged to the Cold War era and should have been dismantled in return for Moscow's relatively peaceful retreat from empire. Zhirinovsky was having a dual effect on the new strategic balance. East European states were desperate for a security umbrella from the West to protect them against future Russian expansionism, and NATO was seen as the only effective such organization. The more progressive of the former Warsaw Pact satellites, Poland, the Czech Republic and Hungary, had already made enquiries about membership. The Russians were shocked when the Lithuanians also asked to sign up. Clinton's response was Partnership for Peace, a toned-down membership scheme that offered joint manoeuvres and close military consultation but studiously avoided committing NATO to extending its remit right up to Russia's borders. The Russians were also invited to join, but they were extremely wary of becoming just another junior member of a Western-dominated club. Hawks in the West accused their governments of running scared of the Russians, of bowing to threats and leaving the East Europeans in the lurch.

The more astute Western policy-makers realized the need to address Russian concerns head on, to eschew the flowery language of partnership and the narrow support of Yeltsin. Russia would not enter the fold if it felt patronized. One concrete measure keenly supported by Moscow was to turn the Group of Seven into the Group of Eight, even though in narrow economic terms, the next place at the table of the richest industrialized nations was not for Russia's taking. 'Russian foreign policy inevitably has to be of an independent and assertive nature,' Kozyrev wrote in an impassioned plea to American policy-makers. 'If Russian democrats fail to achieve it, they will be swept away by a wave of aggressive nationalism, which is now exploiting the need for national and state self-assertion.'

Gaidar put it more bluntly when asked about the future affiliation of Eastern Europe. 'You have a choice. You can have the Baltics in NATO and Zhirinovsky in the Kremlin, or you can have the Baltics out of NATO and Yeltsin in the Kremlin.' Better the devil you know.

19
The Inventor

'Let us drink to the new-born child.' Mikhail Kalashnikov spoke hesitantly into the microphone, his shrill voice wavering. The grand old man of Russian weaponry was addressing hundreds of VIPs – government ministers, military top brass and foreign diplomats. They had gathered in a government guesthouse in Sparrow Hills to celebrate the birth of Rosvooruzheniye, a state company that would promote and coordinate Russian arms sales abroad. It was a glittering affair – trout, salmon, caviar, sucking-pig, washed down with vodka and the best wines from the former Soviet Union – just like the good old days. But not quite. Arms exports from Russia had plummeted from $20 billion a year in the 1980s to $4 billion in 1993. Entire cities were dependent on the industry, and hundreds of thousands of workers, some of the country's most highly qualified, were on part-time labour. Full-time unemployment loomed. Many of the armaments that were going abroad were doing so illegally. Defence officials and soldiers stole the contents of entire depots and sold them off – 10,000 unneeded tanks, thousands of assault rifles and other arms. Kalashnikovs were going for as little as $50 each, well below market value.

There always seemed to be something sanctimonious about the West's objections to the trade. A nation whose industry was contracting by the day was being told by the outside world that it should not be dealing in arms. Russia had already lost its dominance of the market with many of its former allies, who were turning to the West for military imports. When Moscow tried to sell missile technology to India, the Americans turned the affair into a diplomatic incident, warning of the dangers of proliferation. On that occasion, the Russians yielded. But the affair caused bad blood and in future they wouldn't be so amenable to persuasion. Western concerns that disillusioned scientists and experts might turn to all-comers to make a buck or two were not without foundation. But the Russians saw in the warnings a broader conspiracy, that the Westerners wanted to hog the market for themselves.

Rosvooruzheniye was set up in November 1993 with exclusive rights to sell arms abroad. The aim was to end the confusion of previous years when separate government agencies competed against each other. 'The military–industrial complex is living through tough times at the moment. We've got to get out there and sell the stuff,' Kalashnikov said, putting on his best marketing man's voice. He would travel to Moscow from his home town of Izhevsk, in the Ural mountains, to help wherever he could. In a matter of a year or two he had been virtually around the world to arms fairs in Europe, the USA, even Abu Dhabi. He was his own trademark. What Coca-Cola was for America, the Kalashnikov was for Russia. Selling was not what he had dedicated his life to, but duty was duty.

Kalashnikov's story was a microcosm of the tragedy of Soviet industry. For all his inventions, for all his patriotism, he had little to show for his decades of toil. The furniture in his two-bedroomed flat in Soviet Street was paid for out of the Stalin Prize he won before he was thirty. More than 70 million of his assault rifles had been sold around the world, but he had received barely a penny's worth of royalties for them. Only Soviet Communism could have exploited such brilliance with such ruthlessness and disdain. So revolutionary was the AK-47 (literally, Automatic Kalashnikov made in 1947) that for the first years of production it was carried in a special case. Photographs were forbidden, cartridge cases had to be picked up after firing. Young Kalashnikov was sworn to secrecy. He could not tell his parents what he was doing. Even in the early 1980s he was ordered not to reply to a letter from an American academic. Few people recognized him on the streets. Only in his home village of Kurya in the mountainous region of Altai, near the Mongolian border, had a statue been erected to him. Belatedly, the authorities in Izhevsk decided to honour him with a bust in the centre of the city; but the idea became bogged down in bureaucracy.

Kalashnikov was still working at Izhmash, the arms factory to which he devoted most of his life. It was there that many of the Soviet Union's most secret weapons were produced. Izhevsk started making guns more than a century ago. Until the end of 1991 it was a closed city. As soon as it lost its special status it sought foreign orders to keep its hundreds of thousands of workers off the dole. Many were put on short time or enforced 'holiday'. Officially, Kalashnikov retained his title as chief designer. He would go in most days, turning his meticulous attention to a new hunting rifle.

I accompanied Kalashnikov, his son Viktor, and his friends on a hunting expedition. It was the day after his seventy-fourth birthday. We were going to look for elk in pine forests three hours into the countryside from Izhevsk. The thermometer outside the hunting lodge had slipped below minus 20°C. For the hunters conditions were perfect, but little time remained before the sun would go down. In the new free-market society, shooting had become the pastime of the rich. Kalashnikov and his four colleagues warmed themselves by the open fire and gulped down a small glass of cranberry vodka. One quick inspection of their weapons and it was time to get moving. They donned their *valenki*, the felt-lined boots designed a century ago, for which there is no modern match, and their *tulupi*, ankle-length woollen coats.

We clambered on to the back of an army truck, shielding our faces from the biting cold. The vehicle ground into action, drowning out all conversation. For Kalashnikov, it made no difference. A life of firing weapons had left him hard of hearing. The hunters spotted small footprints; the lorry veered down a steep incline in pursuit. On we went, around and around the forest, a veritable maze, but the elk eluded us. Morale began to drop: thoughts turned to the warm lodge and to an evening of jokes and reminiscences. Kalashnikov's face creased up. Suddenly, someone cried 'over there'. A split second later three shots rang out and an animal tumbled to the ground. The truck raced between the trees to the booty. The elk had been shot clean through the neck. They jumped down and tied its body to a rope and the lorry dragged it the remaining mile home across the snow. The mood lightened. It must be Viktor, they decided, who should claim the spoils.

It was pitch dark by the time we made it back. Before the evening meal, Kalashnikov decided to take a sauna, the favoured Russian way of unwinding. He stripped and scampered the twenty yards to the *banya* hut. Inside, he breathed slowly and deeply, his gold teeth glinting through the steam. Alone with him, I asked about his invention. Was he the creator of another Frankenstein? Had his monster grown out of control? Could he really be a maker of widows? His voice creaked. 'When the Germans invaded I saw my comrades in pain. They were being wheeled into hospital, injured in defence of their motherland against the fascists. Courage was not enough. The Nazis had superior armoury. I wanted to redress the balance.' Kalashnikov skipped forty years to a Soviet Union in collapse, where army conscripts and their officers were selling his rifles for a song. 'D'you think it's pleasant seeing all those hoodlums using your gun? Armenians and Azeris killing each other. We all lived so peacefully before.' This was the great 'family of nations' that was the Soviet Union.

He recalled meeting Yeltsin during a presidential visit to Izhevsk towards the end of 1992. 'I told him I saw no reason why he had to get rid of our USSR, our motherland.' What most appalled Kalashnikov, and millions of his fellow countrymen, was the sight of Russian killing Russian during the battle for the White House. 'Look at how much it's cost to repair that building – billions, they say. What was the point of it all? I thought we voted for those people in parliament.' An army man through and through, Kalashnikov was slipping into the murky waters of politics. He quickly brought himself into line with a curt: 'Anyway, politicians aren't worth talking about.' But it was not hard to draw conclusions. Here was a man who loved his country – the Soviet Union – intensely. Even so, he was restrained in his criticism of Yeltsin. Authority, after all, is authority. He was, he said, very obliging when Korzhakov's men came to visit the other day, shortly after the October events, enquiring about the latest guns. They were presumably preparing themselves for another hardline revolt.

What galled Kalashnikov most of all were the spivs who had hijacked his invention. 'Russia, the West, it's basically the same. They're out to make money from you. All they want is some free advice on improving their weapons.' His first visit to the Cold War enemy was to Washington in May 1990 where he was introduced to his American counterpart Eugene Stoner. Kalashnikov's clothes were shabby. The few dollars in his pocket had been given by the factory and by the American institute that was sponsoring the trip. He was dumbfounded by the inequality of the treatment. 'Stoner has his own aircraft, I can't afford my own plane ticket.'

How could one of the great inventions of modern times have been the work of a country boy with barely an education, who could not draw and knew nothing about guns? The beginnings could not have been more humble. After basic secondary schooling he became a technician on the Turkestan–Siberian railway. It was the time of Stalin's crash industrialization. Kalashnikov wanted to play his part in the great experiment. To begin with, he tried his hand at a device to measure fuel consumption in train fuel tanks, but nothing much came of it. Then the war came, and he was drafted as a tank mechanic to the front, near Bryansk. Within months he was injured, and it was in hospital that he became obsessed by his dream. 'I decided to construct a gun of my own which could stand up to the Germans. It was a bit of a crazy escapade, I suppose. I didn't have any specialist education and I couldn't even draw.'

His first designs did not attract much attention, but on release from hospital he went back to his engine workshop in the Altai to try to make a prototype. Nobody seemed to mind that he spent all his time on his 'hobby', and it was not long before he was on his way to Alma Ata, with his first model in his hand. On arrival in the town he was briefly arrested for carrying unauthorized firearms, but the police released him when he told them of his dream project. Kalashnikov went straight to the Party official in charge of defence matters and pleaded for advice. He was sent to the workshop of the prestigious Moscow Aviation Institute, which had been evacuated to the Kazakh capital. But he soon became frustrated. Eventually, after a determined battle with the bureaucrats, he finally made it to Moscow. There he could compete with the best.

The early days were not easy. The diminutive sergeant was scorned by the top brass, generals such as Vasily Degtaryov, the most prominent weapons designer between the wars. So shy was Kalashnikov that he signed his sketches 'MikhTim', the first syllables of his first names. But he persevered, and by 1949 had been awarded the Stalin Prize and made a Hero of Socialist Labour. The same year he was transferred to Izhevsk to supervise production, and by the mid-1950s the AK was standard issue to the Soviet armed forces. General Degtaryov had been usurped. Kalashnikov joined the Communist Party only in 1953. He could not avoid it. He was neither a believer nor a rebel, he simply wanted to get on with his job. Only in the 1960s, when he became a member of the Supreme Soviet, which then met for only a few days a year, did he come out of the shadows.

He met his wife Yekaterina at an army testing range near Moscow. She was a graphic artist and helped him put his designs on paper. They married in 1943 and had four children. He saw little of them. Yekaterina died in 1977 after a long illness and his youngest daughter Natalia moved in to keep him company; but tragedy struck again when she died in a car crash six years later. He has lived alone for the past ten years, although Yelena, his remaining daughter, goes around on Sundays to do the cleaning. 'After a long day together, I get the feeling he wants me to go,' she said. His deafness increased his isolation. Sometimes, it seemed, he pretended he could not hear just to be on his own.

His only perks were a driver and a country *dacha* by the lake, and even these were given by the local authorities only after a friend, a retired Tatar colonel, shouted at a pompous official: 'You think you're God, but they'll write about him, not you, in the history books.' He relied on a small circle of friends, most of them from the military. The exception was Valentin Sokolov, an expert on animal husbandry who became Deputy Prime Minister of the local region for a while. Sokolov has remained at his side, playing the joker, the fall guy in countless hunting reminiscences. 'They always suspected Kalashnikov,' Sokolov recalled. 'He stood out from the bureaucrats, because he had a brain. They were jealous and thought him wilful.' Wherever he travelled within the old USSR, Kalashnikov took Sokolov with him. 'The locals thought I was his bodyguard,' the doctor said with pride.

The post-hunt dinner was ready and the Kalashnikov clan assembled. Sokolov was to his right, Viktor to his left. There was also Yuri, the manager of the hunting lodge, Boris, his assistant, and Nikolai, who used to be the Defence Ministry's representative at the Izhmash plant. We squashed on to two wooden benches in the small kitchen as Yelena dished up the traditional feast – elk's liver fried with onions, and boiled tongue. The toasts commenced: to the motherland, to hospitality, to a meeting with foreigners that until a year or so earlier would have been impossible. Kalashnikov stood up and addressed the assembled. His language was terse. The words seemed strangely rehearsed. Perhaps this time they were. There was much that he wanted to say. 'My life's not been easy. I wanted my invention to serve peace. I didn't want it to make war easier.' Each sentence was received in silence, as if at a confessional. 'You see, constructors have never been given their just deserts in this country. If the politicians had worked as hard as we did, the guns would never have got into the wrong hands.'

20

Guns 'N' Roses

▬▬▬▬▬▬

B y 1994 the killers had come out of the closet. Until then, most of the violence had been confined to shoot-outs between rival gangs. *Razborki*, they called them, the settling of scores. Cars would draw up outside offices or show rooms and open fire liberally on the owners who had refused to pay protection money. Anyone in business was fair game. Two acquaintances of mine were killed in gangland murders within weeks of each other. Robert Vartanian was a disc jockey in St Petersburg, who had been enjoying his job for years. He was shot dead by a professional killer in the small hours of the morning as he walked home from his club, Nevskiye Zvyozdy, Neva Stars. There was no obvious motive, except for his refusal to ally himself with a particular group. His despairing widow, Irina, had to be restrained at the funeral from saying anything untoward, such as that the killers should be brought to trial. Vartanian was a close friend of Troitsky, the rock promoter who had talked of the conspiracy of silence about the mafia only a few days earlier. The other victim, Marat, was a small-time entrepreneur dealing in videos. He had had links with the KGB and presumed he was safe. He was shot at point-blank range by an intruder at a friend's *dacha*. Marat's crime was to have taken on the mob in a business that is highly lucrative and strictly controlled.

So frequent were these murders that one newspaper started a daily column which delved into gory detail on the most interesting killing of the moment. One of the most baffling cases was the discovery of seven corpses. Two lone and poorly armed policemen stumbled on the bodies at dawn after stopping a little Zhiguli car which was incongruously towing a Mercedes. The victims were lying on the back seat and in the boot of the Mercedes, with a pistol-toting Tajik sitting in the front. An unemployed twenty-year-old man was driving the Zhiguli, and the boss of a local firm was in the passenger seat. Investigators later ascertained that the killers had been waiting on the landing outside the flat of one of the victims. They gunned him and several of his associates down in the flat. His bodyguards had been waiting downstairs. Suspecting that something was wrong, they ran up to the flat, walked in, and were gunned down too. The murderers took the bodies down one by one, dumped them in the Mercedes, but found out that it wouldn't start. So they flagged down a *chastnik*, a private driver who was looking to make a bit of money on the side by doubling up as a taxi-driver. The unsuspecting moonlighter asked for 15,000 roubles (just over £5). He didn't ask who, or what, was in the Mercedes, not even when the mafiosi asked him to drive them to a rubbish dump on the edge of the city, a popular spot to deposit corpses, douse them with petrol and set them ablaze. Police had to release him, as his pleas of innocence were impossible to challenge. What remained unclear was why the criminals driving with him didn't take on the police when stopped.

Often the law enforcement agencies and the criminals were in league. In the provinces, the system was far more simple, the spheres of influence more clearly defined. In Vladimir, to the east of Moscow, the GAI traffic police would tip off highwaymen after stopping particular lorries that had not paid them off. The scam continued for months. In Kazan, capital of Tatarstan, criminal gangs insisted on a 'road tax' from drivers of 'smart' cars (that even included Soviet-made Volgas). Failure to pay up would lead the traffic police to find a pretext for confiscating the vehicle.

According to a report early in 1994 by Pyotr Filippov, head of the President's Analytical Centre for Social and Economic Policy, up to 80 per cent of businesses and banks, and all retail outlets, paid protection. Much of their money was spirited out by banks, only for the bankers themselves to be picked off to prevent disclosure. In 1993, the Interior Ministry recorded around 13,000 crimes by government officials, ranging from power abuse to forgery, but these by definition were the small fry. The figures invariably did not take account of the bigger players.

Foreigners often started with good intentions that were soon destroyed. It was extremely difficult to get by without paying protection. The only way around the problem was to have friends in high places who might frighten off the extortionists, or to be such a large enterprise that even they might not have the resources to take it on. As General Mikhail Yegorov, head of the Interior Ministry's department on fighting organized crime, put it: 'They know how to find you. They make it their business to find your business. For them "no" is not an acceptable answer.' Complaints by Westerners about extortion demands rarely aroused sympathy. Resentment and paranoia were emotions fostered under the Communists. A Western company that had done well must, by definition, be cheating someone, and, naturally, raping Mother Russia. There was nothing wrong in taking something back.

Most kept their stories to themselves, for fear of reprisals from the gangs or trouble from the authorities. But the stories often slipped out. There was the case of an American bar manager. When his joint enterprise opened in the centre of Moscow in the spring of 1993 it was hailed as a breakthrough, a moderately priced all-day cafe, not one of the plethora of expensive restaurants or sleazy nightclubs. For the first few months it was packed with 'normal' Russians and foreigners, drinking quietly. Then the heavies began to appear at the door, entrance fees were demanded, the bands playing music became more lurid and tacky, and the clientele changed to the men in the loud sports jackets with their scantily clad 'girlfriends'. One day, after complaining once too often, the American manager was given $2,000 in cash and a one-way plane ticket back home, and told to not to come back. His losses were immense.

As Troitsky and others had lamented, names would be named in private, jokes would be told, but the 'thieves in law' as the godfathers were known, never came to light. Until the murder of Otari Kvantrishvili, that is.

His killers had been staking out the Krasnopresensky *banya*. From the attic of a block of flats in Solyarny Lane there was a clear line of fire. At 5.45 p.m. on 5 April 1994, Kvantrishvili left the *banya* with his bodyguards. *Banyas* had through the years been places where the mobsters could relax. In the old days they were given private rooms. After taking the steam, they would relax, playing cards, eating and drinking, and making deals. With the onset of market forces, the entry price had become so expensive – up to £10 in some cases – that the general public could no longer enjoy one of the most traditional and popular of all pastimes. Sportsman, philanthropist, businessman, politician-in-the-making, Kvantrishvili had no such financial problems. At forty-six he was one of the untouchables, with friends in the Kremlin, parliament, police headquarters, on all sides of the political divide. From 200 yards away he was killed with three shots fired from a German-made rifle.

The funeral, three days later, was a spectacle to behold. Never before had the political and artistic elite and the gangsters come together in such public communion. They came in their thousands to the Vagankovskoye cemetery to bid farewell. Many of the wreaths said simply 'from your friends'. In the pecking order of resting places this cemetery would probably come third, after the Kremlin Wall (the last ashes placed there were Chernenko's in 1984) and Novodevichy (where Khrushchev joined Gogol, Chekhov, Eisenstein and Prokofiev). There were few more prestigious places of interment than Vagankovskoye. From the entrance, where the men in the dark glasses stood alongside their limousines, Kvantrishvili's mourners walked past the memorial to Vladimir Vysotsky, the bard who more than anyone epitomized and illumined the despair of Brezhnev's stagnation years. Further into the compound lay the graves of the three young men killed in the 1991 coup. Alongside them was a more impressive tombstone to the pop star, Igor Talkov, shot as he sang his angry folksy ballads in a theatre in St Petersburg at the end of 1991. He became a martyr to the cause, and word had it that he had been killed by 'Jews'.

Another recent arrival at the cemetery was Oleg Karatayev, boxer and racketeer, who was killed leaving a restaurant in Brighton Beach. For the

American government, the activities of some members of Russia's Jewish diaspora in this small corner of New York state had become embarrassing. It was reluctantly having to come to terms with the realization that some of those 'refuseniks' over whom it fought with the Soviet government during the tense negotiations of the Cold War had become common criminals, and not petty ones, but major international gangland leaders. When Karatayev was cut down, it was Kvantrishvili who naturally arranged his guard of honour and his burial, close to Vysotsky.

Kvantrishvili was born in Zestafoni, western Georgia, in 1948, but grew up in the Krasnopresensky district of Moscow. He and his brother were said to have been brought up by the crime family that ran the area, who led them into underground gambling, mainly on horse races and cards. He was a wrestler of impressive standing. He was jailed for gang rape in 1966 and in 1970 sent to hospital in Lublino, near Moscow, for mild schizophrenia. It was a convenient step to secure his eventual release. By the early 1980s he was working as an Olympic coach at Dynamo sports club, which was run by the KGB and Interior Ministry. There he would meet policemen and sportsmen on the fringes of crime. He and a friend, Iosif Kobzon, started a foundation called Shield and Lyre, designed to help policemen and their families in Moscow. He came to know other 'authorities' in the crime world, figures nicknamed 'the Taiwanese' and 'the Snowball Tree'.

Kvantrishvili began making serious money when he opened the first hard-currency casinos in Moscow. To have done so in the mid-1980s, under Communism, required cooperation from the authorities. He moved on from there to raw materials. The deceptively named Sports Academy, a closed joint-stock company of which Kvantrishvili was director, was agent for the export of hundreds of thousands of tons of cement, aluminium, titanium, fuel oil and various ores, drawn from state reserves. It was also an import agent for consumer goods for many other companies, including kiosk distributors. It was all about licences, and Kvantrishvili had all the ones that mattered. In return, he gave large sums of money to orphanages and Afghan war veterans (a group with which Burbulis was linked). Shortly before Kvantrishvili's death, Yeltsin signed an order giving the Academy freedom from both export and import taxes from 1993 to 1995, a concession worth trillions of roubles.

Who killed Kvantrishvili? There were several versions of the answer – his business partners, rival gang leaders, or the authorities themselves. There had been an unwritten rule that mobsters, however powerful, keep themselves in the shadows. Kvantrishvili had instead become a household name. He created a Fund for the Social Protection of Athletes, named after the famous international goalkeeper, Lev Yashin, to help retired sportsmen. His name was behind the League of Professional Boxers. Not a week went by when his smiling face did not fill the television screens.

He didn't drink or smoke, but he enjoyed the good life. He was seen at the weddings, funerals and parties of famous men and women. He counted among his good friends the head of the Moscow police department. Kvantrishvili, it was said, was one of only a handful of non-employees who could walk into the police's Petrovka headquarters without a permit. He started investing in legal businesses, buying into hotels, factories, oil wells, timber yards. He was on the board of directors of one of Russia's leading banks. Just after the storming of the White House in 1993 he even created his own political party, Athletes of Russia, an amusing front but one that could have become influential. But in the weeks prior to his death Kvantrishvili sensed that the mood was shifting against him. He had asked the police to help his bodyguards with additional protection, but had not received it.

He was buried next to his brother, Amiran, who had been killed the previous August by a Chechen group. On that occasion, Yeltsin had sent him a letter of condolence. This time, the chief pall-bearers were the popular singers Alexander Rozenbaum and Kobzon, who had flown in from Los Angeles, where he had one of his homes. Over 100 other 'thieves in law' were present. One mourner was a close former aide to Rutskoy; another was Bogdan Titomir, Russia's most famous rap artist. The media treated the affair with a circumspection borne of fear, but when one gingerly broke ranks, and stated what everyone knew of the deceased's links with the underworld, the rest followed suit. Russian Television was braver than most, using the soundtrack of *The Godfather* to accompany the report on its news bulletin. 'We have lost a leader,' said Rozenbaum. 'I am not afraid to use that word.'

Kobzon had been one of the many 'unmentionables'. He had made his first money importing carpets and other items while entertaining the troops, Vera Lynn style, in Afghanistan. He then made several strategic trips to East Germany, from where he was allowed to export back Western consumer goods. He was reported to own several buildings in East Berlin. After Kvantrishvili's death, Kobzon said he feared for his life. His friends in the Kremlin tried to put his mind at rest by reinforcing his guard. They persuaded Kobzon to stay, and he entertained them royally. He organized concerts, brought in Western showbiz stars like Liza Minnelli, who beamed all over when joined on stage by Kobzon and Sobchak, the Mayor of St Petersburg, to sing the folk song 'Kalinka' arm-in-arm with her. Kobzon had more money than he had time to spend it. He presented his daughter with a little *pied-à-terre* on Tverskaya Street: five rooms, with a green marbled bathroom the size of the average flat and a state-of-the-art German kitchen. Not bad for a seventeen-year-old schoolchild.

Another friend of Kvantrishvili's was Tarpishev, the President's tennis coach and close confidant. After Yeltsin became a deputy in the Soviet parliament in 1989, when his health was anything but robust, he was persuaded to take up the sport. Tennis was perfect for Yeltsin. It was a modern, vigorous and Western-looking pastime. Yeltsin had a few trainers to start with, but his introduction to Tarpishev by his friend and bodyguard Korzhakov was enough of a recommendation.

In June 1993, in the midst of all the corruption sagas, Yeltsin signed order number 473. So many papers were laid on his desk that this one probably hardly caught his eye. This document established a national sports foundation, not a particularly controversial move given the sorry state into which the once world-beating Soviet sports machine had fallen. Any means of accruing money for the good of sport surely had to be welcomed. Yet, as with so many licences, this one was aimed as much at rewarding loyalty by allowing individuals to profit as at philanthropy. The foundation would become a limited company with two trading arms. It would be freed from all import and export duties for three years, would not have to pay back to the state the usual proportion of hard-currency profits, and would be granted large quotas to export cement, mercury, titanium, aircraft fuel, aluminium and other ores. Apart from Tarpishev, the other main figure in this project was, perhaps inevitably, Kvantrishvili. However indirectly, the President had signed over a series of economic privileges to a man of doubtful repute.

More surprising than the actual revelation of this transaction was the lack of reaction it caused. The newspaper which broke the story, *Novaya Ezhednevnaya Gazeta*, which was allied to the Gorbachev Foundation, said 2.5 trillion roubles (about £800 million) of potential state revenues had been lost overall by the waiving of export duties and other restrictions – invariably granted to political allies. The system of patronage was proving costly, although a small minority were getting very rich. The practice had been pursued with a vengeance by Chernomyrdin, especially in his first year in power. Wherever there was a friend, he would help out, liquidating billion-rouble debts owed by banks and granting long-term loans at fixed rates well below inflation. The government was acting like a charity organization for over 200,000 industrial companies. The Prime Minister was especially forgiving to the gas and oil industry, his power base.

A few days after Kvantrishvili's passing, *Komsomolskaya Pravda* published a taped conversation he had had with one of its journalists. 'They write that I'm the mafia's godfather,' he said. 'It was Vladimir Ilyich Lenin who was the real organizer of the mafia and who set up the criminal state. I'm really an honest man.' He was genuinely popular, among sportsmen, pensioners and others in financial trouble. Also, his kind would help budding entrepreneurs by providing low-interest or interest-free loans to help them start out. The only thing demanded in return was staunch loyalty. Perversely, Kvantrishvili's high profile had given some a sense of security. He had been the public face of the mafia. His death, they feared, might signal the start of a new phase of criminal operations, with the mantle passing on from the semi-official public figures to more sinister, behind-the-scenes gang leaders. Now, for the first time, names could be named. Or so some thought.

Andrei Aizderdzis was a businessman. He was also an exposer of mafia activities. He was further a member of parliament, albeit not a prominent one. He was gunned down on the staircase of his block of flats as he stepped out of his car at his home in the affluent suburb of Khimki. His killer had hidden in the basement of the nine-storey block, firing one blast from a pump-action shotgun into his chest at close range through a ventilation shaft before abandoning his gun and fleeing. It was another highly professional job. Somebody bore a grudge. Was it his work as a member of the New Regional Policy faction in parliament? Hardly, it was one of the least controversial of the groups represented. Was it the work of his private bank, MDK, whose chairmanship he had handed over on election to the Duma? Possibly. Or was it the fact that a magazine put out by his company had published a list of the 266 most famous 'thieves in law', the godfathers, who were ruling Russia? Not to be ruled out.

News of the murder left deputies in parliament stunned and angry. It was one thing for gunmen to go around shooting or blowing up ordinary entrepreneurs, quite another for them to go for a member of the State Duma, who enjoyed full immunity. An emergency closed session of parliament was called in which a resolution was passed demanding the sacking of Yerin, the Interior Minister. He had hardly distinguished himself during the October events, or indeed before or after them. He was in charge of a ministry supposedly at the forefront of the battle against crime; yet by his own admission there had been 250 contract murders stemming from protection disputes in 1993, more than twice as many as in 1992. Yeltsin ignored the calls. Whatever Yerin's competence, he had proven himself staunchly loyal.

No sooner had they got over one drama than another deputy, Sergei Skorochkin, said he had killed a mobster in self-defence after a dispute over extortion rackets. Before joining the Duma he had owned a vodka distillery in his home town of Zaraisk, 100 miles-south east of Moscow. He admitted that he had paid off the mob for some time, the last major instalment being $15,000 dollars to a gang that had threatened to kill him. The visits then became more frequent. The local state prosecutor was in their pocket, so appeals to the authorities were useless. The intimidation came to a head when, driving home from a restaurant, he found his way blocked by seven men and a car. One of them, he said, opened fire. He shot back, killing him. The others fled. 'I have nothing to hide. I don't consider myself guilty of anything.' Skorochkin became a national hero overnight.

Prosecutors, judges, anyone could be bought, for tasks big or small. Many of the bribes were for humdrum business, as in the case of friend of mine, Olga. She had lived with her mother in a room in a *kommunalka*, a communal flat, in the centre of Moscow. Communal flats were Khrushchev's answer to the housing shortage, forcing groups of complete strangers – families, single people, pensioners – to share cramped living quarters. As soon as the housing market was freed up under Gaidar's reforms, *kommunalka* inhabitants were desperate to find one-room flats, even in the back of beyond, to escape the ordeal. The more enterprising stayed put, hoping to be the last remaining residents. Olga was one such example, and after a two-year battle she managed to 'privatize' the entire apartment – at a cost. It was situated in the most chic part of town, close to the Patriarch's Pond that had been made famous by Bulgakov's seminal novel, *The Master and Margarita*. Olga had to bribe the judge hearing the case two million roubles (just over $1,000), and pay her lawyer almost the same amount. She eventually received the required documents. The money was considerable, but with the value of such properties running at over $100,000, and with loans available at low interest, it was a snip. There were countless stories like hers of prospective home-owners, office or shop proprietors. To do anything required paperwork, and paperwork required rewards. Almost none of these transactions ever resulted in prosecution. The police complained of lack of adequate legislation. They were having to use the Russian criminal code of October 1960 which, though it had been amended dozens of times, was anachronistic and unequal to the task, making no distinct reference, for example, to corruption. In 1993, only 236 companies and 423 individuals had their books checked by the tax inspectorate, out of tens of thousands that were operating in the country. By the start of 1994, some 5,700 criminal groups were operating inside Russia, according to Interior Ministry figures; the number of major syndicates with international links was put at more than 300. These organizations are estimated to spend 30 per cent of their profits on bribes, keeping officials sweet.

All over the world, the Russian mafia was becoming hot news. Journalists outdid themselves to track down the most brutal murders. After shootings came kidnaps (seventy-two in Moscow in the first three months of 1993 alone) and car bombs. The reports had a devastating effect on Russia's image abroad. So incensed was Mayor Sobchak at the label given to St Petersburg, the 'mafia capital of Russia', that he used a visit by Prince Charles to try to convince the outside world that the dangers had been exaggerated. The German Embassy submitted an official note to the Russians expressing concern over the crime situation, and made it clear that the local law enforcement agencies were not capable of providing businesses with sufficient protection. The embassy said that if the situation deteriorated further it would consider recommending that German companies withdraw from the Russian market.

Each Western country had its uses. Italy and America provided contacts with other groups; Germany was the first port of call for drugs, arms smuggling and prostitution rackets. The BKA, the German Federal Police, identified about 10,000 women from Eastern Europe and former Soviet states, many aged under sixteen, who had been kidnapped, threatened or lured to the West with false promises by organized criminal gangs. With the closure of the Balkan route as a result of the war in the former Yugoslavia, Russia became one of the most important transit routes for narcotics, with Russian groups forming close alliances with Colombian and other cartels.

According to Italian investigators, crime groups from Italy and Russia held two 'summits' in 1992 and 1993 – one in Prague, the other in Warsaw – to discuss 'drug money laundering, drug trafficking and selling nuclear material'. London, the financial centre, was where much of the money was laundered. It was no wonder that Russia had over 2,000 institutions calling themselves banks. The minimum capital requirement was just 100 million roubles (less than £50,000), a figure that was constantly being devalued in real terms by inflation. Even the Central Bank agreed. 'A situation where entrepreneurs face the choice of either buying a good car or setting up a bank is paradoxical and abnormal,' said one senior official. Many of the banks had been established with only one aim in mind, as a vehicle for laundering dirty money. The gangs had so much money they didn't know how to spend it. One bank fraud alone had brought them $500 million – a third of the size of the loan the Russian government spent months negotiating with the IMF.

By 1994, more than $40 billion had been taken out of the country (twice the sum total of money that the G7 said it could conjure up, long-term, for Russia). Half of that total was swilling about the London financial system. The British government's National Criminal Intelligence Service made no secret of the problem, or of the task it was facing. One of its difficulties was the absence of an effective opposite partner in Moscow. Their fears were confirmed when an Englishwoman, Karen Reed, was murdered on her front doorstep in Woking, Surrey. The commercial hit-men, who were thought to be Israeli, were working on behalf of the Chechens, two of whose senior figures were killed in London the year before. The man sentenced to life imprisonment for their murder, an Armenian, was Karen Reed's brother-in-law. Her sister was taken into police protection. The criminals operated under false passports. Some lived most of the year in the country, having set up UK-registered companies for the transfer of capital from the former USSR to offshore banks. Others would come and go more or less frequently, smuggling in with them weaponry for sale to terrorist groups.

By far the worst nightmare for Western law enforcement agencies was the prospect of Russian organized crime acquiring nuclear material. German police recovered several consignments of plutonium and other substances of low or just below weapons-grade quality. The discoveries were most certainly the thin end of the wedge. The Americans were also taking the 'atom mafia' with the utmost seriousness. Announcing the opening of an FBI office in Moscow, the bureau's director, Louis Freeh, said the worst in Russian crime was still ahead. 'We must focus on the possibility of organized crime, rogue nations or bands of terrorists obtaining nuclear weapons or weapons-grade plutonium and uranium from Russia and any other source,' Freeh told the US Congress. 'There are vast amounts of nuclear weapons and nuclear materials in the former Soviet Union. It is the greatest long-term threat to the security of the United States.' The Russian government acknowledged that North Korea had been actively scouting for components for nuclear weapons from criminal organizations after apparently failing to attract Russian nuclear scientists to work for them. Five North Koreans were expelled. The authorities revealed that as far back as 1992 a group of Russian experts from the strategic rocket forces was stopped as it was about to fly to Pyongyang.

Some Russian politicians, especially the radicals, shrugged off these concerns. Popov, the former Mayor of Moscow, had said from the outset that corruption was not only inevitable, it was laudable. It was the start of the transfer of money, the understanding of the value of money. With time that money would be washed clean, much of it would return from dodgy Swiss bank accounts into respectable Russian corporations. After all, had not many of the big names in America started out in an unsavoury business environment? Did not the descendants of the robber barons of the late nineteenth century become pillars of the establishment?

Presumption of innocence before guilt was another convenient excuse. The débâcle over the Rutskoy investigation had shown that suspicion of a criminal act was not good enough to see off political opponents. The complacency was staggering. Yeltsin tried hard to have Ilyushenko, his more malleable investigator, confirmed as Prosecutor General. For Ilyushenko, the man who should have been leading the hunt, low-level corruption was all down to job insecurity. 'I know the psychology of the civil servant. He's not inclined to take risks. He takes bribes because he's not sure what will happen to him tomorrow. The chair he's sitting on is too rickety. If he had some guarantee from the state about his future he would have less reason to give in to the temptation of corruption.'

Time and again Yeltsin had promised tough action, but little ever seemed to come of these assurances. In May 1994 he unveiled a new strategy, calling for the allocation of five trillion roubles (nearly £2 billion) to the war against organized crime, with better training and equipment for police and surveillance of corruption within their ranks. A few weeks later the authorities launched Operation Hurricane in Moscow, involving 20,000 heavily armed Interior Ministry troops and regular officers. More than 2,200 suspects were detained during two days of raids on companies, banks, hotels and markets. Charges were brought against 750 of them. · Nearly 200 commercial enterprises were suspended, while the government told regional leaders to prepare for a package of emergency measures against mobsters, especially in cities such as St Petersburg, Yekaterinburg and Vladivostok. The authorities claimed the crackdown had been a great success. In reality it hadn't. Most of the mafiosi had been tipped off beforehand by moles inside police headquarters. Those caught were small fry.

The presidential team drew up a decree giving sweeping powers of detention and detection to the police. Yeltsin said he would stake his reputation on the battle to 'cleanse Russia of criminal filth'. The decree gave security forces the right to detain suspects for thirty days without trial and allowed prosecutors to search premises and trawl through bank accounts of anyone suspected of mafia involvement without a court order. In parliament, which only a few weeks earlier had been gripped with hysteria following the murder of Aizderdzis, many deputies opposed the measures, arguing that they endangered civil liberties and violated the constitution. The head of parliament's committee on legal affairs said Yeltsin was treating the constitution like a prostitute, 'using it only when he needs it'. Only a few months earlier, during the state of emergency in October 1993, the police had shown how arbitrary their interpretation of the law was. With considerably reinforced powers, it was feared that the police and the security services could be manipulated by criminal bosses to close down rival firms and use violence against their directors. Such nice scruples, however, cut little ice among a population frightened to leave their homes at night.

Two bomb attacks on one day gave Yeltsin the impulse he needed to overrule parliament and push his decree through. Boris Berezovsky, General Manager of the Logovaz firm in the town of Togliatti, where the Zhiguli was made, escaped with only cuts after an explosion ripped out the front of his car outside Moscow's Paveletsky Station. His driver had his head blown off. Berezovsky had become a target because he had lobbied successfully with the government to impose extra duties on the import of foreign cars, to give the little Zhiguli, or Lada, as it was known in the West, a chance. The people who ran the dealerships weren't too happy.

For once, it looked as if Yeltsin was serious. But even if he was sincere, did he have the power or incentive to persuade the thousands of corrupt officials in the police and elsewhere to sever their links with the criminals? Boldyrev, the man sacked by Yeltsin's delving too deeply into corruption and crime, believed things had already gone too far:

> What we have now is a mafia-controlled state. It's not going to be easier to dislodge than the system of state socialism we had before. And this time a lot more blood is going to be spilt. We're operating

on the principle of grabbing something as quickly as possible, and once we've grabbed what we need we're happy for order to be established. But remember we're talking about a very large country, a very rich country. There's a huge amount still to be grabbed, and that will take a long time.

21
Brezhnev Revisited?

C linton had been gone barely twenty-four hours when the bombshell was dropped. Gaidar had quit, barely four months after returning to the government as Chernomyrdin's number two. The news was acutely embarrassing for the President, a sign that his word was no longer law. Worried about the Zhirinovsky factor, the Americans had probed Yeltsin on his commitment to reform during the summit. Time and again, Yeltsin had told Clinton: 'Gaidar stays.' There would be, as the Americans had acknowledged, more therapy, less shock. But the team would stick together. Yeltsin was forced to accept Gaidar's resignation. On the following day the rouble had one of its worst days on record. There were fears it could go into free fall, scuppering all hope of economic stabilization. Then it was it the turn of Boris Fyodorov. He too said he could no longer work with Chernomyrdin. He told Yeltsin he would stay on only if several other ministers were sacked. Yeltsin consulted Chernomyrdin, who refused point-blank. The only out-and-out radical left in the cabinet was Chubais.

Yeltsin was looking desperately weak. He had not recovered from his narrow escape in October, or from the disaster of the December elections. His actions had an air of incipient panic. His attitude to the reformers was confused. He supported them in principle, but now feared Chernomyrdin. He wanted to remain on friendly terms with the West, but felt the need to bang the nationalist drum. There was no deftness to his touch, only an attempt – and failure – to satisfy all sides that smacked of Gorbachev in his final years.

From early in 1992 to the assault on the White House, the political process had been dominated by the animosities between Yeltsin on one side and Khasbulatov and Rutskoy on the other. Power struggle and policy had been inextricably linked. After going to the brink in October, Yeltsin needed a new agenda. He brought in some fresh faces. Georgy Satarov, the head of the Presidential Council, was the most prominent among their number. With a new constitution in place and a new parliament still finding its feet, the President should no longer take on his critics but woo them, the aides told him. Consensus, national accord, should become the buzzwords.

All this presupposed that the original foes remained locked up. In its first weeks, members of the Duma had repeatedly tried to put the question of an amnesty for the rebels on to the agenda. On each occasion they failed, but it seemed only a matter of time. After coordinated pressure from Zhirinovsky's LDP, the Communists and Agrarians, the new speaker, Ivan Rybkin, agreed to allow the issue to be discussed. The result was devastating for Yeltsin. By an overwhelming majority, deputies voted to free Rutskoy, Khasbulatov, even Barkashov's fascists, from Lefortovo prison. Only Russia's Choice voted against; Yavlinsky's group abstained, while Shakhrai's voted with the hardliners. Yeltsin's team should have been prepared. But when the results came through, they responded characteristically – in panic. Yeltsin phoned Kazannik, the new Prosecutor General on whom he thought he could rely. The diffident lawyer was summoned, and told to do all that it might take to keep the enemies in prison. Kazannik refused. He said he could see no legal reason why he should overrule parliament. Yeltsin was incensed. The following day Satarov went over to the Duma to see Rybkin. There was no time to waste. Rybkin was conciliatory. They discussed the issues earnestly for several hours. Nobody managed to inform them that the rebels had already been released. Had nobody bothered to telephone them, or could they not get through?

Over at Lefortovo, the inmates were preparing their departures. Rutskoy had asked Lyudmila, his wife, to bring over his military uniform. Sporting his fatigues, the Hero of the Soviet Union medal he had won in Afghanistan, and a full beard, Rutskoy looked the very model pre-revolutionary patriot, straight out of Tolstoy. As the crowds cheered 'Rutskoy – President', he walked regally out of the main gate. He was accompanied by Anpilov and Konstantinov, two of the most notorious extremists. By contrast, Khasbulatov skulked out through a side entrance, muttering his 'deep disgust for the current crop of politicians'. 'Machiavelli was a child compared to them,' he said. Khasbulatov pledged to return to academia. If so, he had a strange way of showing it. He was whisked off by a group of Chechens in an awaiting Mercedes.

Kazannik quit the next day, accusing Yeltsin of dirty dealings. 'I resigned because I was asked to break the law, and that is not within my power. Let the people blush who are wiping their feet on the law to lift themselves higher,' Kazannik told his staff in a brief farewell speech. That censorious final flourish only betrayed his ignorance of the political game. Such lofty disinterest was out of tune with the times. For the previous two years, the law had been a political instrument, and nobody – Zorkin, Stepankov or Makarov – had tried to exercise it otherwise. Kazannik was mocked as the country yokel. His pride dented, he went on to the offensive, suggesting that Yeltsin's storming of the White House might be interpreted by future courts as a crime against the state. He also claimed that several top figures, including Korzhakov, had been allowed to issue decrees without the usual clearance procedure.

Unsure of his friends, at least Yeltsin knew his enemies. The Security Ministry had refused to help him during the uprising, often giving him information that was either incomplete or deliberately misleading. His advisers concluded that he had nothing to lose in taking on the entrenched institution. He disbanded the ministry, replacing it with a much smaller Federal Counter-Intelligence Service, which would be directly under his control. All employees, the presidential decree said, would undergo a screening process. The agency was told to confine itself to counter-intelligence and the fights against terrorism, drug trafficking and arms dealing. Yeltsin followed up the gambit by creating a new post of National Security Adviser. Yuri Baturin, a much-respected old Gorbachev hand, was told to keep a close eye on the Service. This was only the latest of many attempts to clip the wings of the former KGB, and each time the President had been thwarted. Yeltsin extracted one benefit from the amnesty. He used it as a pretext to get rid of Golushko, who had no intention of trimming down the new Counter-Intelligence Service.

Yeltsin retreated to Sochi for another of his strategic holidays. His back ailment – the inflammation of the root of the spinal column – had become more acute. Just before disbanding the old parliament, he had invited the Spanish doctors who had operated on him in 1990 to come to Moscow to look at him. They told him to give up tennis, and to swim for half an hour every morning. He followed their instructions, but each time he appeared in public he was looking more in distress, more ungainly, more wooden. It was not for nothing that he was being compared ever more frequently to Brezhnev, the old dodderer, who would skip pages from speeches without noticing.

As Yeltsin was resting on the Black Sea coast, a newspaper in Moscow issued a sensational report. *Obshchaya Gazeta*, which had close links with the Gorbachev Foundation and was edited by Yegor Yakovlev, whom Yeltsin had sacked as television chief, published a document called Version Number One. The memorandum, allegedly signed by four prominent politicians, gave details of how Yeltsin could be removed from power. The four men at the centre of the plot were Oleg Soskovets, the First Deputy Prime Minister and close ally of Chernomyrdin; Mikhail Kolesnikov, Chief of the General Staff; Luzhkov, the Mayor; and Shumeiko, the former Deputy Prime Minister who had become chairman of the upper house, the Federation Council. The report said state television had been planning to screen a film portraying Yeltsin as a man 'in poor health who also is drinking heavily'. At the same time, parliament was to be asked to approve the transfer of powers to Chernomyrdin.

The alleged protagonists furiously denied any thoughts of a coup. As soon as the document was leaked, the prosecutor's office began investigations. If it had been an elaborate hoax, what had been the point? Perhaps to discredit the figures mentioned, perhaps to sow discord between Yeltsin and his more moderate critics. Somebody was feeding the rumour mill, leading an American network to report that Yeltsin had been diagnosed as suffering cirrhosis of the liver. The conspiracies reached fever pitch when Chernomyrdin suddenly broke off talks with the Managing Director of the IMF, Michel Camdessus. He told him he had to fly down to Sochi to see Yeltsin, who was suffering from a bout of flu. 'I have some things to discuss with the President,' Chernomyrdin said cryptically. If the Prime Minister had wanted to talk over with Yeltsin, confidentially, the terms of the loan he had been discussing with Western financiers, why had he simply not said so?

The rumours were adding to the widespread perception that Yeltsin was a lame duck. His allies began a desperate rearguard action, offering television interviews and newspaper articles on the subject of the President's health. Kozyrev said he had seen Yeltsin down in Sochi. 'He gave us so many instructions they will take at least an entire month to be implemented.' Shumeiko, when receiving Western ambassadors or other dignitaries, would take off his mantelpiece a photograph of Yeltsin playing tennis, as if to say 'that proves it'. The situation was so serious that Yeltsin's wife, Naina, was persuaded to talk to the press. 'He works every morning. He has bathed in the sea. He has been going for walks and has made several trips in a helicopter. The fact that he has gone to Sochi, does that mean that he must definitely be undergoing treatment? Are there no doctors in Moscow? All these conversations about illnesses are dirty politics.'

A week after the crisis broke, Yeltsin returned to Moscow. Gradually the questions abated. Yeltsin hoped, when questioned during a visit to Spain shortly afterwards, that he would have the last word.

I wish everyone could have such health as I have. A man who plays a rigorous game of tennis regularly for one and a half hours, with professional tennis players for partners, a man who swims in the Black Sea in March, with the water down just to four degrees, can such a man be of poor health? A man who works sixteen to eighteen hours a day, practically without weekends. The Communists, of course, are constantly spreading rumours. They would like to put me in a bad mood, make up stories, but all this is not serious.

The authority of the President was at rock bottom. Like Brezhnev, he might survive in office for several more years, but he would not be taken seriously. It was not that the political opposition was particularly dangerous. Zhirinovsky was ranting, but to little apparent effect; Rutskoy was talking darkly of conflicts to come. Apart from the amnesty, the Duma had made a lacklustre start. The country seemed to be stumbling about aimlessly. Nobody was really in charge. Nobody seemed to care.

The turnout in December was bad enough; for local elections in March, it was considerably lower. In St Petersburg it didn't reach one voter in four, even after Sobchak had broken the rules by extending the ballot to a second day.

Yeltsin pinned his hopes on reaching a consensus with the Duma. His team came up with the Agreement for Civic Accord, a document bearing all the hallmarks of the Soviet era: the title was lofty, the contents appeared empty. Still, there was nothing offensive in it, and most of the opposition parties that had pledged to boycott it fell into line. More than 200 parties, organizations and regions were invited to the Kremlin's resplendent St George's Hall to sign the accord. The ceremony was choreographed to perfection. The announcer's voice bore an uncanny resemblance to the man at the May Day festivities of old on Red Square, whose every declaration was followed by a taped recording of a crowd chanting 'hurrah'. With characteristic self-importance, Kostikov trumpeted the signing as 'one of the most significant events in Russia's history'. Each participant was presented with equal grandiloquence. For the Union of Women of the Russian Navy and the Association of Metal Workers it was a big day. For the more sceptical party leaders it was not. Yavlinsky refused to show up; the Communists and Agrarians took part but did not sign, while Zhirinovsky once again threatened to steal the show. As he arrived at the Kremlin he said he hadn't made up his mind. He would sign only if Yeltsin smiled at him. Yeltsin smiled, Zhirinovsky signed. At the end they all stood up, applauded themselves, and moved off to the majestic reception room for the most important part of the proceedings – the banquet. It lasted late into the night. With the help of copious amounts of caviar, vodka and champagne, and a relentless series of toasts, enemies became friends again.

Attention was invariably turning to the succession. The next presidential elections were not due until June 1996; but a campaign of sorts had already begun. Yeltsin had already made it clear that he wouldn't stand for re-election. He said he saw up to a dozen possible candidates, but that he was 'grooming' one or two. If he was, he was doing it discreetly.

Chernomyrdin was now the undisputed pretender to the throne. The man who had started so unconvincingly as premier at the end of 1992 had over the following year grown very rapidly in stature. His very greyness became an asset, suggesting stability and continuity after the turbulence of Yeltsin's first years in office. Chernomyrdin was a wily operator. On a personal and professional level his disdain for the radicals was intense. He diluted their influence by bringing his own men in, but he waited before moving against them. The election rout of Russia's Choice gave him that opportunity. Yeltsin was wary of Chernomyrdin, but he was also indebted to him. Here was a man who had stood by the President's side throughout his travails with parliament and who kept the wheels of government moving when everyone else was preoccupied with intrigues. Chernomyrdin developed his power base quietly but steadily. He assumed the final say on most major personnel and policy decisions. His own staff grew almost to the size of the President's.

His great asset was his ability to learn, and to alter his course in midstream. When he took over from Gaidar he poured scorn on the radical's idea of a free market, calling it a bazaar. His views were those of a typical *gosudarstvennik*, a Soviet industrialist who believed in the state's right to control the economic levers. Production was the be-all and end-all. He recited the same mantra day after day. *'Nado rabotats,'* 'We must work.' As long as the brave Soviet labourer dug more deeply, broke more sweat, everything would be all right. By the time of Gaidar's second resignation, in January 1994, Chernomyrdin's priorities had shifted slightly. 'The period of market romanticism is now over,' he said. 'But we will not permit its replacement by a fetishism of production. The current government considers the fight against inflation its utmost aim.' He was pleased to see Gaidar and Fyodorov go. He was even happier to see the back of their Western advisers such as Sachs and Aslund. When asked his reaction to Sachs's resignation, Chernomyrdin replied: 'Jeffrey who?'

The radicals had been a convenient foil for Chernomyrdin in his first year in office. Criticism of the government was invariably directed at them. Now, for the first time, the Prime Minister was to bear full responsibility. The collapse of the rouble on the day after their resignations provided him with his first lesson. A market of sorts was in place; he realized that its confidence had to be won. The remarkable happened. Chernomyrdin became more parsimonious with the state's money than Gaidar had ever had the scope to be. Credits to ailing industries were severely curtailed. In the first five months of the year production fell by a quarter. Thousands of enterprises had stopped work, and thousands more were operating part-time. The profligate Central Bank boss Gerashchenko also applied the squeeze. He was doing everything the monetarists had demanded in 1992, but now he was doing it for his *friends*. Bank interest rates were increased to above the inflation rate, providing a disincentive to borrow commercially. Inflation dropped steadily, down to just over 8 per cent a month – an enormous figure by Western standards, but compared to the near-hyperinflationary 50 per cent of a few months earlier it was a very creditable achievement.

Chernomyrdin had stolen Gaidar's clothes, and it was embarrassing for the radicals to admit it. 'It is an irony of history that the reformists sowed the seeds and that non-reformists are reaping the harvest,' said Gaidar, somewhat disingenuously. Chernomyrdin's political antennae were sharper than the radicals' had been. He accepted the bald facts, that thousands of factories could not be saved and had to go to the wall. Those that could transform themselves and produce goods that had a place in the market would be encouraged. Russia did not need Western engagement for that. Aid and credits, he said, should be confined to social welfare. Alexashenko, the Deputy Finance Minister, who had served in both administrations, said of Chernomyrdin: 'He proved himself receptive to education. I remember when he started off he thought nothing of giving credits to several sectors and tried to freeze prices. Inflation doubled in a week. He was frightened. He asked whether the two factors were interrelated, and when told they were he took stock. He realized that he had very limited space to operate, that he had no other choice.'

By mid-1994 some experts were allowing themselves to make optimistic forecasts. Some said the economy was close to bottoming out, with steady growth to follow. The Centre for Economic Reforms said real incomes and consumption had actually risen compared to the year before. Official figures had tended to paint a gloomier picture than was the reality because they failed to take into account parts of the private sector and the still-large black economy, so any statistics that looked good were all the more surprising. Opposition to the government's economic strategy was muted, partly because so many parties were represented in what was a broad coalition.

The biggest danger was a more transparent one: the lumpenization of a society that had been used to equality in poverty, but now had to come to terms with the emergence of a small but not insignificant number of super-rich, a small middle class, and a large proportion of the disgruntled and displaced. Unemployment was reaching 10 per cent, and rising sharply, even taking into account undeclared jobs on the side. The problem was most desperate in the dozens of one-industry towns that were built as part of the Communist experiment in social engineering and were now facing economic oblivion. Much of the wealth was concentrated in Moscow, St Petersburg and a pocket of other cities. A lumpenized society had already shown itself susceptible to the easy promises of Zhirinovsky. The demographics played into the hands of the extremists. Russia was, literally, dying. It was the only major industrialized state where life expectancy was decreasing. In 1992, 200,000 more people died than were born. That discrepancy rose to 700,000 in 1993. It was hard to persuade the downtrodden that the causes of so much of their misery were not so much the changes of the past few years as the economic negligence and environmental vandalism of the previous seventy. This was all part of the long process of re-education. Chernomyrdin came to understand that, and was wary of making promises of a better life ahead. Yet so closely was he associated with the second phase of the reform programme that his prospects of succeeding Yeltsin would depend largely on improving living standards in the months to come.

A man of similar mould to the Prime Minister was Ivan Rybkin. The Chairman of the Duma had the advantage of relative youth – he was forty-six when he took on the job – and a conventional background. He had run the Communist Party organization at Volgograd Agricultural Institute, kept his head down and avoided problems throughout his career. He stood for election for the Agrarians, and he won the race for speaker because he was seen by the main hardline parties as one of them. Quickly, however, he established a reputation as a conciliator, and secured the qualified trust of Yeltsin and the government despite the fracas caused by the release of the White House rebels. But the historical precedents for Rybkin were not good. In pre-revolutionary times Russia had four Dumas in twelve years and two of their chairmen ended up in prison. The speakers of parliament's day, Lukyanov, and of Yeltsin's, Khasbulatov, suffered the same fate. Rybkin represented the new moderately pro-reform consensus. So did Shumeiko, his counterpart in the upper house. Shumeiko was voraciously ambitious, but his murky reputation in the corruption scandals of 1993 was a considerable handicap.

As the balance shifted, so Russia's Choice moved away from centre stage. Its was often a lone voice in parliament, but Gaidar seemed to be relishing his new role as leader of one side of the opposition. His Institute for Economic Programmes in the Transitional Period became a brains trust for bright young economists. In the Duma he began to flourish. His first motion, to protest against the construction of a new parliament headquarters on a disused football field next door to the White House, at a cost of $500 million, won cross-party support. Chernomyrdin was forced to abandon the project.

When it came to Kremlinology, Russians often cited the satirical novelist, Vladimir Voinovich. Since the revolution, as he pointed out, the country's leaders had alternated between the bald – Lenin, Khrushchev, Andropov, Gorbachev – and those with a full head of hair – Stalin, Brezhnev, Chernenko and Yeltsin. The theory appeared to leave the door open to Chernomyrdin. But there was another possible – Luzhkov, the Mayor of Moscow.

Luzhkov ran the city like the Party chiefs of old. Even Yeltsin, in his ill-fated days as Moscow boss, had not enjoyed such power. In return for his staunch support of the President, Luzhkov was given *carte blanche* over the capital. He rewrote the law book, restoring restrictions on 'immigration' to Moscow to prevent overcrowding and to combat crime. Another of his measures was the reintroduction of the system of *druzhinniki*, volunteer policemen whose red armbands were a symbol of the police state of old. The Mayor ordered the training of 5,000 vigilantes, who would have the right to carry sticks and make arrests. But with no guns at their disposal, the upright young men in their new blue uniforms did not instil fear among the criminals. They concentrated their efforts on drunks.

Not one new building in the city could go up without Luzhkov's personal approval. Everything depended on his signature – and everyone knew what it took to attain that signature. But to impugn his integrity was an expensive business. Each time he sued a newspaper he won. As one journalist put it privately: 'There isn't a judge in the city who'll find against him.' His economic philosophy, to give it a grand title, was the 'managed market economy', a Gorbachevian hybrid. He fought bitterly to scupper Chubais' privatization scheme, arguing that the sales of state property at auctions had been 'the actions of a drunk'. Luzhkov even took to conducting his own 'foreign policy', proclaiming that Moscow recognized Crimea as an integral part of Russian territory. For all his autocratic vagaries, Luzhkov won increasing popularity. Against all the odds, he kept Moscow working, after a fashion.

Zhirinovsky's problem was that more conventional politicians were chipping away at his agenda, such as a crackdown on crime and a tougher foreign policy. The release of Rutskoy and the rebels, which he had advocated in parliament, only added to his troubles. He was no longer the lone voice of populist nationalism. Rutskoy represented a more disciplined and less quixotic alternative and lost no time in denouncing Zhirinovsky as a 'criminal case'. But Rutskoy was also struggling to find a role in the new political order. Shorn of his vice-presidential tag, his vituperative attacks on Yeltsin seemed tired, as did his call for a new 'social patriotic' movement. 'There will be iron discipline, firm order,' Rutskoy proclaimed. 'We have absolutely no need for dissent. We have had enough of experimentation. In the end, the aim of this movement is to come to power.' Whatever Rutskoy's weaknesses, there remained a large constituency receptive to some form of protest; it was a matter of finding the most attractive figurehead.

Solzhenitsyn chose his moment to return. On 27 May 1994, at the age of seventy-five, twenty years after being bundled, handcuffed, on a plane bound for Germany, he touched down on Russian soil. Fittingly his first stop was Magadan, the most notorious of the ports in the network of Soviet labour camps about which he wrote in *The Gulag Archipelago*. 'I know that I am arriving in a Russia tormented, disheartened, in shock, changed beyond recognition, still searching for itself and for its own meaning,' he told the thousands awaiting him in Vladivostok. Solzhenitsyn said he was on a voyage of discovery, to learn from his countrymen. But he seemed clear enough about what was happening. Communism had been superseded by unbridled capitalism: two different systems, but one relationship between the rulers and the ruled. 'Communism has remained in people's hearts, souls and minds.' Revival would come only through reconciliation. 'But first the oppressors and executioners must first repent and say: "Yes, I did it."' In the same breath, Solzhenitsyn likened the old *nomenklatura* to the new rich, 'those who rob the people before our very eyes, who thieve our national wealth. They must repent and give charity as proof of their repentance.' The extraordinary odyssey continued, taking him by special train from the Far East, through the heart of Siberia across the Urals to Moscow. His new home was a *dacha* built under his wife's supervision in Moscow's green belt. The three-storey house was situated on a plot of land once used by Stalin's henchman, Lazar Kaganovich, who sent millions of peasants to their deaths during the collectivization of the 1930s. It was a fitting reminder.

The clarity of the condemnation was disconcerting for Russia's rulers. Solzhenitsyn railed against the free-market philosophy of the radicals, but was careful not to disparage Yeltsin personally. All sides of the political establishment were eager to ingratiate themselves with the new spiritual leader of the opposition, partly in hope of minimizing future attacks and partly in hope of reaping political dividends from association with him. Among the younger generation, his return did not pass unnoticed. The man who had embodied dissidence was worthy of curiosity, and respect. But Russia, it seemed, had moved on. Robbed of the *frisson* of reading them in *samizdat*, Solzhenitsyn's tomes on the crimes of the Communist state were hard to find on the shelves of bookshops. Their place had been taken by pulp fiction, detectives, horror stories, science fiction, business manuals and sex guides.

It had taken him almost three years after the collapse of Communism to abandon his reclusive life in Cavendish, Vermont. He had left it so long to give Russia time to seek out a new path. Perhaps he had left it too late. Instead of finding democracy, he said, his countrymen had allowed in another oligarchy.

The figures bore out Solzhenitsyn's view. Research from the Academy of Sciences showed that 75 per cent of Yeltsin's entourage had made their careers in the Communist Party or in Soviet state structures. With each reshuffle that figure was increasing. In Chernomyrdin's government the proportion was the same. In the regions, not much more than 10 per cent of leadership figures had come from outside the Party hierarchy. They were all doing well for themselves now. Pavlov, the hedgehog, and all those around him who had so disparaged the free market, were running banks or investment houses and making a fortune.

Three years after the collapse of the old, Russia was an unlovable and unloving place. There was a meanness about the streets, a sense of ever-present danger. Old habits, such as visiting friends' houses in the evenings, became more difficult. Many people fell out of the habit of having their friends around. It was too expensive, and guests would want to leave early for fear of the journey home. When putting on their coats, they would often reach inside the pocket to check that the gas pistol was still there. Nothing came cheap any more. Prices for most goods outstripped those in the West. To eat in a very ordinary Georgian or

Russian restaurant and come away with change from $100 for two was an experience to savour. According to official figures such a bill corresponded to over two months' salary. It was not hard to find desperately poor people, hawking their pathetic wares on street corners. If the statistics were taken at face value, almost the entire population would be categorized as below the poverty line. Millions were working on the side to make ends meet.

But by the third year of the reforms, many people were doing considerably better than they cared to admit. A look at any flight to any foreign destination testified to that. The passengers were not all crooks and spivs. An ever-increasing proportion of the population was living in the dollar economy, earning money that while below Western levels was still enough to afford a cheap holiday to the beach on Crete or to visit friends in London. The dollar economy was no longer confined to Western firms. Whatever the origins of their money – perhaps the Communist Party, the KGB or another state institution that had privatized itself overnight – and whatever the moral rectitude of their bosses, Russian firms were finding a niche for themselves and filling a consumer market that had barely begun to form. In the initial period almost all the goods were imported, but at least they were coming. Russians were embarrassed to ask for translations from the English or German of the instructions on how to work washing machines and microwaves. As soon as they had them installed, however, they acted as if they had always been there. Likewise, the timidity they would display on their first trip to Paris or London quickly evaporated on their second. Even in Gorbachev's day, Russians would always joke they could tell foreigners apart. They dressed better, and walked more assertively. Then there were the Soviet shoes, the grey plastic rounded models stranded in the 1950s. The distinction was still drawn in the mid-1990s, only this time it was usually the other way round. If they had designer suits, Westerners would not wear them on Moscow's steets. Russians had no such qualms about showing off their wealth.

In mid-1994 I met up in London with a Russia's Choice delegation led by Gaidar. A week later, back in Moscow, I asked Golovkov, one of the group's coordinators, his impressions of London. 'Loved it,' he said, 'But I can't understand how you put up with all that socialism, those pub laws, all those restrictive practices. In Russia things are much freer.' For anyone who wanted to make money, pure and simple, Russia was one of the freest places in the world. It had its rules, people had to be paid, but after that was done, and the bodyguards were hired, anything went.

Hope for the future lies elsewhere. The entrepreneurial spirit has been found. What is needed now is a sense of civic responsibility, compassion and moderation. The historians will argue that is a forlorn hope. Russia, they say, is a febrile place that is preordained to lurch from tyranny, to

lawlessness, back to tyranny. On one level, the past few years have borne
out such a theory. One extreme, in the hands of the elite, has been
replaced by another extreme, in the hands of the same elite. Yet in terms
of freedoms, this new society cannot be compared to the old dictatorship.
In the frantic rush to come to terms with the new, memories have
shortened. Russians tend to forget how restrictive and miserable was their
old existence, how demeaning were their lifestyles. Out of the charmless,
crude capitalism new opportunities are being created. In the short term
hope lies in the business class, the former Communists, the criminal and
the less criminal, wanting to turn respectable. Theirs are the victors'
spoils, part of which could be ploughed back into the country from their
Swiss bank accounts. This is already happening in places.

Yeltsin has stumbled upon a political and economic consensus, rough
and ready though it may be, that is likely to outlast him. After the initial
love affair and disappointment, he has tried to steer the country along a
middle path of cautious cooperation with the West. He and future leaders
will always have to look over their shoulders and listen to the interests of
the nationalists, but a foreign policy that is both assertive and open-
minded can be built. Economically and politically, the ground has shifted.
The right to private property and monetary prudence have largely been
accepted by all sides, even the President's arch-foes. Yeltsin's own political
survival is, with each passing day, becoming less crucial to Russia's long-
term stability. After the turbulence of recent years, when his removal
could have opened the way to a far more autocratic regime, that is
achievement indeed.

Select Bibliography

Michael Beschloss and Strobe Talbott, *At the Highest Levels*, Little, Brown, London, 1993

Patrick Cockburn, *Getting Russia Wrong*, Verso, London, 1989

Steve Crawshaw, *Goodbye to the USSR*, Bloomsbury, London, 1992

Karen Dawisha and Bruce Parrott, *Russia and the New States of Eurasia*, Cambridge University Press, Cambridge, 1994

Dusko Doder and Louise Branson, *Gorbachev, Heretic in the Kremlin*, Macdonald, London, 1990

Mikhail Gorbachev, *Perestroika*, Collins, London, 1987

Ruslan Khasbulatov, *The Struggle for Russia*, Routledge, London, 1993

Zhores Medvedev, *Gorbachev*, Blackwell, Oxford, 1988

John Morrison, *Boris Yeltsin: From Bolshevik to Democrat*, Penguin, London, 1991

Hilary Pilkington, *Russia's Youth and its Culture*, Routledge, London, 1994

David Remnick, *Lenin's Tomb*, Viking, London, 1993

Angus Roxburgh, *The Second Russian Revolution*, BBC Books, London, 1991

Andrei Sakharov, *Memoirs*, Hutchinson, London, 1990

Christian Schmidt-Hauer, *Russland in Aufruhr*, Piper, Munich, 1993

Eduard Shevardnadze, *The Future Belongs to Freedom*, Sinclair-Stevenson, London, 1986

Hedrick Smith, *The Russians*, Sphere, London, 1986

—— *The New Russians*, Random Century, London, 1990

Anatoly Sobchak, *For a New Russia*, HarperCollins, London, 1992

Vladimir Solovyov and Elena Klepikova, *Boris Yeltsin: A Political Biography*, Weidenfeld and Nicholson, London, 1992

Jonathan Steele, *Eternal Russia*, Faber and Faber, London, 1994

Arkady Vaksberg, *The Soviet Mafia*, Weidenfeld and Nicholson, London, 1991

Boris Yeltsin, *Against the Grain*, Cape, London, 1991

—— *The View from the Kremlin*, HarperCollins, London, 1994

Daniel Yergin and Thane Gustafson, *Russia 2010 and What it Means for the World*, Random House, New York, 1993

Index

under Yeltsin 98–9
see also Kryuchkov; Shebarshin
Khasbulatov, Ruslan xvii, 11, 27, 30, 33,
51, 54–5, 75, 118, 146, 220, 226
and August 1991 coup 44, 50
and *Izvestia* 164
and March 1993 crisis 139, 141, 142,
143
and October 1993 crisis 148, 149–51,
154, 159
and opposition to Yeltsin 78, 107–8
and Thatcher 137
Khrolenko, Viktor 87–8
Kobets, Konstantin xvii, 5
Kobzon, Iosif xvii, 210, 211
Kohl, Helmut 59
Konstantinov, Ilya xviii, 77, 78, 220
Korzhakov, Alexander xviii, 20, 44, 51,
66, 97, 220
in October 1993 crisis 158, 212
Kostikov, Vyacheslav xviii, 87–8, 136,
199, 223
Kovalev, Sergei 172
Kozyrev, Andrei, xviii, 56, 61, 80, 106,
111, 199
'shock' speech to CSCE 111–12
and December 1993 election 172
Krasavchenko, Sergei 181
Kravchuk, Leonid xviii, 58–9, 60, 61, 64,
191
Kruchina, Nikolai 4
Kryuchkov, Vladimir xviii, 2
and August 1991 coup 42, 43–4, 45
Kuchma, Leonid 192
Kvantrishvili, Otari xviii, 209–12

Landsbergis, Vytautas 193
Layard, Richard 73
Liberal Democratic Party 172, 180, 181,
186–7, 220
see also Zhirinovsky
Ligachev, Yegor 84, 85
Lukyanov, Anatoly xviii, 23, 226
and August 1991 coup 43
in December 1993 election 43
and Yakubovsky 3
Luzhkov, Yuri xviii, 76, 152, 226–7
Lyubimov, Alexander 166–7

mafia 18, 35–6, 78, 90, 92–3, 94–5, 123
see also organized crime
Makarov, Andrei xviii, 6–7, 10
Makashov, Albert xviii, 77, 84, 151
Mamyshev, Vladik 91
Medvedev, Roy 77
military
and August 1991 coup 43, 44, 45
and break-up of USSR 64
and Gorbachev 28
and March 1993 crisis 139, 140
and October 1993 crisis 148, 151, 156,
157–8, 196

and opposition to Yeltsin 82
and parliament 106–7
and Soviet assets in Germany 3–4, 126
see also Kalashnikov, Mikhail
Moldova 64
Moskovsky Komsomolets 83
Murashev, Arkady xviii

National Salvation Front xviii, 82–3
NATO, potential expansion of 199, 200
Nazarbayev, Nursultan xviii, 42, 60, 62,
64, 193
Nazdratenko, Yevgeny 129–30
Nekhoroshev, Alexander 166
Nevzorov, Alexander 164–5, 175
Nezavisimaya Gazeta 161–2
night life, in Moscow 89–93
Nikolayev, Yuri 163
nomenklatura (Communist elite) ix–x
financial dealings 3–4
and organized crime x
'privatization' 117
nuclear weapons 64, 192
and organized crime 215–16

Officers' Union 78–9
opposition to Yeltsin 76–83, 153–5
Communist 82, 86
conservative xi
in December 1993 election *see* political
parties/groups
and entrepreneurs 79
fascist 79–81, 82
among military 78–9, 82
nationalist 77–8, 82–3
pursuit of, after White House siege
170–1
see also White House siege
organized crime 123, 134, 207–18
and media 167, 211
and Soviet elite x
and Western countries 214–16
see also black market; mafia
Orthodox Church
and October 1993 crisis 153
and reform 33, 104
Ostalsky, Dmitry 161–2

Pamyat 56, 79, 81
Parkhomenko, Sergei 155–6, 162
parliament, Russian
Agreement for Civic Accord 223
amnesty for October 1993 rebels 220
and constitution 138, 145
and economic reforms 75
and presidential powers 107–10
relocation, after December 1993 election
174
under Yeltsin 28
parliament, Soviet, under Gorbachev
20–1, 25–6
elections to (March 1990) 26